In accordance with the latest syllabus prescribed by the council for the Indian Certificate of Secondary Education Examination, New Delhi.

OSWAL – GURUKUL

MOST LIKELY

ICSE QUESTION BANK

HISTORY & CIVICS

CLASS IX

By

PANEL OF AUTHORS

EDITION : 2022

ISBN : 978-93-92563-00-3

PRICE : ₹ 299.00

PRINTED AT :

PUBLISHED BY

OSWAL PUBLISHERS

Head Office	:	1/12, Sahitya Kunj, M.G. Road, Agra - 282 002
Phone	:	(0562) 2527771-4
Whatsapp	:	+91 74550 77222
E-mail	:	info@oswalpublishers.in
Website	:	www.oswalpublishers.com

The cover of this book has been designed using resources from Freepik.com

PREFACE

It is a matter of immense pride for us to present the 'ICSE MOST LIKELY QUESTION BANK' series, especially prepared for students appearing for Board examinations in the oncoming year.

This book has been created with the specific purpose of making the students' journey of learning, understanding and revising the concepts, effortless and simple. The topical approach with ample questions for every category is adopted to reinforce the students' understanding of each chapter. The category-wise division also allows them to peruse their progress as well as keep a check on their grasp of the theory.

Meticulous care has been taken in writing the book in simple, student-friendly language without compromising with the clarity of style.

We are confident that the book will enable the candidates to develop a better understanding of the curriculum and help them organize their learning process. This book shall definitely prove to be a fruitful tool for the students and encourage them towards scholastic excellence.

Constructive suggestions for further improvement of the book are always welcome.

—Publisher

The global outbreak of the Novel Coronavirus (COVID-19) has impacted all aspects of life including the educational life at schools. Schools across the country have been shut since March, 2020 due to the pandemic. While numbers of CISCE affiliated schools have tried to adapt to this changed scenario and have tried to keep alive the teaching learning process through online classes, there has been a significant shortening of the academic year and loss of the instructional hours.

To make up for the loss in instructional hours during the current session 2020-2021, the CISCE has worked with its subject experts, to reduce the syllabi for all major subjects at the ICSE and ISC levels. Syllabus reduction has been done, keeping in mind the linear progression across classes while ensuring that the core concepts related to the subject are retained.

The following reduced syllabi, for the current Academic Year 2020-2021 have been made available on the CISCE website www.cisce.org under 'Publications':

- ICSE Reduced Syllabus for Class IX
- ICSE Reduced Syllabus for Class X
- ISC Reduced Syllabus for Class XI
- ISC Reduced Syllabus for Class XII

Heads of CISCE affiliated schools have been asked to ensure that the concerned subject teachers at the ICSE and ISC levels transact the syllabus strictly according to sequence of topics, so as to facilitate further reduction in syllabus, if required, depending on the situation of the pandemic in the country.

We at Oswal Publishers, have developed all our books on the basis of the original syllabi with complete subjective knowledge of all the subjects, so that the students have an access to the entire syllabus. However, for the examination purpose, the students are advised to structure their preparations considering the latest alterations by the Council.

Scan this to know the recent changes in Syllabus

CONTENTS

How to choose a
GREAT CAREER

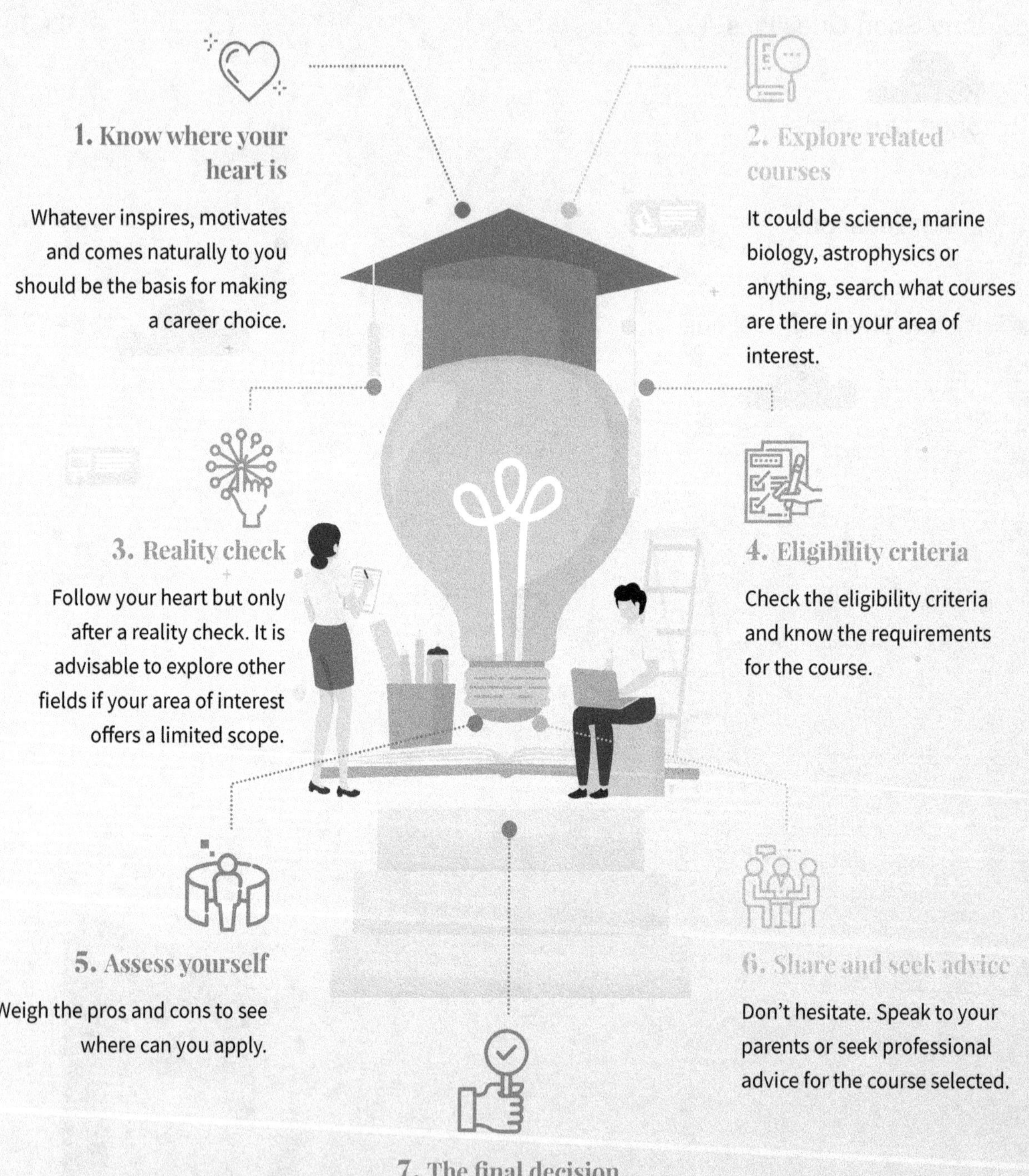

1. Know where your heart is

Whatever inspires, motivates and comes naturally to you should be the basis for making a career choice.

2. Explore related courses

It could be science, marine biology, astrophysics or anything, search what courses are there in your area of interest.

3. Reality check

Follow your heart but only after a reality check. It is advisable to explore other fields if your area of interest offers a limited scope.

4. Eligibility criteria

Check the eligibility criteria and know the requirements for the course.

5. Assess yourself

Weigh the pros and cons to see where can you apply.

6. Share and seek advice

Don't hesitate. Speak to your parents or seek professional advice for the course selected.

7. The final decision

Once you are through with all the steps, you will know where you stand and will be better placed to make the right choice.

Go where your strength is, not where your friends are.

STUDYING ONLINE IN A VIRTUAL GROUP

Virtual study groups are proven to be as effective as the conventional study groups. They are beneficial for each member as they allow individual participation, clearing doubts via meaningful discussions and most importantly provide a friendly support system.

STEPS TO CREATE AN EFFECTIVE VIRTUAL STUDY GROUP

- Before anything else, you need to choose a group of 8-10 people who have the same syllabus and goals as yours.
- Next, fix up a time table that is suitable to all the members. Each day, everyone should come prepared with the topic of discussion in the group.
- After this, you need to find a digital platform where you can organise your study session. ExamTime and Thinkbinder are two of the dedicated web-sites for this use. You can also use common text and video communication apps like WhatsApp or Skype to gather all the members at one place for the purpose of study.
- Avoid going off topic, into idle chat. After a topic has been discussed, all the members should prepare notes for revision and share them in the next session.
- In the final round, you can hold a special quiz session in which all the members can participate and assess their level of understanding of the topic.

So, when you have to prepare for your next test or exam, organise an online group study session with your friends and study smart to obtain the perfect score. You can tell us about your virtual group study experience at contact@oswalpublishers.com . All the best!

WEEKLY SCHEDULE

	MONDAY	TUESDAY	WEDNESDAY	THURSDAY	FRIDAY	SATURDAY	SUNDAY

GOALS

DON'T FORGET!

NOTES

Very Short Questions | Set **1** |

SECTION : A (CIVICS)

Chapter 1. Indian Constitution

Q. 1. What does the word 'Secular' mean?

Ans. The word secular means, 'Not Connected To Any Religion or Faith'.

Q. 2. Name any four eminent members of the Constituent Assembly.

Ans. Four eminent members of the Constituent Assembly were Dr. Rajendra Prasad, Sardar Vallabhbhai Patel, Jawaharlal Nehru and Maulana Azad.

Q. 3. Who was the Chairman of the Drafting Committee of the Constitution of India?

Ans. Dr. B.R. Ambedkar was the Chairman of the Drafting Committee of the Constitution of India.

Q. 4. Who framed the Constitution of India?

Ans. A sever member drafting committee under the chairmanship of Dr. B.R. Ambedkar framed the Constitution of India.

Q. 5. Who gave the idea of an independent Constitution for India?

Ans. The idea of an independent Constitution was first mooted by Pt. Jawaharlal Nehru.

Q. 6. What do you mean by the term 'Republic'?

Ans. The word 'Republic' refers to a state in which power is held by the people through their elected representatives.

Q. 7. Who was appointed as the first permanent President of the Constituent Assembly?

Ans. Dr. Rajendra Prasad was appointed as the first permanent President of the Constituent Assembly.

Q. 8. Is the Preamble a part of the Constitution?

Ans. Yes, the Preamble is a part of the Constitution because it contains the basic structure or framework of the Constitution.

Q. 9. What does the word Fraternity stand for?

Ans. The word Fraternity stands for the spirit of common brotherhood. It ensures the dignity of an individual as well as the unity and integrity of the nation.

Q. 10. Define the term 'Constitution'. [February, 2020]

Ans. The rules and principles which determine how a country is governed and which give its citizens certain rights form the Constitution of a country.

Q. 11. What is meant by the term 'Preamble' to the Constitution?

Ans. The Preamble is an introductory statement, stating the aims and objectives of the Constitution. It describes the 'soul and spirit' of the Constitution of India.

Q. 12. Name the two women who were the members of Constituent Assembly.

Ans. Mrs. Sarojni Naidu and Mrs. Vijaya Lakshmi Pandit were among the women members of the Constituent Assembly.

Q. 13. When was 'Complete Independence Day' celebrated?

Ans. Complete Independence Day was celebrated on 26 January, 1930 and continued to be celebrated till 1947. After India achieved Independence on 15 August, 1947, it came to be known as Independence Day and 26 January as Republic Day of India.

Q. 14. When did the 'Objective Resolution' of the Constitution pass?

Ans. The 'Objective resolution' was passed by the Constituent Assembly on January 22, 1947.

Q. 15. What do the words 'We the people of India' in the Preamble signify?

Ans. These words signify that the people of India are the ultimate source of authority under the Constitution.

Q. 16. Explain the nature of the state that the framers of the constitution sought to establish in India.

Ans. The framers of the constitution sought to establish a welfare state in India.

Q. 17. State one reason, why the Constitution makers intended to establish a Secular policy in India.

Ans. The word 'Secular' means 'Not Connected To Any Religion or Faith.' India is home to many major religions of the world. Therefore, to keep the followers of all religions together the Constitution intended to establish a Secular policy in India. Thus, India has no official religion and is not guided by any religion or religious consideration.

Q. 18. According to the Preamble to the Constitution, who resolved to constitute India into a Sovereign, Democratic and Republic?

Ans. According to the Preamble to the Constitution, people of India resolved to constitute India into a Sovereign, Democratic and Republic.

Q. 19. Whose will is expressed in the Preamble to the Constitution?

Ans. The will of the common people is expressed in the Preamble to the Constitution of India.

Q. 20. What was added to the Preamble by the 42nd Constitutional Amendment Act, 1976?

Ans. The terms 'Socialist', 'Secular', 'Unity' and 'Integrity' were added to the Preamble by the 42nd Constitutional Amendment Act, 1976.

Q. 21. What is the opposite of a secular state? Name any one state that is not secular.

Ans. The opposite of a secular state is a theocratic state. Iran is a theocratic state.

Q. 22. Name three prominent members of the Cabinet Mission.

Ans. Lord Pethick Lawrence, Sir Stafford Cripps and A.V. Alexander were three prominent members of the Cabinet Mission.

Q. 23. Who is a citizen of India?

Ans. Any person who is born in India or either of whose parents was born in India or who has been a resident of India for five years, immediately preceding the commencement of the Constitution is considered as a citizen of India.

Q. 24. What was the number of Articles and Schedules in the original form of Constitution?

Ans. Our Constitution in its original form had 395 Articles in 22 parts and 8 schedules.

Q. 25. What type of liberty does the Preamble want for the Indian citizens?

Ans. The Preamble wants freedom of thought, expression, belief, faith and worship for the Indian citizens.

Q. 26. When was the Constitution of India adopted?   **[November, 2019]**

Ans. The Constitutions of India was adopted on November 26, 1949.

Q. 27. What is meant by a 'Written Constitution'?   **[November, 2019]**

Ans. A Written Constitution is one which sets forth in a single instrument most of the principles under which government shall be organised and conducted.

Chapter 2. Salient Features of the Constitution

Q. 1. What is 'Directive Principles of State Policy'?   **[February, 2020]**

Ans. The Directive Principles of State Policy are guidelines or instructions for central and state governments of India, to be kept in mind while framing laws and policies.

Q. 2. Which Article provides protection of Interests of minorities?

Ans. Article 29 provides that any minority group having a distinct language, script or culture of its own shall have the right to conserve it.

Very Short Questions

Q. 3. If the Directive Principles are non-justiciable, what is the use of incorporating them in the Constitution of India?

Ans. The Directive Principles are incorporated in the Constitution of India as they direct the government to establish economic and social democracy in the country.

Q. 4. Mention the ideal state as envisaged by the Directive Principles of State Policy.

Ans. The ideal state as envisaged by the Directive Principles of State Policy is the one which is committed to ensure to its citizens justice, liberty and dignity.

Q. 5. What is the Directive Principles of State Policy regarding the government of the village?

Ans. Panchayati Raj has been established in the remotest villages and it has been vested with powers to ensure their functioning as units of self-governments.

Q. 6. How does democracy contribute to stability in society?

Ans. Democracy stands for the inalienable rights of citizens, rule of law, independence of judiciary, free and fair elections and freedom of press, etc. thereby contributing stability in society.

Q. 7. What is meant by Equality of Status and Opportunity?

Ans. It implies equal opportunity to all citizens, in matters of public employment irrespective of caste, creed, colour or economic status.

Q. 8. What is meant by Universal Adult Franchise?　　　　　　　　　　**[February, 2020]**

Ans. Universal Adult Franchise means all citizens, aged 18 years and above, irrespective of caste, creed, colour, qualification, etc. have the right to vote.

Q. 9. Which Article ensures social equality and prohibits discrimination against any citizen on the basis of race, religion, sex, birth or caste?

Ans. Article 15 ensures social equality and prohibits discrimination against any citizen on the basis of race, religion, sex, birth or caste.

Q. 10. What do you mean by the term 'Habeas Corpus'?

Ans. In Latin, Habeas Corpus literally means, 'you may have the body'. It protects the safety of any person held in prison or taken into custody.

Q. 11. Which fundamental right prohibits forced labour and 'begar'?

Ans. The right against exploitation prohibits forced labour and begar under Article 23 of the Constitution.

Q. 12. When is the writ of Habeas Corpus issued?

Ans. This writ of Habeas Corpus is issued when a person is illegally detained or restrained.

Q. 13. What is the Article 20 of the Constitution?

Ans. Article 20 provides protection to individuals who are punished or accused of an offence.

Q. 14. Name the Fundamental Right aimed at protecting the interests of the minorities.

Ans. The Fundamental Right aimed at protecting the interests of the minorities comes under Cultural and Educational Rights (Article 29 and 30).

Q. 15. Which writ is issued against a person who has illegally or forcefully occupied a public office?

Ans. The writ of Quo Warranto is issued against a person who has illegally or forcefully occupied a public office.

Q. 16. What is Parliamentary system of government?

Ans. The Parliamentary system of government is a from of goverment in which the power to make and execute laws is held by the Parliament.

Q. 17. Name any two schemes and programmes launched by the government to enhance nutritional level of children.

Ans. Mid-day meal scheme and SABLA are the two schemes and programmes launched by the government to enhance nutritional level of children.

Q. 18. What is meant by 'Preventive Detention'?

Ans. Preventive Detention means to detain a person so as to prevent that person from committing any possible crime.

Q. 19. What is meant by the term 'Right to Equality'?   **[November, 2019]**

Ans. The 'Right to Equality' refers to providing equal treatment to all citizens of a country irrespective of his or her caste, race, gender, religion, economic status and place of birth. This includes Right to Equality before law,' Prohibition of Discrimination' 'Equality of Opportunity', in matters of Public Employment, Abolition of Untouchability and Abolition of Titles.

Q. 20. What is meant by Right to 'Constitutional Remedies'?   **[November, 2019]**

Ans. Fundamental Rights guaranteed in the Constitution cannot serve its purpose until they are safeguarded and enforced by a constitutional method. Article 32 of the Constitution of India gives the citizens the Right to move to the Supreme Court for the enforcement of Fundamental Rights by appropriate proceedings.

Q. 21. State any one Fundamental Right guaranteed to the citizens of India.   **[November, 2019]**

Ans. There are six Fundamental Rights guaranteed in the Constitution of India. They include:

    (i)   Right to Equality (Articles 14-18)

    (ii) Right to Freedom (Articles 19-22)

    (iii) Right against Exploitation (Aricles 23-24)

    (iv) Right to Freedom of Religion (Articles 25-28)

    (v) Cultural and Educational Rights (Articles 29-30)

    (vi) Right to Constitutional Remedies (Article 32)

      (Mention any one Fundamental Right)

Q. 22. Write any one Fundamental Duty of an Indian citizen.   **[February, 2020]**

Ans. One of the Fundamental Duties of an Indian citizen is to protect and improve the natural environment including forests, lakes, rivers and wildlife and have compassion for living creatures.

Q. 23. What is the significance of the Directive Principles of State Policy in the Indian Constitution?

Ans. Directive Principles of State Policy aim to create social and economic conditions under which the citizen can lead a good life. They also aim to establish social and economic democracy through a welfare state.

Chapter 3. Elections

Q. 1. What is an EVM?

Ans. It is an Electronic Voting Machine (EVM) which is used to record votes. The machine shows the names of the candidates and the symbols.   **[February, 2020]**

Q. 2. What is known as General Elections?

Ans. The Lok Sabha election is said to be a General Election.

Q. 3. Who supervises and conducts the elections to the Lok Sabha and Legislative Assemblies of states?

Ans. The Election Commission supervises and conducts the elections to the Lok Sabha and Legislative Assemblies of states.

Q. 4. Define the term 'constituency'.

Ans. A constituency is a well-defined territorial area that includes a body of residents who select a representative amongst them.

Q. 5. Does Election Commission hold the elections to Gram Panchayats and Municipal Corporations?

Ans. The State Election Commission constituted under the Constitution (Seventy-third and Seventy-fourth) Amendments Act, 1992 for each state / Union Territory are vested with the powers to conduct elections for the Gram Panchayats and Municipal Corporations.

Q. 6. Which Articles in the Indian Constitution deal with the composition, powers and functions of the Election Commission?

Ans. Article 324 of the Constitution deals with the composition, powers and functions of the Election Commission.

Q. 7. Who can remove the Chief Election Commissioner before the end of his/her tenure?

Ans. Through impeachment by the Parliament, Chief Election Commissioner can be removed before the end of his/her tenure.

Q. 8. Who has enacted the People's Representation Act?

Ans. People's Representation Act was enacted by the Parliament.

Q. 9. Who can initiate the reforms in our electoral system?

Ans. The Ministry of Law and Justice, Government of India, have constituted a Committee on Electoral Reforms. The main purpose of the Committee is to recommend to the government concrete ways in which our electoral system can be strengthened.

Q. 10. Who decides the disputes on the election symbol of political parties?

Ans. Election Commission decides the disputes on the election symbol of political parties.

Q. 11. Who decides the election disputes?

Ans. All election related disputes are handled by the Election Commission.

Q. 12. Under whose control and discipline is the staff on polling duty?

Ans. The staff on polling duty is under the control and discipline of the Election Commission.

Q. 13. Who appoints the Chief Election Commissioner of India?

Ans. The President of India appoints the Chief Election Commissioner of India.

Q. 14. Who appoints the Election Commissioners?   **[February, 2020]**

Ans. The Election Commissioners are appointed by the President of India.

Q. 15. Who acts as the Chairman of the Election Commission?

Ans. The Chief Election Commissioner acts as the Chairman of the Election Commission.

Q. 16. Mention any one need for elections.

Ans. Elections give common people the right to choose their leaders. The government is hence answerable to the common masses.

Q. 17. What do you mean by the term 'Election'?

Ans. Election is the process where the representatives are chosen to run the government by voting.

Q. 18. What is the term of office of the Chief Election Commissioner?

Ans. The term of office of the Chief Election Commissioner is six years or upto the age of 65 years, whichever is earlier.

Q. 19. What are the two kinds of elections in India?

Ans. The two kinds of elections are:

   (ii) Direct elections

   (ii) Indirect elections

Q. 20. Name the system of election to the office of the President of India.   **[February, 2020]**

Ans. The President of India is elected through indirect election by an Electoral College consisting of the elected members of both the Houses of the Parliament and the elected members of the Legislative Assemblies of the States.

Q. 21. Under what circumstances are Mid-term elections held?

Ans. Mid-term elections are held when a State Legislative Assembly or the Lok Sabha is dissolved before the completion of its full term of five years.

Q. 22. When was the Election Commission established in India?

Ans. Election Commission was established in India on 25th January, 1950.

Q. 23. What is an Electoral roll?

Ans. The electoral roll is a list of persons who are eligible to vote in a particular electoral district and who are registered to vote, if required in a particular jurisdiction.

Q. 24. What is voters list?

Ans. A voter list is a detailed record of every person who is registered and eligible to vote.

Q. 25. Who allots symbols to the political parties?

Ans. The Election Commission allots symbols to political parties.

Q. 26. By whom and on whose recommendations can a Regional Election Commissioner be removed?

Ans. Regional Election Commissioners can be removed by the President of India on the recommendation of the Chief Election Commissioner.

Q. 27. What do you mean by secret ballot?

Ans. A secret ballot system is a voting method in which all votes are cast in secret.

Q. 28. State any one importance of joint electorates.

Ans. Joint electorates promote communal harmony and goodwill. It also discourages communal politics.

Q. 29. Name any two bodies whose members are elected by indirect election.

Ans. Rajya Sabha and council of ministers are the two bodies whose members are elected by indirect election.

Q. 30. Define Election Commission.

Ans. An Election Commission is a body entrusted with the responsibility of implementing election mechanisms.

Q. 31. What is an Election Manifesto?

Ans. An election manifesto is a formal statement of the programme and objectives of a political party. It contains programmes and promises for all sections of the society.

Q. 32. Who allots the symbols to political parties? **[November, 2019]**

Ans. The Election Commission allots symbols to political parties.

Chapter 4. Rural Local Self Government

Q. 1. Name the highest organ of rural local self-government at the district level.

Ans. The highest organ of rural local self-government at the district level is Zila Parishad.

Q. 2. Mention any two limitations in efficient working of local self-governments.

Ans. Two limitations in efficient working of local self-government are:

    (i) Unethical means adopted in elections.

    (ii) Low rate of literacy.

Q. 3. Name three rural local self-government bodies.

Ans. The three rural local self-government bodies are Gram Sabha, Gram Panchayat and Nyaya Panchayat.

Q. 4. Who is the head of the Zila Parishad?

Ans. Every Zila parished is headed by a chair person, who is elected by the members of Parishads among themselves.

Q. 5. What is Nyaya Panchayat?

Ans. A Nyaya Panchayat is a system of dispute resolution at the village level. It is responsible for meeting out justice to the villagers in a speedy and economical manner.

Q. 6. Name the local bodies in rural areas that work at the block level.

Ans. Panchayat Samiti in rural areas work at the block level.

Q. 7. How much gap can be there between the dissolution of the panchayat and fresh elections?

Ans. The gap between the dissolution of the panchayat and holding of fresh elections can be six months or less.

Q. 8. How does the state government supervise the work of the Panchayat Samiti?

Ans. The working of the Panchayat Samiti is supervised by the state government through the Block Development Officer.

Q. 9. What is the head of a Village Panchayat called?

Ans. The head of the Village Panchayat is called the Sarpanch.

Q. 10. Mention any one function of the Zila Parishad. **[February, 2020]**

Ans. The Zila Parishad is responsible for undertaking many developmental functions like poverty eradication programmes, irrigation schemes, rural electrification, public distribution system and more.

Q. 11. Name the three-tier system of the Panchayati Raj. **[February, 2020]**

Ans. The three-tier system of the Panchayati Raj is known as the Panchayati Raj institutions.

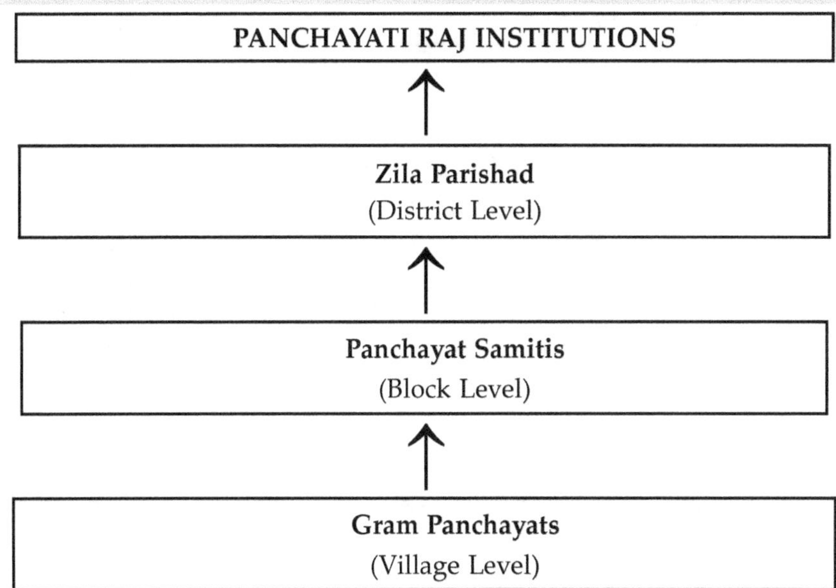

Q. 12. When and in which state was the Panchayati Raj System implemented for the first time in India?

Ans. Rajasthan was the first state to implement the Panchayati Raj System on 2nd October, 1959 at the village Nagaav.

Q. 13. Name the only political institution in India in which direct democracy is practised.

Ans. Gram Sabha is the only political institution in India in which direct democracy is practised.

Q. 14. What is the term of office of the Gram Panchayat?

Ans. The Gram Panchayat is elected for the term of five years.

Q. 15. What is Gram Sabha?

Ans. Gram Sabha is a sort of village assembly. It is a meeting of all adults who live in the area covered by a panchayat. Anyone who is 18 years old or more and who has the right to vote is a member of Gram Sabha.

Q. 16. What is Gram Panchayat?

Ans. The Gram Panchayat is the executive wing of the Gram Sabha. It is the focal point of a local self-governing institution in India.

Q. 17. What is the jurisdiction of a Nyaya Panchayat?

Ans. Nyaya Panchayat can impose monetary fine of ₹ 100 or ₹ 200 but cannot award a sentence of imprisonment.

Q. 18. What is the Chief Administrative Officer of the Panchayat Samiti known as?

Ans. The Chief Administrative Officer of the Panchayat Samiti is known as the Block Development Officer (BDO).

Q. 19. How and by whom can a Panchayat be removed from power?

Ans. A Panchayat can be removed from power by the Gram Sabha with the support of two-third of its members.

Q. 20. Name the committee that recommended the establishment of three-tier system of Panchayati Raj institutions.

Ans. Balwant Rai Mehta Committee recommended the establishment of three-tier system of Panchayati Raj institutions.

Q. 21. How much gap can there be between the dissolution of the Panchayat and fresh elections?

Ans. The gap between the dissolution of the Panchayat and holding of fresh elections can be six months or less.

Q. 22. Name the apex body under the Panchayati Raj System.   **[November, 2019]**

Ans. Zila Parishad is the apex body under the Panchayati Raj System.

Chapter 5. Urban Local Self Government

Q. 1. What is a Municipal Corporation? **[February, 2020]**

Ans. A Municipal Corporation is an elected body that is established in big cities with a population of 8 lakhs or more for running the civic affairs and looking after the needs of the people living in the area. Cities like Delhi, Kolkata, Chennai, Mumbai, Ahmedabad, Lucknow, Patna, Amritsar, Kanpur, Bengaluru, Bhopal, Jaipur, Thiruvananthapuram, etc. have Municipal Corporations. The functions of the municipal bodies are mentioned in the 12th Schedule of the Indian Constitution. It lists 18 subjects. These include town planning, roads, water supply, public health, slum redevelopment and provision and maintenance of public amenities like street lighting, public parks, conveniences, etc.

Q. 2. Who elects the members of Municipal Corporation?

Ans. Members of the Municipal Corporations are elected by the people through elections for a term of five years.

Q. 3. Which committee of the corporation takes policy decision?

Ans. Standing Committee of the corporation takes policy decisions.

Q. 4. Who are Aldermen? How are they elected?

Ans. Aldermen are renowned and respected people of the city who are elected to be members of the Municipal Corporation by the elected representatives of the people.

Q. 5. State any one function of the Mayor of a Municipal Corporation.

Ans. The Mayor presides over the meetings of the corporation and regulates the conduct of business.

Q. 6. By whom are the Municipal Corporations set up?

Ans. Municipal Corporations are set up under a special statute passed by the respective state's legislature. However, in an exception, in Delhi the power to set up a Municipal Corporation lies with the Union Parliament.

Q. 7. How are the members of the General Council of a Municipal Corporation elected? What is the term of their office?

Ans. Members of the General Council of a Municipal Corporation are elected directly based on Universal Adult Franchise via secret ballot for a period of five years and they are known as Municipal Councillors.

Q. 8. Mention any one important function of the Municipal Commissioner of a Municipal Corporation.

Ans. Municipal Commissioner implements the rules, policies and decisions of the Corporation.

Q. 9. Where are the Municipal Corporations established?

Ans. Municipal Corporations are established in big urban areas like Delhi, Mumbai, Chennai and Kolkata.

Q. 10. What is the role of the Standing Committee in a Municipal Corporation?

Ans. The General Council performs various functions through its standing committees. Each Standing Committee handles a specific area, such as, finance, taxation, budgets, public works, health, education, transport, electricity, water supply and sewerage.

Q. 11. What is a Municipal Committee? **[February, 2020]**

Ans. A Municipal Committee is an urban local body which is set up in smaller towns with a population above 20,000.

Q. 12. Mention any one function of the President of the Municipal Committee.

Ans. He/She presides over all the meetings of the Board and regulates how business is to be conducted in these meetings.

Q. 13. Who is the Chief Executive Officer of a Municipal Committee?

Ans. Chief Executive Officer is an appointee of the State Government. He looks after the administrative wing of the Municipal Committee.

Q. 14. According to which Act have urban local self-governing bodies been set up?

Ans. Urban local self-governing units have been set up according to the Nagar Palika Act of 1993.

Q. 15. Who is a Mayor?

Ans. Mayor is the head of the Municipal Corporation.

Q. 16. How many seats are reserved for women in Municipal Corporation?

Ans. One-third of the seats are reserved for women in Municipal Corporation.

Q. 17. In which areas were the first Municipal Corporations set up?

Ans. In the later half of the 19th Century, Municipal Corporations were set up in the Presidency towns of Kolkata, Mumbai and Chennai.

SECTION : B (HISTORY)

Chapter 1. The Harappan Civilisation

Q. 1. What is meant by the 'Chalcolithic Period'?

Ans. The period of history in which both stone and copper tools were used is known as the 'Chalcolithic Period'.

Q. 2. In which period of history was the Indus Valley Civilisation developed?

Ans. The Indus valley civilisation was developed during the Chalcolithic or Bronze Age.

Q. 3. Besides which river did Harappa flourish?

Ans. Harappa Flourished besides the Indus river.

Q. 4. Who discovered the Harappa city?

Ans. The city of Harappa was discovered by Daya Ram Sahni in 1921.

Q. 5. Why the Indus Valley Civilisation was named so?

Ans. The Indus Valley Civilisation was named so because the ruins of earliest cities were found in the valley of river Indus and its tributaries.

Q. 6. Why modern historians prefer to use the term Harappan Civilisation?

Ans. Modern historians prefer to use the word Harappan Civilisation because Harappa was the first site to be discovered and developed much before the Indus Valley Civilisation.

Q. 7. Name any four sites of Indus Valley Civilisation.

Ans. (i) Harappa
(iii) Kalibangan

(ii) Mohenjo-Daro
(iv) Lothal.

Q. 8. Who dugout the ruins of Mohenjo-Daro?

Ans. Mr. R. D. Banerjee dug out the ruins of Mohenjo-Daro in 1922.

Q. 9. What was the duration of Indus Civilisation?

Ans. From 2500 BCE to 1900 BCE.

Q. 10. Name the crops grown by the Harappan people.

Ans. Wheat, barley and rice were probably grown by the Harappan people.

Q. 11. Which animals were domesticated by the people of Harappa?

Ans. The people of Harappa reared animals like oxen, buffaloes, pigs, goats, sheep, camels, dogs and cats.

Q. 12. How do we know about the foreign trade prevalent in Harappa?

Ans. Many seals of Harappa found in Mesopotamia reveal that trade existed between two countries during the civilisation.

Q. 13. Mention one piece of art in stone discovered at Mohenjo-Daro which suggests that men wore a small trimmed beard.

Ans. A stone image of a yogi, draped in a shawl worn over the left shoulder is found in Mohenjo-Daro. His beard is well kept which shows that men wore a small trimmed beard.

Q. 14. Mention any four occupations of the Indus Valley people. (Frank)

Ans. (i)   Agriculture   (ii) Animal rearing
     (iii) Craft   (iv) Trade.

Q. 15. Name any two stone objects of sculpture recovered from the ruins of Mohenjo-Daro?

Ans. (i)   A figure of a nobleman or a 'priest king' draped in a shawl.
     (ii) Another figure is a male torso in red stone with socket holes in the neck and shoulders.

Q. 16. Where was the Great Granary discovered?

Ans. About six granaries have been discovered at Harappa.

Q. 17. What is the importance of seals excavated at various Harappan sites?

Ans. The seals highlighted the people's beliefs, script artistic skill, their physical features, ornaments, dresses, etc.

Q. 18. State any one features of the drainage system of Indus Valley people.

Ans. The drains of the houses were joined to the underground sewers in the streets which transported the waste to the large wells situated on the outskirts of the city.

Q. 19. Give any one evidence which suggests that the Indus Valley people knew the art of painting.

Ans. A painted pot from Lothal shows the paintings of a crow-like bird sitting on the branch of a tree.

Q. 20. "The Harappan Culture" was a highly developed urban civilisation. Give one example.

Ans. The ruins of drains, wells, the Great Bath, etc. found at Mohenjo-Daro evident the highly developed urban civilisation of the Harappan culture.

Q. 21. Why is the Indus Valley Civilisation called the 'Harappan Culture' or 'Harappan Civilisation'?

Ans. The Indus Valley Civilisation called the 'Harappan culture' or 'Harappan civilisation' because the first site of the Indus Valley Civilisation was discovered at Harappa.

Chapter 2. The Vedic Period

Q. 1. What do you mean by the term Aryan?

Ans. The term Aryan is derived from the Sanskrit word 'Arya' that means civilised or noble. As per German scholar Max Muller, the word 'Arya' literally signifies a language, not a race.

Q. 2. When did Aryans settle in India?

Ans. It is believed that the Aryans were first settled in India between 1500 to 1000 BC.

Q. 3. What do you understand by the term Veda?

Ans. (i)   The term 'Veda' comes from the word 'Ved' which signifies 'knowledge'.
     (ii) The hymns of Vedas were addressed to gods and passed down to generations in the form of oral-recitation.

Q. 4. Name the four Vedas, which one is the oldest?

Ans. The Rigveda, the Sama Veda, the Yajurveda and the Atharva Veda. The Rigveda is the oldest among the four.

Q. 5. How many hymns are there in the Rigveda?

Ans. There are 1028 hymns (Suktas) contained in the Rigveda and they in turn divided into mandalas.

Q. 6. How do you explain the term 'vedic literature'?

Ans. The term 'Vedic Literature' simply means to the four Vedas and their collections along with the allied literature derived from the Vedas.

Q. 7. Mention the names of any five gods, personified as forces of nature in the Vedic texts.

Ans. Indra, Agni, Varun, Surya and Yama.

Q. 8. What were the main occupations of the people in the early vedic period?

Ans. Agriculture and cattle rearing were the main occupations in the early vedic period.

Q. 9. Write the names of any two female deities mentioned in the Vedas.

Ans. Aditi and Usha.

Q. 10. Name the Veda which contains the Gayatri Mantra.

Ans. The Rigveda.

Q. 11. Name the Veda that comprises hymns to be chanted during the Vedic sacrifices.

Ans. The Yajurveda comprises 2086 hymns chanted during sacrifices.

Q. 12. What do you understand by the term 'upanishad'?

Ans. The term Upanishad has been derived from the root Upanishad which means 'to sit down near someone'. It signifies the knowledge imparted by the guru to his selected disciples or shishyas.

Q. 13. Give evidence to show that early vedic people worshipped their gods in the open air.

Ans. The early vedic people had no temple and images. The gods were worshipped through prayers in the form of chanting hymns and by performing sacrifices.

Q. 14. Name the epic of which Bhagwad Gita forms a part.

Ans. Mahabharat.

Q. 15. Mention any one feature of the religious sacrifices in the later Vedic Period.

Ans. Sacrifices were performed to please the gods which included offerings of milk, juice of soma plant, grains, ghee and flesh.

Q. 16. What do you understand by Vedangas?

Ans. (i) The Vedangas means limbs of the Vedas that are six in numbers.

(ii) The Vedangas interpret the Vedas in simple language and deal with the pronunciation of words, grammar, astronomy as well as rituals.

Q. 17. What do you know about Brahmanas?

Ans. The Brahmanas are written in prose explaining hymns of the Vedas.

Q. 18. Which Vedic text gives reference to the Varna System? What are these four Varnas?

Ans. (i) The Purusha Sukta, in the tenth mandala of the Rigveda, gives reference to the four-fold Varna System.

(ii) This four-fold Varna System comprised four castes namely the Brahmanas, Kshatriya, Vaishyas and Shudras.

Q. 19. Which kind of government existed in the Rigvedic Age?

Ans. Monarchy was the system of government which prevailed in the Rigvedic Age.

Q. 20. What was the important role of 'Rajan' in the Vedic Age?

Ans. The most important duty of the 'Rajan' or 'King' was to protect the tribe from internal troubles and external dangers.

Chapter 3. Jainism And Buddhism

Q. 1. Who was Vardhmana Mahavira?

Ans. Vardhmana Mahavira was the twenty fourth and last tirthankara of Jainism.

Q. 2. When and where was Lord Mahavira born?

Ans. Lord Mahavira is believed to have been born in 599 BC at Kundagrama, in Vaishali Bihar.

Q. 3. Name the two sects of Jainism.

Ans. Digambaras and Swetambaras.

Q. 4. In which language most of the Jain books were written?

Ans. Ardh-Magadhi and Prakrit.

Q. 5. Who was the founder of the Buddhism?

Ans. Gautama Buddha was the founder of Buddhism.

Q. 6. When and where was Gautama Buddha born?

Ans. Gautama Buddha was born about 567 BC at Lumbini near Kapilvastu.

Q. 7. Name the 'Four Great Sights'.

Very Short Questions

Ans. The four Great Sights that influence the Gautam Buddha were:

   (i) An old man   (ii) A sick man

   (iii) A corpse   (iv) An ascetic seeking salvation.

Q. 8. What is the Ashtangika Marg?

Ans. In Buddhism the way that leads to Nirvana is known as the Ashtangika Marg or the Eightfold path.

Q. 9. In which language was the early Buddhist literature written?

Ans. The holy Buddhist literature was written in languages of Pali, Sanskrit and mixed Sanskrit.

Q. 10. When and where did Gautam Buddha get enlightenment?

Ans. Buddha got enlightenment at the age of 35 under a Pipal tree situated in Bodh Gaya in Bihar.

Q. 11. Name two rulers of North India who helped to spread Buddhism.

Ans. Ashoka, Kanishka.

Q. 12. Name two places known for Buddhist Chaityas.

Ans. (i) Karle in Pune district of Maharashtra.

      (ii) Ajanta Caves near Aurangabad in Maharashtra.

Q. 13. Name three places where Ashokan pillars are found.

Ans. Sarnath, Sanchi and Allahabad.

Q. 14. Which was the earliest school of art that made entirely Indian representation of the Buddha in human form?

Ans. Mathura School of Art.

Q. 15. Name the two sects in which Buddhism was later divided.

Ans. Hinayana and Mahayana.

Chapter 4. The Mauryan Empire

Q. 1. Which famous book was written by Megasthenes?

Ans. Indika.

Q. 2. What are the two foreign literary sources of information of the Mauryan period?

Ans. (i) Megasthenes' Indika   (ii) Vishakhadatta's Mudrarakshasa.

Q. 3. Name the two important archaeological sources that provide description of Ashoka's reign.

Ans. (i) The Rock Edicts of Ashoka.   (2) The 'Great Stupa' at Sanchi.

Q. 4. Who founded the Mauryan Empire?

Ans. Chandragupta Maurya founded the Mauryan Empire.

Q. 5. Which dynasty ruled Magadha before the advent of Chandragupta?

Ans. Before Chandragupta come to power, Magadha was ruled by the Nanda dynasty.

Q. 6. Which of the two titles were assumed by Ashoka after his coronation?

Ans. After ascending the throne, Ashoka took the titles of 'Priyadarshi' meaning 'The Beautiful one' and 'Devanamapriya' that means 'The Beloved of the Gods'.

Q. 7. When was the Kalinga War fought?

Ans. The Kalinga War was fought in 261 BC.

Q. 8. What do you understand by the term 'Dhamma'?

Ans. As explained in the Ashokan Edicts, the 'Dhamma' was to be a moral law or an 'ethical order', which was a common meeting ground of all religions.

Q. 9. When was the Mauryan Empire found?

Ans. The Mauryan Empire was founded in 324 BC by removing the Nandas.

Q. 10. Who was the last Nanda ruler?

Ans. Dhanananda was the last Nanda ruler.

Q. 11. Who was Megasthenes?

Ans. Megasthenes was the Greek diplomat of Seleucus Nicator who visited India during Chandragupta reign.

Q. 12. Name the four provinces that were won by Chandragupta Maurya after defeating Seleucus.

Ans. Herat, Kabul, Baluchistan and Kandhar.

Q. 13. What was the duration of Ashoka's reign?

Ans. The emperor Ashoka ruled the Indian sub-continent from 269 BC to 232 BC.

Q. 14. What were Janapadas?

Ans. During ancient period the huge provinces were subdivided into many districts which were called as Janapadas.

Q. 15. Name the four provinces in which the Mauryan empire was divided.

Ans. Magadha, Avanti, Gandhara and the Southern Province.

Q. 16. How did Mauryan Empire come to an end?

Ans. Pushya Mitra Sunga, the Mauryan General killed the last Mauryan king, Brihadratha in about 187 BC. This incident marked the end of Mauryan Empire.

Q. 17. Why governors were appointed in the capitals of provinces?

Ans. The governors who were known as Aryaputra were appointed in the capitals to manage their provinces properly.

Chapter 5. The Sangam Age

Q. 1. Which period of the Indian History is called as the Sangam Age?

Ans. The duration in southern India from 600 BC to AD 300 is called as the Sangam Age.

Q. 2. What do you understand by the term 'Sangam'?

Ans. The word 'Sangam' is a Sanskrit word which literally means assemblies or association.

Q. 3. Name two groups into which the Sangam literature was divided.

Ans. (i) The Melkannakku or Eighteen Major Works is narrative.

(ii) The Kilkanakku or Eighteen Minor Works is didactic.

Q. 4. What are Megaliths?

Ans. Megaliths are large stones that form a prehistoric monument or part of one. The graves of earliest people were known as Megaliths.

Q. 5. Name the two tamil epics written during the Sangam period.

Ans. Silappadikaram and Manimekalai.

Q. 6. What was the chief occupation of the people dwelling in the Sangam Age?

Ans. Agriculture was the chief occupation of the people dwelling in the Sangam Age.

Q. 7. What is Tolkappiyam?

Ans. Tolkappiyam is the earliest literary work of Tamil literature written by Tolkappiyar.

Q. 8. What were the four divisions of the Sangam society?

Ans. According to Tolkappiyam, the Sangam society was divided into four castes named Anthanar, Arasar, Vaishyas and Vellalas.

Q. 9. Name the chief deities worshipped by Tamil people.

Ans. The chief deities worshipped by Tamil people were Murugan (son of shiva), Mayon (Vishnu), Vendhan (Indira), Varunan and Kotrravai.

Q. 10. Name the crops cultivated by the Tamil people.

Ans. The major crops cultivated by the Tamil people were paddy, ragi, millet, cotton, sweet potato, pepper, ginger, sugarcane and jackfruit.

Q. 11. What were the artificial sources of water in the Sangam Age during the dry season?

Ans. Ring wells and tanks were the artificial sources of water supply during the dry season for irrigation.

Q. 12. Name three items that were exported during the Sangam Age.

Ans. (i) Precious stones, (ii) Spices and (iii) Silk and Cotton textile.

Q. 13. Name any two important centres of Sangam Age for the manufacture of cotton fabrics.

Ans. Uraiyar and Madurai were the main centres for the manufacture of cotton fabrics.

Q. 14. List the different sources of revenue for the kingdoms of the Sangam Age.

Ans. Karai, profits from trade, transit duties and spoils of war were the main sources of revenue during the Sangam Age.

Q. 15. What was Karai in the Sangam Age?

Ans. In the Sangam Age, revenue from agriculture was called 'Karai' which was raised on one-sixth of the total produce.

Q. 16. Why were herostones installed?

Ans. Herostones were installed to honour the heroes who sacrificed for the community.

Q. 17. Why were the graves of the earliest people called the Megaliths?

Ans. The graves of the earliest people are called Megaliths because they were encircled by huge pieces of stones.

Chapter 6. The Age of Guptas

Q. 1. Which period is regarded as the Golden Age of Indian culture?

Ans. AD 320 to AD 480 is regarded as the Golden Age of Indian culture.

Q. 2. Who is regarded as the real founder of the Gupta Empire?

Ans. Chandragupta I is regarded as the real founder of the Gupta Empire.

Q. 3. Where was the Mauryan capital set up by Chandragupta?

Ans. Chandragupta set up his capital at Pataliputra (Patna), Bihar.

Q. 4. Who wrote the Allahabad pillar inscription?

Ans. Harisena wrote the Allahabad pillar inscription.

Q. 5. From where do we get the information about Samudragupta?

Ans. The inscriptions of Allahabad pillar provide a vivid account for Samudragupta.

Q. 6. Name the two main sects of Hinduism during the Gupta period.

Ans. (i) Vaishnavism (Worship of God Vishnu)　　　(ii) Shaivism (Worship of God Shiva)

Q. 7. What was the official language of the Gupta empire?

Ans. The official language of Guptas was Sanskrit.

Q. 8. Who is called the Shakespeare of India?

Ans. Kalidas, the most briliant leminary in the literary firmament is called the Shakespeare of India.

Q. 9. Who was the great grammarian of the Gupta period?

Ans. Panini was the great grammarian of the Gupta period.

Q. 10. Name two schools of sculpture that flourished during the Gupta period.

Ans. (i) Mathura school of Art　　　(ii) Gandhara school of Art

Q. 11. Name the astronomer of the Gupta period after whose name the first Indian satellite was named.

Ans. Aryabhatta.

Q. 12. Name any two educational institutions that flourished during Gupta period.

Ans. (i) Nalanda University　　　(ii) Taxila University.

Q. 13. Name the author of Mrichchakatikan.

Ans. Shudraka.

Q. 14. Who wrote Brahmasphuta Siddhanta?

Ans. Brahmagupta a noted mathematician wrote the Brahmasphuta Siddhanta.

Q. 15. Write one example to justify that theft was rare in the Gupta empire.

Ans. Gold left on road could be recovered after days which justifies that people were content and prospered and theft was rare in the Gupta empire.

Q. 16. How do inscriptions prove the charitable nature of the Gupta kings?

Ans. The Sanchi inscription, Tumain inscription, the Katni copperplate of Jayantha, the Tosham rock inscriptions proved that Gupta kings donated generously for religious and charity purposes.

Q. 17. After whose death did the Gupta Empire gradually fade into obscurity?

Ans. The Gupta Empire gradually faded into obscurity after the death of Skandagupta.

Q. 18. To which dynasty did Harshavardhana belong?

Ans. Pushyabhuti dynasty or Varadhan dynasty.

Q. 19. Name the Chinese pilgrim who visited India during the reign of Harsha.

Ans. Hiuen Tsang.

Q. 20. Who wrote Harshacharita?

Ans. Banabhatta.

Chapter 7. The Cholas

Q. 1. Name the three major ruling kingdoms of South India.

Ans. The Cholas, the Pandyas and the Cheras were the major ruling kingdoms of South India.

Q. 2. Mention any two victories of Cholas under Rajaraja I.

Ans. Cholas annexed the kingdoms of Kalinga and Maldives under Rajaraja I.

Q. 3. What is a Garbhagriha?

Ans. The main shrine of the temple where the image of the main deity is kept is called a Garbhagriha.

Q. 4. Define the term Devadana?

Ans. The lands donated to the temples were called Devadana or Devadaya. The benefit of revenue from that land went to the temple.

Q. 5. What is a Mandapa?

Ans. Mandapa is the audience hall in front of the main shrine. People gather here for prayers.

Q. 6. In which languages were the copper plates and pillars engraved by the Chola rulers?

Ans. Most of the copper plates and pillar were written in Tamil but some were bilingual and were written in Sanskrit as well.

Q. 7. List the four major dynasties of South India from the middle of the 8th century CE to the 10th century CE.

Ans. (i) Chalukyas   (ii) Rashtrakutas
(iii) Pallavas   (iv) Cholas

Q. 8. Which temple is considered to be the best example of Chola temples?

Ans. Brihadeshwara temple is considered to be one of the best examples of Chola temples.

Q. 9. Which two languages were promoted by the Cholas?

Ans. Cholas promoted Tamil and Sanskrit.

Q. 10. Name the two important Chola kings.

Ans. Two important Chola kings were Rajaraja I and Rajendra Chola.

Q. 11. Where can we find the best examples of the Chola paintings?

Ans. The best examples of Chola paintings are found in the pradakshina of the Rajarajeshwara temple.

Q. 12. What is considered the masterpiece of Chola sculpture?

Ans. The bronze image of Shiva as Nataraj is a masterpiece of the Chola sculpture.

Q. 13. Name the main deity that the Chola kings worshipped.

Ans. The Chola emperors worshipped Lord Shiva.

Q. 14. Where did Rajendra I built an artificial lake?

Ans. Rajendra I built an artificial lake near his capital Gangaikondacholapuram.

Q. 15. Who was the first Chola ruler?

Ans. Karikala was the first Chola ruler.

Q. 16. Name the new capital founded by Rajendra I.

Ans. Gangaikondacholapuram was the new capital founded by Rajendra I.

Q. 17. What were the Chola Temples known for?

Ans. The Chola temples were known for their massive vimanas or towers and spacious courtyards.

Q. 18. Who was Vijayalya?

Ans. Vijayalya was known as the founder of the later Chola Empire who captured Tanjore from Pandayas and made Tanjore his capital.

Q. 19. Which Chola ruler was given the title of 'Gangaikonda'?

Ans. Rajendra Chola was given the title of 'Gangaikonda'.

Q. 20. Who wrote the Tamil Ramayana?

Ans. Kamban wrote the Tamil Ramayana.

Chapter 8. The Delhi Sultanate

Q. 1. Why did Ala-ud-din Khalji start the practice of branding horses?

Ans. Ala-ud-din Khalji started the practice of branding horses or, dagh so that the soldiers cannot replace them with horses of substandard quality.

Q. 2. Who laid the foundation of Tughluq dynasty and when?

Ans. Ghiyas-ud-din Tughluq was the founder of Tughluq dynasty in 1320 AD.

Q. 3. Which two coins were introduced by Iltutmish?

Ans. Iltutmish introduced two types of coins- the silver tankas and the copper jittals.

Q. 4. Which Tughluq ruler is known as the 'Man of Opposites'?

Ans. Muhammad bin Tughluq is known as the 'Man of Opposites'.

Q. 5. Who was the last Turkish conqueror of North India?

Ans. Muhammad Ghori was the last Turkish conqueror of North India.

Q. 6. Which five dynasties formed the Sultanate of Delhi?

Ans. The five dynasties that formed the Sultanate of Delhi were, Ilbari or Slave dynasty, Khalji dynasty, Tughluq dynasty, Sayyid dynasty and the Lodhi dynasty.

Q. 7. Who laid the foundation of Qutb Minar?

Ans. Qutbuddin Aibak laid the foundation of Qutb Minar.

Q. 8. Name the first woman ruler of Medieval India.

Ans. Razia Sultan was the first woman ruler of Medieval India.

Q. 9. Who was Balban?

Ans. Balban was the last powerful ruler of the Slave dynasty. His reign marked the beginning of the rule of the Khalji dynasty.

Q. 10. Who was the founder of the Khalji dynasty?

Ans. Jalaluddin Firuz Khalji was the founder of the Khalji dynasty.

Q. 11. Name the places Ala-ud-din Khalji conquered.

Ans. Ala-ud-din Khalji conquered Gujarat, Ranthambhor, Chittor, Malwa, Siwana and Jalore.

Q. 12. What was Barani's most famous work?

Ans. Barani's Tarikh-i-Firuz Shahi, named after Firuz Tughluq I was the most valuable historical work written during the Sultanate period.

Q. 13. What were the provinces divided into?

Ans. The provinces were divided into smaller units of administration called shiqs, each placed under a Shiqdar.

Q. 14. Name the last Delhi Sultan who was defeated by Babur in the Battle of Panipat.

Ans. Ibrahim Lodhi was the last Delhi Sultan who was defeated by Babur in the Battle of Panipat.

Q. 15. Mention the period of Delhi Sultanate in India.

Ans. The period of the Delhi Sultanate in India was from 1206 AD to 1526 AD.

Q. 16. Who was Ala-ud-din Khalji's capable general?

Ans. Malik Kafur was Ala-ud-din Khalji's Capable general.

Q. 17. Mention two dynasties which came up after the decline of Tughluq dynasty?

Ans. Sayyid and Lodhi dynasty came up after the decline of Tughluq dynasty.

Q. 18. Who was the first Muslim invader of India?

Ans. Muhammad bin Qasim was the first Muslim invader of India.

Q. 19. Which sultan considered himself as God's shadow on earth?

Ans. Balban considered himself as God's shadow on earth.

Q. 20. Who invited Babur to invade India?

Ans. Daulat Khan Lodhi invited Babur to invade India.

Chapter 9. The Mughal Empire

Q. 1. Who wrote Ain-i-Akbari?

Ans. Abul Fazl wrote Ain-i-Akbari.

Q. 2. Who was the founder of Mughal Empire in India?

Ans. Zahir-ud-din Muhammad Babur was the founder of Mughal Empire in India.

Q. 3. Why did the Mughals call themselves Timurids?

Ans. Mughals called themselves Timurids because of their connection with Timur.

Q. 4. When and between whom was the first battle of Panipat fought?

Ans. First battle of Panipat was fought in the year 1526 between Babur and Ibrahim Lodhi.

Q. 5. Which were the important departments of the central government under Akbar?

Ans. Revenue and finance, defence, religious endowment and charity, and the imperial household were the important departments of Akbar's central government.

Q. 6. Who were the principle powers against whom Babur won his victories?

Ans. Babur won his victories against the Afghans and Rajputs who were the principle power in India at that time.

Q. 7. Which Mughal ruler has been called the 'Prince of builders'?

Ans. Shah Jahan has been called the 'Prince of builders'.

Q. 8. What is the Akbarnama?

Ans. Akbarnama is the official history of the Mughals commissioned by Akbar. It was written by Abul Fazl.

Q. 9. Who was known as the 'keeper of the King's purse' in Akbar's court?

Ans. Diwan was known as the 'keeper of the King's purse' in Akbar's court.

Q. 10. What was Jaziya? Which Mughal ruler reimposed it?

Ans. Jaziya was the tax collected from the non-Muslims. It was reimposed by Aurangzeb.

Q. 11. What is the autobiography of Babur called?

Ans. Babur's autobiography is called Tuzuk-i-Baburi.

Q. 12. What is the autobiography of Jahangir called?

Ans. Jahangir's autobiography is called Tuzuk-i-Jahangiri.

Q. 13. Why did Humayun spend 15 years in exile?

Ans. Sher Shah, an Afghan ruler, defeated Humayun at Chausa and Kannauj in 1539 CE and 1540 CE, respectively. Following this defeat, Humayun fled to Persia and remained in exile for fifteen years.

Q. 14. What was the basic principle of Sulh-i-Kul?

Ans. Sulh-i-Kul meant 'universal peace'. Its objective was not to discriminate between people belonging to different religions in Akbar's kingdom.

Q. 15. Where was the Ibadatkhana situated? What was its purpose?

Ans. Akbar built a hall of worship called Ibadatkhana at Fatehpur Sikri in 1575, where he invited selected theologians and mystics to foster philosophical discussions.

Q. 16. Which proved to be the last conquest of Akbar and why?

Ans. In 1601 CE, Asirgarh, a fort in the Deccan, proved to be the last conquest of Akbar's life. Akbar had to leave the Deccan for the North where his son, prince Salim had revolted. In 1605, Akbar died.

Q. 17. Who was the last Mughal ruler?

Ans. Bahadur Shah Zafar was the last Mughal ruler.

Q. 18. Who was Nur Jahan?

Ans. Nur Jahan was the queen of Jahangir. She was the daughter of a Persian noble, Mirza Ghiyas Beg.

Q. 19. What do you mean by the term 'mansab'?

Ans. The word 'mansab' means a place or position and therefore, it means a rank in the mansab system under the Mughals.

Q. 20. Name any two taxes abolished by Aurangzeb in the year 1659.

Ans. On being officially crowned in 1659, Aurangzeb abolished octroi tax (pandari) and the inland transit duties (rahdari).

Chapter 10. Emergence of Composite Culture

Q. 1. Whose dargah is situated in Ajmer?

Ans. The dargah of sufi saint Moinuddin Chisti is situated in Ajmer.

Q. 2. Which famous explorer was buried in the St Francis Assisi Church , Kochi?

Ans. The Portuguese explorer Vasco da Gama was buried in the St Francis Assisi Church , Kochi.

Q. 3. Name two important sufi saints.

Ans. Two important sufi saints were Hazrat Khwaja Nizamuddin Auliya and Hazrat Khwaja Moinuddin Chisti.

Q. 4. Mention how Sufism encouraged the growth of vernacular literature?

Ans. Sufism also influenced the poets of that period. Amir Khusrau and Malik Muhammad Jayasi wrote poems in Persian and Hindi praising Sufi principles. They played a great role in promoting vernacular literature.

Q. 5. Who emphasised the concept of Ik Onkar?

Ans. Guru Nanak emphasised concept of Ik Onkar.

Q. 6. What do you understand by the term 'Bhakti'?

Ans. The word 'Bhakti' means 'Devotion to God'.

Q. 7. What is meant by Bhakti cult?

Ans. Bhakti cult was a reform movement within Hinduism. It stressed on the unity of God and brotherhood of man without any consideration of caste, creed or race distinctions.

Q. 8. Name a few famous Bhakti saints.

Ans. A few famous Bhakti saints were Madhavacharya, Kabir, Mira Bai, Chaitanya Mahaprabhu, Ramananda and Ramanujacharya.

Q. 9. Who was St Francis Xavier?

Ans. St Francis was one of the 12 apostles of Christ and had all the virtues necessary for a missionary. He was born in Xavier, Spain and was the co-founder of the Society of Jesus.

Q. 10. What were Khanqahs?

Ans. Khanqahs were like hospices. It was a place where the Sufi masters held their assemblies.

Q. 11. What is Bijak?

Ans. Bijak is the compilation of teachings and philosophy of Kabir. It is the holy scripture for the followers of the Kabirpanthis.

Q. 12. Name any two Sikh Gurus whose hymns are included in the Adi Granth.

Ans. Adi Granth is vast collection of sermons and hymns of the five Sikh Gurus-Guru Nanak, Guru Angad, Guru Amardas, Guru Ramdas and Guru Arjun Devji.

Q. 13. Who sought the Raja's permission to build a fort at Kochi?

Ans. Alfonsa de Albuquerque sought the Raja's permission to build a fort at Kochi.

Q. 14. Mention any two literary sources which throw light on the composite culture.

Ans. Bijak and Guru Granth Sahib are two literary sources which throw light on the composite culture.

Q. 15. Who founded the Sikh religion?

Ans. Guru Nanak Dev was the founder of Sikh religion.

Q. 16. Who followed St Francis Xavier in 1605 after his death?

Ans. Robert de Nobili followed Francis Xavier after his death in 1605.

Q. 17. Name two poets who were influenced by Sufism.

Ans. Malik Muhammad Jayasi and Amir Khusrau were influenced by Sufism.

Q. 18. Who founded the Chisti order (silsilah)?

Ans. Hazrat Khwaja Moinuddin Chisti founded the Chisti order.

Q. 19. Name two famous Sufi saints of the Suhrawardi order.

Ans. Sheikh Shahabuddin Suhrawardi and Khwaja Hamiduddin Nagori were two famous Sufi saints of the Suhrawardi order.

Q. 20. Which Sikh Guru announced the end of personal guruship and named Guru Granth Sahib as the Guru of the Sikhs?

Ans. Guru Gobind Singh, the tenth Guru, announced the end of personal guruship and named Guru Granth Sahib as the Guru of the Sikhs.

Chapter 11. The Modern Age in Europe Renaissance

Q. 1. In what way did the spread of education contribute to liberal thinking?

Ans. The spread of education in the later middle ages changed the outlook of the people in Europe. It made the people to think rationally.

Q. 2. What was feudalism?

Ans. Feudalism is a system of land ownership and duties. In this system, the society functioned through the means of land tenure which bound everyone, right from the king to the smallest landowner through a series of defences and obligations.

Q. 3. Name two thinkers who challenged the age-old beliefs.

Ans. Roger Bacon and Giordano Bruno challenged the age-old beliefs.

Q. 4. Who encouraged art and learning in Europe?

Ans. Popes, emperors, kings, princes and rich merchants of Europe encouraged art and learning in Europe.

Q. 5. Name one Italian city which became a great centre of art and learning in the 15th century CE.

Ans. Venice became a great centre of art and learning in the 15th century.

Q. 6. What role did the printing press play in ushering the spirit of Renaissance?

Ans. The invention of printing press made the books easily available and cheap, thus education began to spread among the masses. So, printing press played an important role in ushering the spirit of Renaissance.

Q. 7. Who set out to discover a western sea route to the East Indies and reached the Americas in 1492 CE?

Ans. Christopher Columbus set out to discover a western sea route to the East Indies and reached the Americas in 1492 CE.

Q. 8. Why did the Renaissance artists pay great attention to the physical aspects of human existence?

Ans. Renaissance artists looked upon art as an imitation of life. For them world was a place of beauty and the purpose of art was to provide pleasure to the senses. Therefore, they paid great attention to the physical aspects of human existence.

Q. 9. What did the Renaissance artist do to show that perfection can be human without being exclusively divine?

Ans. They painted human figures as more beautiful than any other object in nature.

Q. 10. Name two of the famous Renaissance painters.

Ans. Michelangelo and Leonardo da Vinci were two famous Renaissance painters.

Q. 11. What is meant by optimism?

Ans. Optimism means to be positive in thought. It implies that man can improve his own destiny.

Q. 12. What inspired Leonardo da Vinci to paint his objects of art beautifully?

Ans. Leonardo believed that painting should be an imitation of nature and that living things are but a testimony to the presence of the divine spirit in them.

Q. 13. What did Copernicus think about the planetary system?

Ans. According to Copernicus, the Sun was the centre of the universe and the Earth and the stars all revolved around the Sun. This is called the heliocentric idea of the universe.

Q. 14. Why is Renaissance considered as an Intellectual Movement?

Ans. Renaissance brought developments in the field of art, literature, science, politics, religion and philosophy. Therefore, it is considered as an Intellectual movement.

Q. 15. Mention the country where the scholars took refuge after the siege of Constantinople.

Ans. The scholars took refuge in Italy after the siege of Constantinople.

Q. 16. What is the main feature of humanism?

Ans. The main feature of humanism is that 'man' is central to the aims of thought and civilisation.

Q. 17. Name the explorer who reached Kerala's coast of Calicut in 1498.

Ans. Vasco-da-Gama, a Portuguese explorer reached Kerala's coastal town of Calicut in 1498.

Q. 18. Name the English writer who is regarded as 'Bard to Avon'.

Ans. William Shakespeare is regarded as England's national poet and is known as the 'Bard to Avon'.

Q. 19. Name one piece of painting by Michelangelo.

Ans. The Last Judgement and The Fall of Man are among the most beautiful frescoes on the ceilings of the Sistine Chapel in Vatican.

Q. 20. Define Renaissance. **[November, 2019]**

Ans. The term Renaissance is derived from the Latin world 'renascere'. It was the period in Europe between the 14th and 17th centuries when there was a surge of interest in productions of art and literature.

It signifies "the rebirth of the freedom-loving thought", which during the Middle Ages had been fettered and imprisoned by religious authority.

Chapter 12. The Modern Age in Europe Reformation

Q. 1. What is meant by Reformation?

Ans. Reformation is a general name that is given to a set of religious movements that aimed at reforming the Church. It was initiated by a Christian priest name Martin Luther in Europe.

Q. 2. Name two groups into which Christianity was divided in the 16th century CE.

Ans. In the 16th century, Christianity was divided into two groups-the Roman Catholics and Protestants.

Q. 3. Who was Martin Luther?

Ans. Martin Luther was a German Monk of the order of Saint Augustine. He was a professor of philosophy and religion at the University of Wittenberg in Germany. He started Reformation Movement.

Q. 4. What were Martin Luther's views on the sale of Indulgences?

Ans. He turned strongly against the church and openly criticised the papacy for selling indulgences. He pointed out that no one on earth was capable of forgiving sins.

Q. 5. Who were Anabaptists?

Ans. Anabaptists didn't believe in infant baptism because they thought that only those who truly understood and accepted the teachings of God could be legitimately baptized. For them, baptism required a public acknowledgement of their faith.

Q.6. Name the Pope who wanted to build St. Peter's Basiliec with the new architectural designs.

Ans. Pope Leo X wanted to build St. Peter's Basilica with the new architectural designs.

Q. 7. Why did Luther not support the Anabaptist's doctrine?

Ans. Due to the fear of losing the support of the German Princes, Martin Luther did not support the Anabaptist doctrine.

Q. 8. Who was responsible for the spread of Protestantism in Switzerland?

Ans. Ulrich Zwingli spread Protestantism in Switzerland.

Q. 9. Name the leading Protestant reformer in France.

Ans. John Calvin was a leading Protestant reformer in France.

Q. 10. Who were known as Jesuits?

Ans. A great step towards strengthening the Catholic Church was taken by a band of selfless workers known as Jesuits.

Q. 11. Name the Pope who first organised an attempt at making the Catholic Church corruption-free.

Ans. The first organised an attempt to make the Catholic Church corruption-free was made by Pope Paul III.

Q. 12. What was the importance of the Council of Trent?

Ans. The Council of Trent took up strict measures to maintain discipline among the Church officials.

Q. 13. Who was the author of the Ninety-Five Theses?

Ans. Martin Luther was the author of Ninety-Five Theses.

Q. 14. What was the Inquisition?

Ans. It was a special tribunal instituted by the Church to suppress heresy. It was started in 12th-century France to combat religious dissent.

Q. 15. Who founded the Society of Jesus?

Ans. Ignatius Loyola, an invalid soldier from Spain, founded an organisation known as the Society of Jesus.

Q. 16. Mention the name of the pamphlet in which Martin Luther condemned the practices of the Church.

Ans. Martin Luther condemned the practices of the Church in a Pamphlet titled 'The Babylonian Captivity of the Church'.

Q. 17. What did the Society of Jesus do for the Church?

Ans. It rendered selfless service to the Church and humanity.

Q. 18. Who translated the Holy Bible into German language?

Ans. Martin Luther translated the Holy Bible into German language.

Q. 19. What was the Act of Supremacy?

Ans. According to this Act the English monarchs became the clergy and the supreme head of the Church of England.

Q. 20. What was the main focus of the book 'In Praise of Folly' written by Erasmus?

Ans. In his book, Erasmus denounced the evil practices of the Church and emphasised on the return of Bible as a source of authority.

Q. 21. Who founded the Society of Jesus?

Ans. The Society of Jesus was founded by a Spanish noble, Ignatius Loyola in AD 1534.

Q. 22. Who has been called the 'Morning Star' of Reformation?

Ans. John Wycliffe has been called the 'Morning Star' of Reformation.

Q. 23. Name the English monarch who broke connections with the Pope of Rome.

Ans. Henry VIII, the King of England, broke connections with the Pope of Rome.

Q. 24. According to Thomas Moore, what was the concept of the term 'Utopia'?

Ans. 'Utopia' was the name he gave to the ideal and imaginary island nation, where there is no exploitation and no class distinction.

Chapter 13. The Modern Age in Europe Industrial Revolution

Q. 1. The inventions of which machines helped the Industrial Revolution?

Ans. Inventions of Flying Shuttle, Spinning Jenny and Steam Engine helped the Industrial Revolution.

Q. 2. How did the Industrial Revolution widen the gap between the rich and the poor?

Ans. The economic disparity between the rich capitalists and the poor workers led to social inequalities. There was a wide gulf between the social status of the capitalists and the workers.

Q. 3. Who was Karl Marx?

Ans. Karl Marx was a German philosopher and economist and was the most outstanding figure in whole socialist movement.

Q. 4. When was the Communist Manifesto published?

Ans. On February 21, 1848, The Communist Manifesto, written by Karl Marx with the assistance of Friedrich Engels, was published in London.

Q. 5. With which invention is James Hargreaves associated?

Ans. James Hargreaves is associated with the invention of Spinning Jenny.

Q. 6. Name the author of the book 'Das Capital'.

Ans. Karl Marx wrote and published Volume One, but his friend and political ally, Friedrich Engels, edited and published Volumes Two and Three.

Q. 7. What is meant by Socialism?

Ans. Socialism means social or communal control over the means of production.

Q. 8. What is meant by capitalism?

Ans. Capitalism is the economic system in which individuals or groups of individuals own and controls the means of production.

Q. 9. When and in which country did Industrial revolution begin?

Ans. Industrial Revolution began in England in about 1750 AD.

Q. 10. Mention any two famous early inventions in the field of power.

Ans. Steam Engine by James Watt and Locomotive by George Stephenson are the two famous early inventions in the field of power.

Q. 11. When and by whom was the term Industrial Revolution first used?

Ans. The term Industrial Revolution was first used in 1837 by Blanqui.

Q. 12. What do you mean by the term 'Industrial Revolution'?

Ans. Industrial Revolution signifies a series of revolutionary changes that took place in the fields of industry and production.

●●

Short Questions | Set 2 |

SECTION : A (CIVICS)

Chapter 1. Indian Constitution

Q. 1. Mention any two significance of the Preamble to the Constitution.

Ans. The Preamble to the Constitution is significant in many ways. Two significances are:
  (i) The Preamble declares that the source of the Constitution is the People of India.
  (ii) It indicates the secular, socialist and democratic basis of the Constitution.

Q. 2. Mention what the Preamble states about each of the principles of Equality and Fraternity.

Ans. Preamble states about each of the principles of Equality and Fraternity as follows:
  (i) The Preamble assures the citizens' social, political and economic equality for the development of what is best in them.
  (ii) The Preamble emphasises the objective of fraternity to ensure the dignity of the individual as well as the unity and integrity of the nation. The spirit of fraternity is the common factor that unites people from varied backgrounds.

Q. 3. When did the Constitution of India come into force? Why was that date chosen for the enforcement of the Constitution?

Ans. The Constitution of India came into force on 26 January, 1950. This date was especially chosen for the enforcement of the constitution because of its special significance in our freedom struggle. In 1930, this day was observed as the Complete Independence Day for the first time.

Q. 4. The Preamble to the Constitution describes India a Socialist State. What does the expression 'Socialist' mean here?

Ans. The expression 'Socialist' signifies the meaning of 'fair distribution of wealth' and 'securing decent standard of life to the people'. India which is a socialist state does provide equal opportunities to all, irrespective of birth, sex and religion in all aspects of life.

Q. 5. State the significance of January 26 in the Constitution of India.

Ans. In the Congress Session at Lahore it was decided that 26 January should be observed as the 'Purna Swaraj Day' meaning complete independence. For the first time the Complete Independence Day was celebrated on 26 January 1930 and continued to be celebrated till 1947. But after India achieved Independence on 15th August 1947, it came to be known as Independence Day and 26 January as the Republic Day of India.

Q. 6. How is the Indian Republic different from that of the USA?

Ans. In the United States, the President is directly elected by the people whereas in the Indian Republic, the President is indirectly elected by the elected representatives of the people.

Q. 7. The Preamble to the Constitution describes India as a Republic. What is the main feature of a Republican form of government?

Ans. In a Republican form of government the President is the elected head of the State of India, who holds office for a term of five years. He/She has no hereditary right to public office. He/She derives his authority from the people of the country.

Q. 8. Give two examples to indicate that the Preamble to the Constitution has ensured political justice for all.

Ans. Two examples to indicate that the Preamble to the Constitution has ensured political justice for all are :

(i) All Indian citizens have the freedom to express their political views as long as such views do not go against the interest of the country.

(ii) All Indian citizens have the freedom to vote for any recognised political party in the country.

Q. 9. What are the main ideas contained in the Preamble to the Constitution?

Ans. The Preamble to the Constitution declares India to be a sovereign, socialist, secular and democratic republic. The objectives stated by the Preamble are to secure justice, liberty, equality to all citizens and promote fraternity to maintain unity and integrity of the nation.

Q. 10. What does the present day Constitution comprise of?

Ans. Presently, the Indian Constitution comprises of 448 articles in 25 parts and 12 schedules. There are 104 amendments (took place on 25th January 2020 to extend the reservation of seats for SCs and STs in the Lok Sabha and State Assemblies) that have been made in the Indian Constitution so far.

Q. 11. Why did Cabinet Mission come to India and what did it recommend?

Ans. Cabinet Mission came to India with the object of setting up complete self-government in India. It recommended constituting a Constituent Assembly to draw up the future Constitution of India.

Q. 12. Give one fact each in evidence that suggests that India is Sovereign and Socialist.

Ans. Following facts suggests that India is Sovereign and Socialist :

(i) India is neither a dependent nor a dominion of any other nation and is free from foreign interference.

(ii) The Government of India has adopted a mixed economy, introduced five years plans to achieve the value of socialism in a democratic set up.

Q. 13. Give one fact each in evidence that suggests that India is Secular and Democratic Republic.

Ans. Following facts suggests that India is a Secular, Democratic Republic:

(i) India has no official religion and it allows all people to profess, preach and propagate any religion of their choice.

(ii) The Constitution introduced adult franchise which allows people to elect representatives for the Union Parliament, the State Legislatures and the local bodies. In India, President is the elected head of the State of India, who holds office for a term of five years.

Q. 14. The Preamble resolves to secure to all citizens of India "Justice and Liberty". State what the Preamble says about each of them.

Ans. The Preamble resolves to secure to all citizens of India "Justice and Liberty".

(i) Justice ensures equal opportunities to every citizen of India. The Preamble ensures to all people of India what is due to them in all fairness in social, political and economic field.

(ii) The Preamble ensures the citizens freedom of thought, expression, belief, faith and worship.

(iii) Every Indian citizen has the right to hold any belief and express his views freely.

Q. 15. When was the 'body that framed the Constitution of India' constituted? How can you say that such a body represented all sections of the Indian community?

Ans. (i) The body that framed the Constitution of India was constituted in 1946.

(ii) This body represented all communities and classes of the Indian people, such as Hindus, Muslims, Sikhs, Parsis, Anglo-Indians, etc.

(iii) Dr HC Mookerji represented all Indian christians, Dr HP Modi represented the Parsis and Anglo-Indians were represented by Mr Frank Anthony.

Q. 16. How can say that the Constituent Assembly was Mini India?

Ans. It can be said that the Constituent Assembly was Mini India because of the following reasons:

(i) After Independence, the Constituent Assembly of India became a fully sovereign body.

(ii) The Constituent Assembly represented all major sections and communities of India and all shades of opinion.

(iii) Mr Frank Anthony represented the Anglo-Indian community, Sikhs were represented by Mr Hukam Singh, Parsis were represented by Mr Homi Mody whereas Christians and Indian muslims were represented by Mr John Mathai and Saiyed Mohammed Sadullah, respectively. Dr B.R. Ambedkar was from the depressed class. Pandit Jawaharlal Nehru, Sardar Patel and Dr Rajendra Prasad were among the other prominent members of the Assembly.

Chapter 2. Salient Features of the Constitution

Q. 1. Explain why a citizen of India cannot move the court to plead for employment under the Directive Principles of State Policy.

Ans. The Directive Principles are non-justiciable in nature because they are not legally enforceable by the courts for their violation. Therefore, citizen of India cannot move the court to plead for employment under the Directive Principles of State Policy.

Q. 2. What are the two prominent features of the Constitution of India?

Ans. The two prominent features of the Constitution of India are:

(i)   It is the lengthiest Constitution in the world.

(ii) It establishes a parliamentary form of government both at the centre and at the state.

Q. 3. Define the term 'Democracy'.

Ans. Democracy is defined as 'government of the people, by the people and for the people'. It is that system of government in which people choose their rulers by voting for them in elections and the latter remains accountable to the people.

Q. 4. Mention any two Fundamental Duties.

Ans. Two Fundamental Duties are:

(i)   To abide by the Constitution and respect its ideals and institutions, the National Flag and the National Anthem.

(ii) To uphold and protect the sovereignty, unity and integrity of India.

Q. 5. State the Directive Principles relating to the promotion of International Peace and Security.

Ans. The Directive Principles relating to the promotion of International Peace and Security are:

(i)   Maintain just and honorable relations.

(ii) Encourage settlement of international disputes by arbitration.

Q. 6. Mention any three non-justiciable rights of the Indian citizens.

Ans. Three non-justiciable rights of Indian citizens are:

(i)   Equal pay for equal work.

(ii) Just and humane conditions of work and maternity relief.

(iii) Right to education and to public assistance.

Q. 7. Name Two Fundamental Rights that the Constitution confers on the minorities:

Ans. Two fundamental Rights that the Constitution confers on the minorities are :

(i)   Right to establish Educational Institutions.

(ii) Right to conserve the Language, Script and Culture.

Q. 8. Name any two essential freedoms guaranteed to the citizens under Article 19.

Ans. Two essential freedoms guaranteed to the citizens under Article 19 are:

(i)   Freedom of speech and expression.

(ii) Freedom to practice any profession, trade or business.

Q. 9. Mention two Fundamental Rights strengthening the Right to Equality.

Ans. Two Fundamental Rights strengthening the Right to Equality are:

(i)   Prohibition of Discrimination

(ii) Abolition of Untouchability

Q. 10. Mention any two reasons why the Directive Principles of State Policy are a part of the Constitution when they cannot be enforced by law.

Ans. Directive Principles of State Policy are a part of the constitution because:

    (a) They direct the government to accomplish these ideals.

    (b) The fulfillment of these ideals would set up a welfare state in the country.

Q. 11. Mention two Directive Principles which have been implemented by the central or state government.

Ans. Both the state and central governments have made provisions to implement some of these directive principles relating to social and economic justice. Some of these are:

    (i) Most states provide free and compulsory education to children upto the age of 14 years in all government and government aided schools.

    (ii) Reservations are provided to the socially and economically weaker sections of the society like the scheduled castes, scheduled tribes in government services and educational institutions.

Q. 12. What was the precedent which the framers of the Constitution followed in order to include the principles in the Indian Constitution?

Ans. The Irish Constitution was the first to include both the Fundamental Rights and Directive Principles as distinct entities by making the former enforceable and the latter non-enforceable by the courts. While articulating the Directive Principle the framers of the Indian Constitution got inspired by the Irish Constitution of 1937.

Q. 13. Under what categories can Directive Principles be classified?

Ans. There are various types of Directive Principles. They can be classified under the following categories:

    (i) Some Directive Principles promote economic justice and Gandhian or socialist values.

    (ii) Some Directives are related to the protection of the environment and monuments.

    (iii) Some others uphold law, justice and administration.

Q. 14. On what grounds are Directive Principles criticised?

Ans. The Directive Principles have been criticised for the following reasons:

    (i) They are of non-justiciable character. So, this means the violation of Directive Principles of State Policy cannot be challenged in any court.

    (ii) The Directive Principles of State Policy from Articles 36 to 51 in Chapter IV have not been properly classified.

    (iii) There are many elements in these Directive Principles. They have not produced tangible results.

Q. 15. Mention two Directive Principles in respect of each of the following:

    (i) Economic equality   **(ii) Social equality**

    (iii) A social pattern of society

Ans. **(i) Economic equality :**

        1. Provision of equal pay for equal work for men as well as women.

        2. Provisions to prevent concentration of wealth in the hands of a few and exploitation of women and children.

    (ii) Social equality :

        1. Directives aim to raise the standard of living of the people and to improve public health.

        2. Promotion of educational and economic interests of scheduled castes, scheduled tribes and other weaker sections.

    (iii) A social pattern of society:

        1. The state should provide for citizens, a proper adequate means of livelihood through securing for all its citizens, men and women, equal rights.

        2. The state shall endeavor to secure for the citizens a uniform civil code throughout the territory of India.

Q. 16. Mention how Directive Principles act as a measuring rod to assess the success or failure of a government.

Ans. Directive Principles act as a measuring rod to assess the success or failure of a government. Success or failure of a government can be judged to the extent to which it has implemented the provisions of the Directive Principles. Alert citizens can make it difficult for the government to ignore these directives. If the government fails to work for the welfare of the people, public will go against the government. They may not vote for the party in power in the next general elections and may not re-elect the government.

Q. 17. Mention two Directive Principles which aim at the following:
   (i)   Preservation of the ancient cultural heritage of India
   (ii) Strengthening democracy
   (iii) Promoting public health

Ans. (i)   **Preservation of the ancient cultural heritage of India :** Directive Principles also want to create awareness for protection of our national heritage. They want the government to :
   1.   Protect our environment and safeguard the forests and wildlife of the country.
   2.   Protect all monuments, places and objects of national importance.

   (ii) **Strengthening democracy :** Directive Principles which aim at strengthening democracy are:
   1.   A uniform civil code throughout the country.
   2.   Separation of the judiciary from the executive and enable the judiciary to be independent and impartial.

   (iii) **Promoting public health :** Directive Principles which aim at promoting public health are:
   1.   Prohibition of consumption of intoxicating drinks and drugs.
   2.   To raise the level of nutrition and the standard of living and to improve public health.

Q. 18. How do the Directive Principles exercise influence on the working of the government in power?

Ans. In a democracy, directive principles can become the basis of judging a government's performance. Alert citizens can make it difficult for the government to ignore these directives. If the government fails to work for the welfare of the people, they may not re-elect the government.

Q. 19. What is meant by the term 'Welfare State'?

Ans. A welfare state is a form of government in which the state protects and promotes the economic and social well-being of the citizens. It is based upon the principles of equal opportunity, equitable distribution of wealth, and public responsibility for citizens unable to avail themselves of the minimal provisions for a good life.

Q. 20. What is meant by Equality before Law in the context of Fundamental Rights?

Ans. As per Article 14, the Constitution of India guaranteed that all its citizens will be treated equally before the law irrespective of their social and economic status. The Constitution prohibits discrimination between two persons placed in similar circumstances or conditions.

Q. 21. How can we say that the Directive Principles supplement the Fundamental Rights?

Ans. Directive Principles are considered to be fundamental basis of good governance. Fundamental Rights are the most basic human rights. Both supplement each other because the latter is imperative for the people to enjoy liberty, justice and freedom. However, the former is responsible on ensuring that we get these rights. Directive Principles link ideas with reality.

Q. 22. What is the significance of the Directive Principles of State Policy in the Indian Constitution?

Ans. Directive Principles of State Policy aim to create social and economic conditions under which the citizens can lead a good life. They also aim to establish social and economic democracy through a welfare state.

Q. 23. Mention any one importance of the Right to Information granted by an Act enacted in 2005.

Ans. Right to Information act gives citizens of India access to records of the central government and state records. This right helps to curb corruption and promotes transparency in Government departments.

Q.24. With reference to the Indian Constitution, answer the following questions :

    (i) Define 'Welfare State'.

    (ii) State any three differences beween Fundamental Rights and Directive Prindiples of State Policy.

    (iii) Explain the importance of 'Single Citizenship' and 'Universal Adult Franchise' as important features the Constitution. **[November, 2019]**

Ans. (i) The Constitution of India declares India as a welfare state.

    1. A Welfare State provides for its citizens a wide range of social services, such as education, medical care and financial aid down during old age, sickness or unemployment.

    2. The Constitution of India lays down that "the State shall strive to promote the welfare of the people".

    3. Under Part IV of the Constitution, which includes Directive Principles of State Policy, the State is directed to ensure to the people:

        (a) Employment   (b) Education

        (c) Assistance in case of old age, sickness and disablement

(ii) Three differences between Fundamental rights and Directive Principles of State Policy:

    1. **Fundamental Right are justiciable but Directive principles are not:** Fundamental Rights are enforceable. The Supreme Court or the High Court have the power to issue writs or order for the enforcement of Fundamental Rights. The Directive Principles cannot be enforced in a court of law. No worker can secure "a living wage" by means of proceedings in court.

    2. **Fundamental Rights protect our civil liberties while Directive Principles lay down the 'Economic Democracy' as our ideal:** Fundamental Rights protect life and civil liberties, such as freedom of speech and expression, and the right to profess any religion. The Directive Principles indicate as to what our economic idea or social order ought to be.

    3. **Rights constitute limitations upon State action while the Directive Principles are in the nature of positive directions:** Fundamental Rights are mostly negative in character as they indicate the things the State must not do. However, the Directive Principles are positive in character as they direct the State to support the citizens in cases of economic unemployment, old age sickness.

(iii) 1. Under a federal system there is a dual citizenship, which means a citizenship of the State to which a person belongs and that of the Nation, which includes all the States.

    2. For example, in America, all persons are citizens of the United States and of the States they reside in.

    3. However, in India, all citizens have a single identity, that of beings Indians, no matter which State they belong to.

    4. The Constitution of India recognises a single citizenship.

Chapter 3. Elections

Q. 1. Mention any two functions of the Election Commission.

Ans. Two functions of the Election Commission are :

    (i) Preparation of the Electoral rolls.

    (ii) Conduct of elections.

Q. 2. Mention any one advantage and disadvantage of 'Direct Elections'.

Ans. **Advantage of 'Direct Elections':** The elected representatives are accountable to the voters for their actions.

Disadvantage of 'Direct Elections': The voters may develop partial attitude towards the wrong candidates based on the caste, religion or emotions.

Q. 3. What are the two stages in the election process before the election campaign begins?

Ans. Two stages in the election process before the election campaign begins are:

(i) Nomination of candidates.

(ii) Scrutiny of nominations.

Q. 4. Mention one main advantage and one disadvantage of Indirect Election?

Ans. **Advantage of Indirect election:** It reduces the role of people as the choice is made by a handful of representatives.

Disadvantage of Indirect Election: This is less democratic as what the people want to say is to be inferred from their representatives.

Q. 5. Mention any two circumstances in which a Ballot Paper can become invalid.

Ans. Under the following circumstances a ballot paper becomes invalid:

(i) It is not marked at all.

(ii) Choice for more than one candidate is indicated by the voter.

Q. 6. What is security deposit?

Ans. In an electoral system, a deposit is the sum of money that a candidate for an elected office, such as a seat in a legislature, is required to pay to an electoral authority before he or she is permitted to stand for election. If the candidate does not achieve the refund threshold, the deposit is forfeited.

Q. 7. What is Model Code of Conduct?

Ans. The Model Code of Conduct is a set of guidelines and instructions on campaigning, general conduct and meetings, etc. during elections. The Model Code of Conduct remains effective until the entire election process is not completed.

Q. 8. What is the importance of voter identity cards?

Ans. A voter's identity card, also known as Electors Photo Identity Card (EPIC) is a photo identity card, which is issued by the Election commission of India to all citizens of India who are entitled to vote.

Q. 9. What is the difference between a voter and a candidate?

Ans.

S.No.	Voter	Candidate
(i)	A person who elects the candidates is a voter.	A person who contests the election is known as a candidate.
(ii)	All the citizens who attain the age of 18 become a voter.	In order to contest elections a person must attain the age of 25 years.

Q. 10. State any one reason why Universal Adult Franchise is adopted in India.

Ans. Universal Adult Franchise is adopted in India to:

(i) Empower people to indirectly participate in the administration of the country.

(ii) Ensure legal and political equality in the society.

Q. 11. Who is eligible to cast a vote in India?

Ans. The Constitution of India permits every person who:

(i) is a citizen of India.

(ii) is not less than 18 years of age.

(iii) is not otherwise disqualified under any law.

Q. 12. What are the different types of constituency?

Ans. There are two types of constituencies:

(i) **Single-Member Constituency:** When the coustituency is entitled to only one representative, it is called a single-Member constituency. India and England have Single Member Constituency.

(ii) **Multi-Member Constituency:** Constituecies sending more than one representative are called Multi-Member constituencies, for example Germany, France and Italy.

Q. 13. What is the basis of elections in India?

Ans. In India, the following are the basis of elections:

    (i) Universal Adult Franchise   (ii) Secret Ballot

    (iii) Joint electorates

Q. 14. What is the significance of Universal Adult Franchise in a democracy?

Ans. Universal Adult Franchise plays an important role in a democracy because it states that every individual irrespective of their caste, colour, religion, gender, or status has right to vote and each vote has equal value *i.e.*, "one vote one value".

Q. 15. Which important amendment was done in the Indian Constitution in 1988?

Ans. An important amendment to the Indian Constitution in 1988 was done by lowering the eligibility age of adult universal franchise from 21 to 18.

Q. 16. What is meant by a direct democracy? Give one example of direct democracy from the ancient world history.

Ans. A direct democracy is one where the citizens directly participate in the day-to-day decision making and in the running of the government. The ancient city-states in Greece were considered good example of direct democracy.

Q. 17. In the event of violence or malpractice in the poll, what measures can the Commission adopt?

Ans. In the event of violence or malpractice in the poll the Commission can adopt the following measures:

    (i) Elections are considered invalid in those constituencies, where unfair means are used.

    (ii) In case of rigging and booth-capturing, severe penalities are inflicted on the accused.

Q. 18. Who defines what is free and fair elections?

Ans. Free and fair elections refers to those elections which happen in a democratic and social way in which everybody has the right to choose their representatives according to their choices and their wishes. In fair elections the competing political parties do not try to influence the choice of the people.

Q. 19. What is the main purpose of allotting symbols to political parties?

Ans. Political parties are allotted reserved common symbols, while the independent candidates may select them from a list of free symbols. Main purpose is that these symbols may be easily recognised by illiterate people.

Q. 20. Mention any two comparative disadvantages of direct and indirect election.

Ans.

S.No.	Disadvantages of Direct Elections	Disadvantages of Indirect Elections
(i)	The voters may develop partial attitude towards the wrong candidates based on caste, religion or emotions.	This is less democratic as what the people want to say is to be inferred from their representatives.
(ii)	The accurate public opinion that is expressed through the voting ballots may get disfigured as all voters do not vote.	As the number of voters is quite low, there are chances of corruption, horse-trading and bribery to secure votes.
(iii)	A huge amount of time, energy and money is involved in direct elections.	Some voters may even disobey orders from their party and cast their vote in favour or against a specific representative.

Q. 21. Under what circumstances can a 'Mid-Term Election' be held?

Ans. Mid-term elections are held to bring new house to power when the full term of five years of State Assemblies or Lok Sabha has not been completed and the house has to be dissolved. Legally, the expression 'Mid-term Election' has no importance as only Lok Sabha elections are called General Elections, regardless of the fact whether the last house completed its term or was dissolved midway.

Q. 22. On what grounds can the Returning Officer reject the nomination paper of a candidate?

Ans. (i) It is the duty of the Returning Officer to scrutinise the nomination papers of each candidate thoroughly. This responsibility cannot be passed down to the Assistant Returning Officer by the Returning Officer.

(ii) The nomination of any candidate with incomplete and invalid papers is rejected by the Commission.

(iii) The candidates have to be genuine, qualified and fulfilling all criteria like election symbol, deposit money, etc.

Q. 23. The Election Commission has only supervisory role and not the legislative one with regard to the conduct of free and fair elections. Examine it.

Ans. (i) The Constitution of India has vested in the Election Commission of India the superintendence, direction and control of the entire process for conduct of elections to Parliament and Legislature of every State and to the offices of President and Vice-President of India.

(ii) The Commission has no power to make rules and regulations. It can only enforce existing laws.

(iii) Therefore, we can say that Election Commission has only supervisory role and not the legislative one with regard to the conduct of free and fair elections.

Q. 24. Why is an independent Election Commission important?

Ans. An independent Election Commission is important for the following reasons:

(i) To ensure that no party candidate uses unethical and unfair means in name of caste or religion.

(ii) To ensure that no one party or several parties can influence the conduct of elections.

(iii) To supervise the machinery of the elections throughout the country to ensure free and fair elections.

Q. 25. Mention any three provisions taken to ensure independence of Election Commission?

Ans. The independence of the Election Commission is secured by the following provisions:

(i) The Chief Election Commissioner is appointed by the President of India. But once appointed he/she is not answerable to the President or the Government.

(ii) During the election period, the EC can order the government to follow some guidelines, to prevent use and misuse of governmental power to enhance its chances to win elections, or to transfer some government officials.

(iii) When on election duty, government officers work under the control of the EC and not the government.

Q. 26. Mention any three comparative advantages of direct and indirect elections?

Ans.

S.No.	Advantages of Direct Elections	Advantages of Indirect Elections
(i)	It stimulates the interest of the masses in various affairs related to public welfare and the nation.	It reduces the role of people as the choice is made by a handful of representatives.
(ii)	The elected representatives are accountable to the voters for their actions.	It is more appropriate for elections in extremely large constituencies.
(iii)	Depending upon their judgement, the voters can select as well as reject representatives.	It mostly involves low cost campaigns.

Q. 27. What is the method to remove the Chief Election Commissioner?

Ans. (i) To remove the Chief Election Commissioner the resolution is introduced in either House of Parliament by two third majority of the House.

(ii) He/She can be removed from the service if the resolution for such a removal is passed in each House of the Parliament by majority of the total membership of each House and also by a two third majority of its members present and voting.

(iii) The Chief Election Commissioner is allowed to defend himself. If both Houses pass the resolution, then the address is sent to the president for removing the officer. In case, either or no House passes the resolution, the matter is dropped.

Chapter 4. Rural Local Self-Government

Q. 1. Mention any two limitations in efficient working of local self-governments.

Ans. Two limitations in efficient working of local self-government are:

(i) Unethical means adopted in elections.

(ii) Low rate of literacy.

Q. 2. (a) What is Gram Panchayat ? State any two functions of the Gram Panchayat.

(b) List any three functions of Panchayat Samiti.   **[February, 2020]**

Ans. (a) The Gram Panchayat is the executive wing of the Gram Sabha. The Gram Panchayat members are elected by the members of the Gram Sabha.

The two functions of the Gram Panchayat are:

(i) Civic duties such as provision of safe drinking water including maintenance of public wells and tanks; health care facilities by setting up dispensaries; upkeep of roads, footpaths and culverts; good drains and provision of street lights.

(ii) Administrative and regulatory functions include registration of births, deaths and marriages; maintenance of and ward services; maintenance of common property in the village; and helping the government to maintain law and order.

(b) Three functions of Panchayat Samiti are :

(i) Civic facilities and development functions include rural health programme, rural water supply, to develop and maintain rural roads, regulation of markets; functions relating to agriculture, animal husbandry and fisheries, development of cottage industries; social welfare and rural employment.

(ii) Supervisory functions include supervising the work of the Gram Panchayat in the Block, examining the budget of the Panchayat, exercising control over the functioning of the Block Development Officer and his assistants, and to draw plans for development of the Block in coordination with the development plans of the Panchayat of the Block.

(iii) Delegated functions include to arrange for funds from the government for the various activities mentioned above, and to carry forward the Integrated Rural Development Programmes (IRDP) of Central and State governments under the directions of the District Boards.

Q. 3. Mention any two qualifications required to be elected as member of Gram Panchayat.

Ans. Two qualifications required to be elected as member of Gram Panchayat are:

(i) Person should be a registered voter in the electoral roll of that Gram Panchayat.

(ii) He/She must not be less than 21 years of age.

Q. 4. What are the kinds of problems these local self-government deals with?

Ans. Local self-government looks after the needs and issues of a village, town, a district or a city. It deals with local problems such as water supply, health, sanitation, primary education, maintenance of roads, street lights, drainage, upkeep of parks, libraries, etc.

Q. 5. Mention any two Civic and Developmental functions of a Panchayat Samiti.

Ans. Two Civic and Developmental functions of a Panchayat Samiti are:

(i) Providing hospital and health care services.

(ii) Providing improved quality of agricultural equipment, undertaking small irrigation schemes, provide chemical fertilisers, etc.

Q. 6. Apart from local self-government in India, what are the other two levels of government?

Ans. Apart from local self-government in India, the other two levels of government are:

  (i) On the national level, there is union government.

  (ii) State government forms the second tier of the government. It looks after the interests of the people in state.

Q. 7. What is the need of Local Self-Government?

Ans. Local self-government is required because problems at the local level are best solved by the local governments. Local people tend to know best about the problems that are related to their areas like water supply, sanitation, education, electricity and public works. These problems cannot be properly dealt with by state and central government.

Q. 8. How does local self-government prove to be beneficial in relieving the burden of state government?

Ans. The local bodies handle problems locally and assume responsibility for developmental work. As a result, the state administration can have time to look into bigger problems at the state level.

Q. 9. Mention two socio-economic functions of the village panchayat?

Ans. Two socio-economic functions of the village panchayats are as follows:

  (i) For providing primary education village panchayats set up elementary schools.

  (ii) Village panchayats take initiatives to set up dispensaries and medical centres, clear wells and ponds and help in the prevention of outbreak of contagious diseases.

Q. 10. Mention any two important functions of the gram sabha.

Ans. Two important functions of the gram sabha are:

  (i) Keeping an eye on the working of Gram Panchayat.

  (ii) Implementing governmental schemes related to generation of employment in the village.

Q. 11. State two welfare functions of a village panchayat.

Ans. Two welfare functions of a village panchayat are:

  (i) Introducing welfare programmes for children and women.

  (ii) Introducing community development programmes.

Q. 12. What are the sources of income of a Panchayat Samiti?

Ans. Sources of income of a Panchayat Samiti are as follows:

  (i) Grants by the state government.

  (ii) Income from taxes levied by the Samiti.

Q. 13. When did the new Panchayati Raj Act come into force?

Ans. The new Panchayati Raj Act came into force on 24 April 1993 via the 73rd Amendment Act which added a new Part IX consisting of 16 Articles and the Eleventh Schedule to the Constitution.

Q. 14. Briefly state the composition of the Zila Parishad.

Ans. The composition of the Zila Parishad varies from state to state. Zila Parishad generally consists of 40-60 members comprising of the following:

  (i)   Pradhans or Chairmen of all the Panchayat Samitis in the districts.

  (ii) Members of Parliament and Members of the State Legislatures elected from the district.

  (iii) Chairmen of Municipalities in the district.

  (iv) Deputy Commissioner of the district.

  (v)   Representative of women, scheduled castes and Scheduled Tribes. Supervisor of all Government Departments in the district.

Q. 15. How can we say that the institution of local self-government train people to be leaders in a democratic society?

Ans. The local institutions act as training grounds to prepare its members to manage state or national affairs in later years. The experience gained in local self-government bodies help them to accept bigger challenges at the level of state or nation. Many leaders like Dadabhai Naoroji, Bal Gangadhar Tilak, etc. started their careers from local self-government bodies to reach higher platforms regionally and nationally.

Q. 16. How are the members of the village panchayat elected?

Ans. Members of the Village Panchayat are directly elected by the Gram Sabha. Village Panchayat is headed by a Sarpanch. In some states, Panchas (elected members of the Gram Sabha) elects a Sarpanch from amongst themselves. While in other states Sarpanch is directly elected by all members of the Gram Sabha. Elections to a Panchayat are held on the basis of secret ballot and adult franchise.

Q. 17. Mention any one function of Gram Sabha. **[November, 2019]**

Ans. The function of Gram Sabha are as follows:

(i) To approve the budget for the year.

(ii) To consider new taxes which the Gram Panchayat may like to levy.

(iii) To review the audit report of the last year's accounts of the Panchayat.

(iv) To elect the Gram Pradhan as well as the members of the Gram Panchayat.

(v) To remove the President and the Vice-President of the Gram Panchayat from their offices if they are not working properly, with two-thirds resolution of the members of the Gram Sabha.

(vi) To oversee all other activities of the village.

(Mention any one function of Gram Sabha)

Q. 18. State any function of Panchayat Samiti. **[November, 2019]**

Ans. The functions of a Panchayat Samiti are of three kinds :

(i) **Civic facilities and developmental function:** The panchayat samiti is responsible for implementing rural health programme; rural water supply, rural roads and regulation of markets.

(ii) **Supervisory functions :** The Panchayat Samiti supervises the work of the Gram Panchayats.

(iii) **Delegated functions :** Panchayat samiti work to improve the quality of rural life through schemes like Integrated Rural Development Programme (IRDP), etc.

(Mention any one function of Panchayat Samiti)

Q. 19. What are different levels of the Panchayati Raj ? **[November, 2019]**

Ans. Panchayati system was introduced in Nagaur at Rajasthan on October 2, 1959. However, the 73rd Amendment of 1992 provided the three-tier Panchayati Raj system. The new Panchayati Raj Act came into force on April 24, 1993.

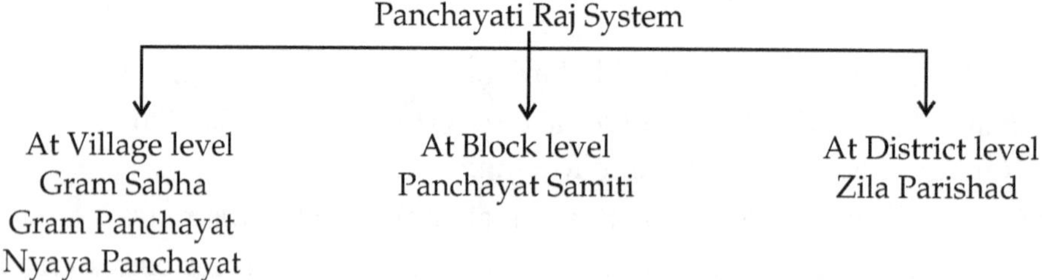

(i) The Village Panchayat cosisting of a Gram sabha, a Gram Panchayat and a Nyaya Panchayat functions only at the village level.

(ii) The Panchayat Samiti, placed in the second tier of the Panchayati Raj system, manages all the activities of the Gram Panchayat within the block covering several villages.

(iii) Zila Parishad is an apex body under the Panchayati Raj System. It coordinates the activities of various Panchayat Samitis.

Chapter 5. Urban Local Self Government

Q. 1. Give any two functions of a Municipal Corporation in the field of public health.

Ans. Functions of a Municipal Corporation in the field of public health are:

(i) It is the duty of the corporation to maintain hospitals, centres of welfare, maternity homes and dispensaries.

(ii) It is the duty of the Municipal Corporation to organise vaccinations and inoculation camps for eradication of infectious diseases.

Q. 2. What does a Municipal Corporation do in the field of education?

Ans. The Corporation is responsible for setting up schools up to primary and secondary levels, along with centres for educating adults, setting up libraries, museums, and night schools. The Corporation ensures that children below the age of 14 go to schools.

Q. 3. Name any two local self-governing bodies in urban areas.

Ans. Two local self-governing bodies in urban areas are as follows:

(i) Municipal Corporations

(ii) Municipal Committees (Municipalities)

Q. 4. Mention any one point of difference between a Municipal Corporation and Municipal Committee.

Ans.

Municipal Corporation	Municipal Committee
Large metropolitan cities with a population of one lakh or more are governed by the Municipal Corporations.	Smaller cities and towns are governed by the Municipal Committee.

Q. 5. Name the three important constituents of a municipality.

Ans. Three important constituents of a municipality are:

(i) General Body (ii) Chairman/President

(iii) Chief Executive Officer

Q. 6. Mention any two functions of the mayor of a city corporation.

Ans. Two functions of a city corporation are:

(i) To preside over the meeting of the corporation and to regulate the conduct of business in such meetings.

(ii) To maintain decorum and discipline in the meetings.

Q. 7. Why is the mayor more of a figure head than an active functionary?

Ans. The mayor is the head of the Municipal Corporation, but the role is largely ceremonial as executive powers are vested in the Municipal Commissioner. The office of the Mayor combines a functional role of chairing the Corporation meeting as well as ceremonial role associated with being the first citizen of the city.

Q. 8. Mention any one obligatory and one discretionary function of a Municipal Corporation.

Ans. One obligatory and one discretionary function of a Municipal Corporation are as follows:

(i) **Obligatory function:** Public Health and Sanitation.

(ii) **Discretionary function:** Transport facility.

Q. 9. Who is the head of the Municipal Corporation? What is his/her normal term of office?

Ans. The mayor is the head of the Municipal Corporation. The mayor is usually elected for a term of one year and can also be re-elected after the expiry of that period.

Q. 10. State two important functions of a Municipal Corporation in the field of education.

Ans. Important functions of a Municipal Corporation in the field of education are:

   (i) The Municipal Corporation establishes primary and secondary schools, night schools and adult education centres.

   (ii) It provides free education in primary schools.

Q. 11. In which urban area is a Nagar Panchayat constituted? Why it is also called as Notified Area Council?

Ans. A Nagar Panchayat is set up in town having a population of less than 10 thousand. It is so called because its formation was notified by the government in the State Gazette.

Q. 12. Mention any two functions of a Municipal Corporation with respect to the Public Conveniences.

Ans. Two functions of a Municipal Corporation with respect to the Public Conveniences are as follows:

   (i) Construction and maintenance of roads and streets.

   (ii) Construction of public urinals and toilets at public centres.

Q. 13. Mention any two functions of a Municipal Corporation with respect to safety, sanitation and garbage disposal.

Ans. Two functions of a Municipal Corporation with respect to safety, sanitation and garbage disposal are as follows:

   (i) Making arrangement for proper disposal of garbage outside the city.

   (ii) Maintaining fire bridges at convenient centres in the city for the safety of the people and their property from calamity caused by fire.

Q. 14. State the three wings in the administrative set-up of a Municipality. How are they elected?

Ans. Three wings in the administrative set-up of a Municipality are:

   (i) **The General Body or Council:** The members of General body or Council are called Councillors and the adult citizens residing in a particular Municipal ward elect them.

   (ii) **The President :** The Councillors of a Municipal Committee directly elect their President, a senior Vice President and a Junior Vice President from amongst themselves.

   (iii) **The Executive Officers and other officers:** In most states, the Municipal Committee appoints their own Chief Executive Officers while in some states the state government appoints them.

Q. 15. What qualifications are needed to contest for the Municipal Council's election?

Ans. A citizen can contest its municipal election if he or she possesses the following qualifications:

   (i) He/She should be a registered voter in the area of the Municipal Corporation.

   (ii) He/She should be at least 21 years of age and not more than 25 years as prescribed under the Corporation Act.

   (iii) He/She should not hold any office of profit under state government or any of the local bodies of the state government.

Q. 16. State the powers of a Municipal Commissioner.

Ans. A Municipal Commissioner has the following powers:

   (i) To grant or cancel licenses or contracts for various jobs.

   (ii) To issue order for the payment of municipal taxes.

   (iii) To sanction leave to the employees of the Municipal Council.

Q. 17. With reference to the Urban Local Self Government, answer the following questions:

[November, 2019]

   (i) List any three Discretionary functions of the Municipal Corporation.

   (ii) State any four functions of a Municipal Committee.

Ans. (i) The following are some discretionary functions of the Municipal Corporation:

     1. **Transport facilities:** Local authorities may manage a bus service for carrying people from one place to another.

     2. **Cultural activities:** Municipal Corporations may estabilish libraries and museums. Cultural activities like drama, music and painting are also encouraged by Corporations.

3. **Sports and recreation:** The Municipal Corporation organises fairs, exhibitions and wrestling events. Recreational facilities may also be provided.

4. **Welfare services:** Municipal Corporations are expected to launch family welfare schemes and to undertake poverty alleviation programmes, etc. The Corporation can also look after the public distribution system. **(Mention three points)**

(ii) The functions of a Municipal Committee are:

1. **Public health and sanitation:** The Municipality has the responsibility of maintaining hospital and dispensaries, cleaning public lanes and preventing the sale of rotten foodstuffs and adulterated milk, etc.

2. **Electricity and water supply:** It is the duty of the Municipal Committees to provides safe drinking water and electricity for domestic and commercial use.

3. **Education and sports:** The Municipalities establish primary and secondary schools. They provide facilities to young boys and girls to develop an aptitude for sports.

4. **Public works:** This includes construction of roads, shopping centres and community halls.

5. **Registration of births and deaths:** The Municipal Boards maintain an account of births and deaths in the city.

Discretionary functions include establishing libraries and reading rooms, constructing stadiums for sports and games, organising fairs and exhibitions, providing transport facilities and other amenities for people's convenience. **(Mention any four points)**

SECTION : B (HISTORY)

Chapter 1. The Harappan Civilisation

Q. 1. What do you mean by the term civilisation?

Ans. (i) The word 'civilsation' comes from the Latin word 'Civis' that means someone who resides in a town.

(ii) Thus, civilisation refers to the process by which a society or place reaches an advanced stage of social and cultural development.

Q. 2. State any two features of the Great Bath.

Ans. (i) The Great Bath discovered at Mohen jo-Daro resembles a huge swimming pool.

(ii) It is 12 metres long, 7 metres wide and 2.5 metres deep.

Q. 3. State any two ways in which the script of the Indus Valley Civilisation provides us with valuable historical information.

Ans. (i) The seals excavated at Harappa and Mohenjo-Daro were inscribed with pictorial writing which revealed us an idea that the Harappan people had their own language.

(ii) The script is compilation of symbols and signs but remains undeciphered.

Q. 4. What was the purpose of the rooms surrounding the Great Bath?

Ans. (i) These rooms were probably utilized for religious activities.

(ii) Some historians believe that these rooms were built for changing clothes.

Q. 5. Give the evidences to show that Harappan people trade with Sumerians.

Ans. An engraved steatite vessel, a model ram, an adze, small pottery rings excavated from Indus Valley were imported from Sumer, thus indicate international trade with Sumerians.

Q. 6. Write a note on the style and pattern of script during Harappan Civilisation.

Ans. (i) Inspite of regular documents on stone or baked clay tablets, numerous seals unearthed at Harappan sites which had pictographic writing.

(ii) About four hundred inscriptions have been found in which people used phonetic script initially but later evolved as alphabetic pattern.

Q. 7. Throw a light on the granaries used by the Indus Valley people.

Ans. (i) The granaries were used to storing grains.

(ii) Alongwith granaries, working floors and room barracks for accommodating labourers were also found.

(iii) The existence of the Great Granary shows the prevalence of a centralized tax collecting unit. **(Any Two)**

Q. 8. State any two features of urban town planning in the Harappan Civilizations.

[February, 2020]

Ans. The Harappan people were skilled in town planning:

(i) The streets: The streets and lanes of the Indus Valley divided the entire city into rectangular blocks. The streets were straight, wide and cut each other at right angles. The roads were rounded at the corners so that heavy carts could move easily. Fire-burnt bricks were used to pave the streets. The houses did not encroach upon the streets.

(ii) The drainage system: The most unique feature of the Harappan city was the drainage system. A brick-lined drainage channel was there along all the streets. The drains at home were connected to the drains on the streets. The drains were covered with bricks or stones and had manholes at regular intervals for inspection and cleaning. This reflected that people of Harappa paid great attention to sanitation and health.

Q. 9. Write short note on the Great Bath.

Ans. (i) The Great Bath was a large open four-sided building surrounded by galleries and rooms from all sides.

(ii) The pool was connected to the well, built nearby for supplying water to the pool.

Q. 10. Illustrate the Lothal's dockyard developed during the Indus Valley Civilisation.

Ans. (i) The great Dockyard at Lothal discovered in 1954 proved the long distance trade connection of Harappan cities with Mesopotamian and Egyptian cities.

(ii) The Dockyard was enclosed by a massive brick wall to protect the structure from massive flood.

Q. 11. Enlist two important features of 'Dancing girl' excavated at Harappan site.

Ans. (i) The bronze figure of a 'dancing girl' excavated from Mohanjo-Daro depicts the symbol of vitality, variety and originality.

(ii) The right hand of the girl rested on her back and left hand is fully covered with bangles made of ivory or bones.

Q. 12. Throw a light on the food consumed by the Harappan people.

Ans. (i) The staple diet of the Harappan people was wheat and barley.

(ii) Besides rice, fish, poultry, milk and mutton were also commonly eaten.

Q. 13. Give the evidences to show that Indus Valley people use ornaments and cosmetic.

Ans. (i) Ornaments like armlets, finger rings and necklaces have been discovered which depict that both men and women were fond of wearing ornaments of gold, silver, copper and precious stones.

(ii) A number of fixtures made of ivory and metal combs, oval bronze mirrors and small dressing tables have been unearthed at the sites that suggest that the harappan women were aware of face make up and coilleries.

Q. 14. How did Harappan people amuse themselves?

Ans. (i) Generally, Harappan people amused themselves through indoor games, dancing and listening music.

(ii) A large number of clay and terracotta models of men, women, animals, carts, whistles in the shape of birds and animals have been unearthed from the sites suggesting their use as toys in daily life.

Q. 15. Throw a light on the furniture and utensils used by the Harappan people?

Ans. (i) The furniture and utensils excavated at Mohenjo-Daro indicate a high standard of civilisation because of their various types and designs.

(ii) The beautifully painted grey and red ware pottery, vessels for the kitchen, chairs and beds made of wood, lamps were excavated that show what people manufactured in those days.

Q. 16. What were the means of transport for the Harappan people?

Ans. (i) A copper specimen of Ekka (Cart) with a top-cover has been found at Harappa.

(ii) It indicates that bullock carts with or without the top-cover was used as the chief mode of transport.

Q. 17. State two examples as evidence to prove that the Harappans paid greater attention to health and sanitation.   **[November, 2019]**

Ans. Two examples that show that the Harappans paid greater attention to health and sanitation are :

(i) A brick-lined drainage channel flowed alongside every street and the house drains were connected to the underground main drains.

(ii) The drains were provided with manholes at regular intervals for proper inspection and cleaning.

Q. 18. Give the evidence that suggests that the people of the Harappan Civilisation had :

(i) concern for sanitation   (ii) an efficient civic organisation

(iii) engineering skill

Ans. (i) Elaborate drainage system suggests that Harappan people had concern for sanitation.

(ii) Dwelling houses were situated on either side of the road and were provided with covered drains connected with the streets drains. The bathroom's floor sloped to the corner where the drain carried off the waste water. This suggests that Harappan people had an efficient civic organisation.

(iii) The existence of the Great Bath reveals the engineering skill of the Indus people.

Q. 19. State any three valuable pieces of information that the Seals provide about the Harappan Civilization.   **[February, 2020]**

Ans. The seals provide valuable evidence about the social, economic, political and cultural life of the people of Harappa.

(i) The figures on the seal reflect the dress, hair style and ornaments worn by the people of Harappa.

(ii) They throw light on the religious beliefs and faith of the Harappan people. They tell us about the commercial activities and trade relations of the people of those times.

(iii) They show the artistic skill of the Harappans.

(iv) They give us knowledge about the Harappan script.

Q. 20. When and how did the Harappan Civilisation come to light?

Ans. Alexander Cunningham, a British officer in India, gets credit for preliminary excavations in Harappa. In 1921, under the supervision of RB Daya Ram Sahni, a number of seals were found from the site of Harappa in west Punjab. In 1922, a huge city of Harappa was excavated. This was followed by the discovery of big mound by RD Banerjee in the Larkana District of Sindh, which was named as Mohenjo-Daro.

Q. 21. The Indus Valley Civilisation came to an abrupt and sudden end in about 1500 BC. List 1 reason for this end.

Ans. The following were the probable reasons for the decline of Harappan Civilisation :

(i) Regular floods   (ii) Foreign invasions

(iii) Earthquakes and grasslands   (iv) Overgrazing of grasslands

(v) Destruction of forests   (vi) Change in the course of Indus.

Q. 22. Differentiate between the Harappa and Mohenjo-Daro sites of the Indus Valley Civilisation.

Ans.

	Harappa	Mohenjo-Daro
(i)	It was located in the Larkana district of Sindh (Now in Pakistan).	It was situated on the bank of river Ravi in the Montgomery district of West Punjab (Now in Pakistan.)
(ii)	It is bigger in area than Mohenjo-Daro.	It is comperatively smaller.
(iii)	It was discovered by Daya Ram Sahni in 1921.	It was discovered by R. D. Banerjee in 1922.

Q. 23. Why is the religion of the Indus Valley people considered to be the foundation of the present day Hinduism?

Ans. Because the religious faiths such as the worship of Shiva, animals and trees show that the religious belief of the Harappan people were the foundation on which Hinduism grew up.

Q. 24. State the reasons behind the development of civilisation.

Ans. (i) With the introduction of agriculture the primitive man transformed from food gatherers to food producers.

(ii) Subsequently, man started to build permanent shelters and also learnt the art of spinning, weaving and formed a society of farmers, weavers, potters and carpenters.

(iii) Thus the process of social evolution started gradually and led to the formation of civilisation.

Q. 25. Why the Indus people maintained a close commercial relation with the outside world?

Ans. For the import of precious stones, different metals and other articles, the Indus people had to establish trade connections with certain Central Asian and West Asian countries alongwith Sumeru (Mesopotamia) and Egypt.

Chapter 2. The Vedic Period

Q.1. What do you understand by the term Sapta Sindhu ?

Ans. (i) Sapta Sindhu was a region of India in which Aryans were lived during the Vedic Age.

(ii) It is the land of seven rivers comprising the River Sindhu (Indus) , River Chenab (Asikni) River Beas (Vipas) , River Jhelum (Vilasta), River Ravi (Parusni), River Satluj (Satadru) and River Saraswati.

(iii) It covers the present day Punjab, Eastern Afghanistan and parts of Western Uttar Pradesh.

Q. 2. Write any three sacrifices performed by the king to strengthen his position during the later Vedic Period ?

Ans. During Vedic Period the sacrifices performed by King include :

(i) Rajasuya (consecration ceremony)   (ii) Asvamedha (horse sacrifices)
(iii) Vajapeya (chariot race)

Q. 3. What is the subject matter of Upanishad ?

Ans. (i) Basically the Upanishads are anti-ritualistic.

(ii) They discuss the theories of creation of the universe and define karma , the doctrine of action, and hold Brahma (creator) and atma (soul) as identical.

Q. 4. Write any two features of the education system imparted in Gurukulas.

Ans. (i) At the gurukulas the gurus provided knowledge not only about religion, but also in arts of warfare, statecraft, medicines and astrology.

(ii) The young disciples lived with the guru till they learnt enough to lead decent life.

Q. 5. State any three changes that took place in the religious life of Aryans during the later Vedic Period.

Ans. (i) Brahmins emerged as powerful priestly class and they transformed the simple vedic religion into a complicated rituals with superstitions.

(ii) The rituals and sacrifices became costly and beyond the reach of an average man.

(iii) Brahma, Vishnu and Shiva became prominent in place of nature gods like Indra and Varuna.

Short Questions

Q. 6. Write any two features of 'Sama Veda'.

Ans. (i)   The word Sama Veda is derived from the root 'Saman' that means melody. It is a collection of melodies.

    (ii) It contains verses which are supposed to be sung by the priest while performing Yajnas.

Q. 7. What do you know about Yajurveda?

Ans. (i)   The Yajurveda consists the rituals to be observed while having sacrificial ceremonies.

    (ii) It has to be partitioned into two main texts; White or Shukla Yajurved which contains hymns (mantras) and the Black or Krishna Yajurveda that has commentary in prose.

Q. 8. Name the oldest Veda composed during early Vedic period. What does it contain ?

[February, 2020]

Ans. The oldest Veda composed during the early Vedic period is the Rig Veda. It is a collection of 1028 hymns that highlight the political, social, economic and religious conditions of the early Vedic period.

Q. 9. Give two features of the political organisation of the Aryans during the Rigvedic Civilisation.

Ans. (i)   The early Aryans lived in tribes called 'Janas' headed by its own chief or king.

    (ii) The king sought the advice of the two assemblies named as Sabha and Samiti.

Q. 10. What is the importance of Upanishad ?

Ans. (i)   Upanishads are anti-ritualistic and specify philosophical knowledge and spiritual learning.

    (ii) They are of great importance as they contain valuable information about the social and religious condition of the Aryan.

Q. 11. Give two important features of the economy activity during the Rigvedic civilisation.

Ans. (i)   Agriculture was the chief occupation of the Aryans which includes cultivations.

    (ii) Barter system of trade was flourished through which general commodities were exchange against each other.

Q. 12. What do you know about Sutras?

Ans. (i)   Sutras explain the customs and rituals of the later Vedic period.

    (ii) They dealt especially with the rituals relating to soma sacrifice.

Q. 13. Give two feature of the political organisation of the Aryans during the vedic period.

Ans. (i)   In both the early and later vedic period, the kings were always prepared to serve their subjects.

    (ii) In both the cases local self government was an important institution.

Q. 14. What are the sources of information regarding the vedic age?

Ans. (i)   The sources of information regarding the early vedic age comprises of the four principal vedas, the Brahmanas, the Aranyakas and the Upanishads, etc.

    (ii) The sources for later vedic period includes the Sutras, the Vedangas, the Upavedas, the Darshanas, the Puranas, the Mahakavyas and the Dharmashastras, etc.

Q. 15. Give any two religious features of the early Vedic period.

Ans. (i)   Aryans worshipped several Nature-gods, however they believed in monotheism who is the source of all powers vetted with the nature god.

    (ii) The way of worship was very simple as they recited several hymns in the open air to praise the God.

Q. 16. Write any two important changes in the political field during the Later Vedic Period?

Ans. (i)   In comparison to the Rigvedic Period, the Later Vedic Period has big kingdoms and empires such as kuru, Panchal, Kosala, Magadha, Kashi, etc.

    (ii) Instead of king himself, their armies led by their commanders to fight battles.

Q. 17. Differentiate between the following :

    (a) Position of women during the Early Vedic Period and Later Vedic Period.

    (b) Trade during the Early Vedic Period and Later Vedic Period.

    (c) Worship during the Early Vedic Period and Later Vedic Period.

    (d) Sabha and Samiti

    (e) Ramayan and Mahabharat.

Ans.

(a)   **Position of Woman:**

S.No.	Early Vedic Period	Later Vedic Period
(i)	Women had equal status as men.	The position of women declined.
(ii)	They could participate in assemblies.	They were not allowed in assemblies or yajnas.
(iii)	They could receive education.	Fewer women could receive education.
(iv)	Widow remarriage was allowed.	Widow remarriage was looked down.

(b)   **Trade:**

S.No.	Early Vedic Period	Later Vedic Period
(i)	Trade was carried out by exchanging bullocks and horses.	Silver coins were used.
(ii)	Guilds and associations did not exist.	Guilds and associations were prevalent.

(c)   **Worship:**

S.No.	Early Vedic Period	Later Vedic Period
(i)	Early Vedic Aryans worshipped natural forces.	Natural gods lost their importance.
(ii)	Religious practices were simple.	Religous practices became highly complex.
(iii)	Chanting hymns was important.	Rituals were given more importance than chanting mantras.

(d)	Sabha	Samiti
(i)	It was composed of only the distinguished members.	It was a body which represented the whole tribe.
(ii)	Its members were called sabhasad and headed by sabhapati.	No such proclamation were used.

(e)	Ramayana	Mahabharata
(i)	It contains 24,000 couplets.	It is written in 16 volumes containing 1,00,000 couplets.
(ii)	It is the life story of Lord Rama and his virtues.	It is the story of the battle fought between the Pandavas and Kauravas.

Q. 18. Why is the Vedic literature known as 'shruti'?

Ans. (a) The word 'shruti' means to hear.

    (b) The vedas were passed down the generations in the form of oral recitation. Therefore, they are also known as 'shruti' or 'relevations'.

Q. 19. Why is the discovery of iron consider an important event in the Later Vedic Period?

Ans. (i) The discovery of iron helped the Aryan people to clear forests and bring new lands under cultivation.

    (ii) With the discovery of iron, metal and leather work, carpentry and pottery made great progress which gave rise to trade.

    (iii) Agriculture grew in importance and metal tools and iron plough shares were used instead of the wooden.

Q. 20. Describe two reasons for the importance of the Vedic literature in Indian Society.

Ans. (i) The vedas throw much light on the social, political, religious and economic life of the Aryans.

(ii) Vedas were considered the store-house of the Aryan wisdom as it consists of not only the four vedas but also other allied books like the Brahmanas, the Aranyakas, the Upanishads, etc.

Q. 21. Describe the reasons for importance of epics for Indian Society.

Ans. (i) The Bhagwat Gita is held sacred and continues to mould the lives of many Indians till today.

(ii) Both the Ramayan and Mahabharat help in reconstructing the history of ancient India.

(iii) Based on themes of these epics, India's magic dance and drama developed through the countries and inspired the life and the culture of Indians.

Q. 22. Give reasons for the impact of Aryan culture for Indian society.

Ans. (i) The Aryans gave to India the Sanskrit language which served as the mother language for many regional languages.

(ii) The Vedas and the Upanishads became the basis for the present day Hindu religion.

(iii) Vedic hymns are still chanted at Hindu ceremonies connected with birth, marriage and death.

Q. 23. State any two changes in the caste systems that were evident in the Later Vedic period.   **[November, 2019]**

Ans. Two changes in the caste system that were evident in the Later Vedic period were :

(i)   There was a fixation of occupations on the basis of one's caste.

(ii) The position of the Shudras was made miserable by depriving them of the rights of learning the sacred texts and performing sacrifices. They were forced to live in separate settlements outside the village or the town boundaries.

Q. 24. Write any two features of the Gurukul system of Education.   **[November, 2019]**

Ans. Two features of the Gurukul system of Education were :

(i)   No fees were charged for this type of education, but the pupils paid a voluntary contribution known as Gurudakshina when they completed their education.

(ii) Children from both the rich and poor families stayed together and rendered various duties in the running of the Gurukul.

Chapter 3. Jainism And Buddhism

Q. 1. What are the five vows for the Jains?

Ans. Five vows for the Jains are :

(i)   Not to injure life,   (ii) Not to tell a lie,

(iii) Not to steal,   (iv) Not to possess any property and

(v)   To practice chastity.

Q. 2. Mention two features of the Chaitya Hall, Karle.

Ans. (i) The Chaitya Hall, Karle was made in the beginning of the Christian era in the Satavahana period.

(ii) It served the purpose of a meeting hall or a service hall.

Q. 3. Who was the founder of Jainism? Name the twenty third Tirthankara.

Ans. (i) Vardhman Mahavira is considered as the real founder of Jainism.

(ii) The first tirthankara of Jainism was Rishabhdeva and the twenty-third Tirthankara was Parshvanath.

Q. 4. What is known as the 'Great Renunciation'?

Ans. (i) The event when Buddha left his home and kindgom at the age of 29 and went in search for truth is known as the 'Great Renunciation'.

(ii) For two years, he became the disciple of a Brahman and studied the Vedas and Shastras.

Q. 5. State any two effects of Buddhism on the Indian sculpture.

Ans. (i) Gautam Buddha was totally against idol-worship but gradually people began to make his stone images, raising him to the position of a god.

(ii) Several historians confirm that the practice of making images and idol-worship did not exist in India previous to the rise of Buddhism.

Q. 6. Write any three contributions which Jainism made to Indian architecture.

Ans. (i) Jain followers built stupas, monasteries and temples to perpetuate the memory of their saints and sages.

(ii) They built beautiful temples and images at their pilgrimage centres such as Purshavan Hill, Pawapuri, Rajgrih, Girnar and Mount Abu.

(iii) The Jains also built rock cut cave temples like Hathi Gumpha or Cave in Orissa, the Indra Sabha Cave at Ellora and the Lion Cave in Udaygiri.

Q. 7. What are the contribution of Jainism in the field of religion?

Ans. (i) Jainism did a praise-worthy job to remove several evils of Hinduism.

(ii) It saved the people from rigidity of Yajna and sacrifices and simplified the complex ideas.

Q. 8. Mention the literary works of Jainism.

Ans. (i) The chief works of Jains called the Anges, that were written in Prakrit.

(ii) The original teachings of Lord Mahavira were compiled in fourteen books called Purvas.

Q. 9. How one can achieve the salvation as per the Jain philosophy?

Ans. (i) Like Hindus, Jains also believe that chief goal of a man's life is to attain salvation or moksha from the cycle of births and rebirths.

(ii) This moksha can be achieved by following the three jewels or Triratnas of right faith, right knowledge and right conduct.

Q. 10. What is the belief of Jainism about the idea of the caste system?

Ans. (i) Jainism does not believe in the caste system and preached equality in all human beings.

(ii) All who have faith in Jainism are brothers without any class distinction.

Q. 11. State any three causes that led to the rise of Jainism and Buddhism in the 6th century B.C. in India.   **[February, 2020]**

Ans. During the 5th and 6th centuries, the rigid caste system, the complex system of religion and the existing social and economic inequalities made the people look out for a different kind of society and religious system. The three causes that led to the rise of Jainism and Buddhism in the 6th century B.C. in India were :

(i) Difficult vedic language: The Vedic texts were written in Sanskrit which was beyond the comprehension of the common man. The common people were unable to understand. They did not follow the rituals and mantras of Brahmin priests.

(ii) Rigid caste system: Caste was decided according to birth and not according to profession. People could not change their profession and it was fixed. People of lower castes were ill-treated by the people of higher castes. Untouchability came into practice. People of lower castes were forbidden from entering temples and following rituals. These discriminations and caste division were resented by the intellectuals and many common men. The Buddhist Sangha was open to all equally.

(iii) Complex vedic religion: Earlier the rituals were simple and people were able to understand, follow and perform them. However, gradually the rituals became complex and meaningless. Also the rituals became costly for the general public to perform. People could not comprehend and were discontented with the religious beliefs and practices of that age.

Q. 12. What is Nirvana?

Ans. (i) As per the Buddhism philosophy one should live a noble life and attain Nirvana that means ultimate salvation.

(ii) In the 'Nirvana' state, the soul becomes free from the eternal cycle of life and death.

Q. 13. Write the contributions of Buddhism in the Education sphere.

Ans. (i) The Buddhist monasteries were transformed into vital centres of learning.

(ii) The renowned universities of Taxila, Nalanda and Vikramsila drew the attention of many students from abroad.

Q. 14. State two points of similarity between Jainism and Buddhism.

Ans. (i) Both religions denied the existence of God.

(ii) Both religions opposed the authenticity of the Vedas and the necessity of performing animal sacrifices.

Q. 15. What was the impact of Buddhism on social life of the people?

Ans. (i) Buddhism revealed society's weaknesses and promoted intellectual tradition.

(ii) It aimed at the upliftment and betterment of the deprived section of society.

Q. 16. Write any two factors for the decline of Jainism.

Ans. (i) The rigid principles of Jainism found very difficult to follow.

(ii) Jainism was restricted to India and didn't spread to foreign countries due to lack of efforts by missionaries.

Q. 17. Why the Buddhism declined in India?

Ans. Buddhism declined in India because of the following reasons:

(i) As time passed the royal patronage made the Buddhist monasteries rich and the monks and nuns began to lead a life of luxury subsequently the common man lost faith in Buddhism.

(ii) The split in Buddhism caused quarrels and differences among them which took away the spirit of unity in Buddhism and made the people to convert the religion.

Q. 18. Why is the place shravanabelagola important for Jains?

Ans. The colossal statue of Gomateshwara is situated at Shravan Belagola in Karnataka and is known for its huge height and grandeur. Hence, it become an important Jain pilgrimage site.

Q. 19. Why was Buddha's teaching called the Middle Path?

Ans. At one side the Buddha condemned the priests while on the other side he opposed the life of severe austerity as preached by the Jains. Thus his teaching was called the Middle Path.

Q. 20. Why were images of the Buddha introduced in art?

Ans. The Buddha was totally against idol-worship but gradually people began raise him to the position of a god and thus people started to make his images.

Q. 21. What are the Jatakas ? **[February, 2020]**

Ans. The Jataka tales, written in Pali, is a Buddhist sacred literature. It describes the previous births of Lord Buddha. They also throw light on political, economic and social conditions of the society between fifth and second century BC.

Q. 22. (a) Differentiate between the Hinayana and Mahayana sect of Buddhism.

(b) Differentiate between the Swetambaras and Digambar as sects of Jainism.

(c) Differentiate between tripitaka and Jatakas.

(d) Differentiate between Jainism and Buddhism.

Ans. (a) **Hinayana:**

(i) The followers of Hinayana or lesser vehicle strictly followed the doctrine of Buddha and denied the existence of God.

(ii) They do not believe in idol worship nor that Buddha was God.

(iii) They believe in the Eight-Fold Path as the only means of Salvation.

Mahayana:

(i) The followers of Mahayana or Greater Vehicle followed the combine doctrine of Buddhism.

(ii) They believe that Buddha was an incarnation of God and worship his statues and Boddhisattvas.

(iii) Instead of keeping their goal of attaining salvation, they made their aim to attain swarg.

(b)

S.No.	Digambaras	Swetambaras
(i)	They were the orthodox followers of Mahavira.	They were not the orthodox followers of Mahavira.
(ii)	They kept long fast and led an extreme austere life.	They kept fast but did not believe in extreme austerity.
(iii)	They discard clothes.	They wear white tunics.

(c) **The Tripitaka :**

(i) It is Buddhist sacred literature comprises three volumes or baskets.

(ii) The Vinayapitaka, the Sutrapitaka and Abhidhammapitaka are three baskets of this literature.

(iii) It contains Buddhist philosophical principles, lectures of Buddha and guidence for monks to manage buddhist monastries.

The Jatakas :

(i) The Jatakas are the stories of Buddha's birth and his life before achieving enlightenment.

(ii) The stories provided the glimpse of Indian life in the 3rd and 4th century.

(d)

S.No.	Jainism	Buddhism
(i)	Jainism was founded even before the appearance of 24th tirthankara, Mahavira.	Buddhism was founded by Buddha around 6th century BC.
(ii)	Jainism believes in the existence of soul in every living being.	Buddhism does not believe in the existence of soul.
(iii)	Jainism remained restricted within the Indian sub-continent.	Buddhism extended beyond the boundaries of India.

Chapter 4. The Mauryan Empire

Q. 1. Who wrote Arthashastra ? What is it about?   **[February, 2020]**

Ans. Arthashastra was written by Kautilya is an extremely sophisticated and detailed treaties on state-craft.

(i) It was one of the greatest treaties by Kautilya on economics, politics, foreign affairs, administration, military and war, arts and religion of Mauryan Empire.

(ii) It discusses the life and society of Mauryan people.

(iii) It describes in detail the qualities and discipline required to be a wise and virtuous king.

Q. 2. Who was Chanakya and which famous book did he write?

Ans. (i) Chanakya was an ancient philosopher, economist, and royal adviser of Chandragupta Maurya.

(ii) He wrote the Arthashastra.

Q. 3. State the importance of Ashoka's Edicts.

Ans. (i) The Ashokan Rock Edicts are the most reliable source of information about Ashoka's reign.

(ii) The inscriptions on these edicts describe the Buddhist concept of dharma.

Q. 4. State any two features of the Sanchi Stupa.

Ans. (i) The Sanchi stupa in Madhya Pradesh is the oldest stone structure built by emperor Ashoka in the 3rd centrury BC preserving the ruins of Buddha.

(ii) The four gateways that were added later on the four sides of this stupa depict scenes from the life of Buddha.

Q. 5. What were the reasons that led Ashoka to conquer Kalinga?

Ans. The main reasons that led Ashoka to conquer Kalinga were as follows:

(i) Kalinga was the only Kingdom which was controlled by the Nandas.

(ii) It was important from military point of view as it controlled the land and sea routes to South India and South-East Asia.

Q. 6. Briefly describe the extent of Mauryan empire under Ashoka.

Ans. (i) Under Ashoka the Mauryan Empire extended from the North Western Mountains of Hindukush that consists Kashmir, parts of Indus valley, the entire Gangetic delta and the foothills of Nepal to the Mysore.

(ii) Outside India the empire includes Kabul, Herat and Kandhar.

Q. 7. Name the boards of five members in which the Mauryan army was divided.

Ans. (i) Board of Infantry,   (ii) Board of Cavalry

(iii) Board of War Chariots   (iv) Board of War Elephants

(v) Board for Navy   (vi) Board for managing transport

Q. 8. Discuss the provincial government under the Mauryan administrations.

Ans. (i) Till the Ashoka's reign the Mauryan Kingdom was divided into Magadha, Avanti, Gandhara, Southern Province and Kalinga.

(ii) Governors were appointed to the capitals to manage the provinces.

(iii) The head of these provinces were known as Aryaputra or kumar.

Q. 9. State any two factors that led to the decline of the Mauryan Empire.

Ans. (i) It was believed that Ashoka's peaceful policies were the root cause of the decline of the empire because it gave a chance to Pushyamitra Sunga to revolt and end the dynasty.

(ii) The successors of Ashoka were weak and failed to hold the reins of such a huge empire.

Q. 10. Describe the role of king in the Mauryan Empire.

Ans. (i) The king was the supreme authority of the government whose throne passed on to the next successor by hereditary.

(ii) He was not only the head of the state but also the head of the Judiciary and Military administration.

Q. 11. Write in brief the system of spies in the Mauryan Empire.

Ans. (i) The system of spies was an excellent aspect of Mauryan administration where the emperor employed spies to get regular information about the working of his state.

(ii) The king had to be aware of all matters concerning the burea cracy, thus these spies collected all valuable information for the king about his state, his army and the performance of his officials.

Q. 12. What was the role of the council of Ministers in the Mauryan administration?

Ans. (i) In the Mauryan Empire the king was assisted by a council called the 'mantriparishad' and its ministers were called as 'mantris'.

(ii) The mantriparishad consisted of Purohit (high priest), senapati (commonder-in-chief), Yuvaraj (heir appurent) and few other members.

Q. 13. Discuss the revenue system of the Mauryan Empire.

Ans. (i) The taxes were raised both in cash and in kind by the local officers called Agronomoi.

(ii) The chief sources of revenue was the land tax which was one-sixth to one-fourth of the produce while the second major source of income was toll tax that was levied on all articles excepted grain and cattle, etc.

Q. 14. What do you understand by the term Bali and Bhaga?

Ans. (i) Among the two kind of taxes Bali and Bhaga, the Bali was a religions tribute.

(ii) Bhaga was called the king's share and was levied on agricultural produce at the rate of one-sixth to one-fourth.

Q. 15. Who were exempted from paying tax in the Mauryan Empire?

Ans. (i) As per the Rummindei Edict the birth place of the Buddha *i.e.* Lumbini was exempted from bali and was to pay only one-eighth of Bhaga.

    (ii) The Brahmins, women, children, the blind and other physically and mentally challenged persons were not liable to pay any kind of tax.

Q. 16. Write any two characteristics of the Mauryan Empire.

Ans. (i)   In the Mauryan Empire the society was divided into classes still the happiness and peace existed in the kingdom.

    (ii) Trade, agriculture, art and architecture, all flourishad in the Mauryan Empire.

Q. 17. Why Ashoka wanted to fight the Kalinga War?

Ans. Ashoka wanted to fight the Kalinga War because it was the only kingdom that was not under the Mauryan Empire.

Q. 18. Give reason why the coronation ceremony of Ashoka took place after four years of his father's death in 273 BC?

Ans. Ashoka's coronation ceremony took place in 269 BC after four years of his father's death because the war of succession took place among the sons of Bindusara and Ashoka took 4 years to won this war.

Q. 19. Differentiate between Pulsias and Prativedaka.

Ans. (i)   The Pulsias were like public relation officers who kept the emperor updated about public opinion about his rule.

    (ii) On the other side, the prativedakas were special reporters of the king and had direct access to him.

Q. 20. What was the difference between bali and bhaga?

Ans. Bali was a tax paid on the religious grounds whereas Bhaga was a tax charged on the agricultural products and cattle.

Q. 21. Differentiate between Susrusa and Apichiti.

Ans. Both Susrusa and Apichiti are the code of duties of Dhamma. The term susrusa means to obedient towards elders and parents while Apichiti means to respect teachers.

Q. 22. What is the importance of the 'Ashoka's Edicts'?   **[November, 2019]**

Ans. The importance of Ashoka's Edicts are :

    (i)   The Ashoka's edicts are the most reliable source of information about Ashoka's reign.

    (ii) They provide an insight into the life and ideals of Ashoka in particular and about the history of the Mauryans in general.

Chapter 5. The Sangam Age

Q. 1. Name the three state that flourished during the Sangam Age.

Ans. (i)   The Pandyas (Capital Madurai)

    (ii) The Cholas (Capital Kaveripattanam)

    (iii) The Cheras (Capital Vajji)

Q. 2. What do you understand by the term Ettutogai?

Ans. (i)   Ettutogai stands for eight anthologies in the Sangam literature.

    (ii) The main test of Ettutogai is a Tamil work of poetry known as the purananuru which reflects the statecraft, kingship and governance.

Q. 3. State any two superstitious beliefs of the people dwelling in the Sangam Age.

Ans. (i)   A women with untidy hair was considered a bad omen.

    (ii) A Banyan tree was considered the abode of gods.

Q. 4. What was the condition of widows during the Sangam Age?

Ans. (i)   The life of widows was miserable during the Sangam Age.

    (ii) They had to shave their head, abandon all ornaments and consume only the tasteless, and tedious food.

Q. 5. What was the five-fold divisions of land during the Sangam Age?

Ans. The five-fold divisions of land during the Sangam Age were as follows :

    (i) Kurinji (hilly tracks)   (ii) Mullai (pastoral)

    (iii) Murudam (agricultural)   (iv) Neydal (coastal)

    (v) Palai (desert)

Q. 6. Write any two food habits of the ancient Tamils.

Ans. (i) The food-habits ranged among the people according to their economic status.

    (ii) Offering betel leaves to guests had become a social formality.

Q. 7. What were the archaeological sources of the Sangam Age?

Ans. Archaeological sources for the Sangam Age were consisted megaliths, herostones and Brahmanical inscriptions that have thrown a lot of light on the ancient Tamil society, religion and economy.

Q. 8. How did the ancient Tamil dress themselves?

Ans. (i) In the Sangam society, the rich wore silk and fine cotton garments while middle class people wore two pieces of cotton clothes.

    (ii) Women used flowers to decorate their hairstyles.

    (iii) Both men and women used perfumes made of sandal and flowers.

Q. 9. How do we know about the trade guilds of the Sangam Age?

Ans. (i) A number of inscriptions have been found which evident the existence of several trade guilds of metal workers, potters, blacksmiths, carpenters, goldsmiths hydraulic engineers, corn-dealers, etc.

    (ii) These guilds usually act as financiers and bankers as well.

Q. 10. Define 'Megaliths'.   **[February, 2020]**

Ans. (i) Megaliths are large stones carefully arranged by people and used to mark burial sites. They were prevalent in the upland portions of the peninsula of India in eastern Andhra and Tamil Nadu and in Kashmir.

    (ii) The megaliths contain not only the skeleton of people who were burried but also pottery, iron tools and weapons, arrows, spearheads, sickles, ornaments of gold and stone, and fragments of rice and other grains. Few burial sites of the Chalcolithic age and early Iron age are marked by megaliths.

Q. 11. What were the local markets in the Sangam Society?

Ans. Local markets in the Sangam Age were called 'Anagadis' along with day markets called 'Nalangadis' and evening markets called 'Allangadis'.

Q. 12. Differentiate between Silappadikaram and Manimegalai.

Ans. (i) Silappadikaram and Manimegalai both were Tamil epics written by Adigal and Saathanar respectively.

    (ii) The first one describes the detailed life style of the Tamil people, language, religious practices and myths while later describes the Buddhist culture.

    (iii) Silappadikaram focuses the story of a merchant Kovalan and his wife Kannagi whereas Manimegalai is the story of Manimegalai the daughter of Madhavi and Kovalan who becomes a Buddhist nun.

Q.13. What is meant by the term 'Sangam' ?   **[November, 2019]**

Ans. The word 'Sangam' means 'Assembly'. According to early traditions three Sangams or Assemblies of literary men were held at Madurai, the center of great literary activity in the Tamil Country.

Chapter 6. The Age of Guptas

Q. 1. Give two important aspects of the Bhakti cult during the Gupta period.

Ans. (i) During the Gupta period the Bhakti cult gave importance to devotion rather than to knowledge.

(i) The people devoted themselves to one's personal god with love and surrender.

Q. 2. How did Sanskrit become an important language during the Gupta period?

Ans. (i) Sanskrit was recognized as the court language and was used in their inscription.

(ii) Gradually it became the accent of India.

Q. 3. Name three dramatists and three poets of the Gupta period.

Ans. Three Dramatists: (i) Kalidas (ii) Vishakhadutta (iii) Shudraka.

Three Poets: (i) Harisena (ii) Bharavi (iii) Subhandhu.

Q. 4. What is the importance of Prayag Prashasti?

Ans. (i) Prayag Prashasti is written in praise of Samudragupta by Harisena.

(ii) It provides an impressive list of kings and tribal republic conquered by Samudragupta.

(iii) It also indicates the information about different kings and people who populated India in the first half of the 4th century AD.

Q. 5. State any two major contributions of Aryabhatta.

Ans. (i) Aryabhatta was the first to hold that earth is a sphere rotating on its axis and that eclipses were the shadow of earth falling on the Sun or the Moon.

(ii) In his book, Aryabhatiyam, he has dealt with different branches of the subject including Algebric identities.

Q. 6. How did Chandragupta enhance his power and prestige?

Ans. (i) Chandragupta enhanced his power and prestige by entering into alliance with the Lichchhavi tribe, which had taken control of pataliputra during the unsettled period after the fall of the Kushana power.

(ii) With the help of Lichchhavis, Chandragupta I was able to establish a kingdom, which covered modern Bihar, Jharkhand and eastern uttar pradesh.

Q. 7. State the uniqueness of the Panchatantra.

Ans. (i) In the stories of Panchatantra, animals and birds play the part of king's ministers and common men.

(ii) The Panchatantra has been translated into many languages and no other book except the Bible has been translated into so many languages as this famous book.

Q. 8. In what way did Gupta period make progress in the field of Education.   **[February, 2020]**

Ans. Significant progress was made in the field of education during the Gupta period :

(i) Besides the Pathshala, there were world renowned universities such as Nalanda and Taxila. Nalanda was situated near Rajgriha, near Patna in Bihar. Taxila was located near Rawalpindi, now in Pakistan.

(ii) Students from all over the country and from abroad came for higher education. These universities came to be known for its research and advanced studies.

Q. 9. Give evidence to show that India had become a great centre of learning during the Gupta period.

Ans. (i) The Guptas were great patrons of education.

(ii) The names Nalanda, Takshila, Ujjain, Vikramshila and valabhi were evident that these universities became great centre of higher studies by attracting scholars from all parts of India and abroad.

Q. 10. Mention two important features of Ajanta paintings.

Ans. (i) The frescos on Ajanta paintings illustrate episodes from the life of Buddha as depicted in the jataka stories.

(ii) Some of the Ajanta murals reflect Buddhist values such as love and understanding.

Q. 11. What is metallurgy? Name the finest example of metallurgical skills that developed during Gupta period.

Ans. (i) The scientific study of metals is called metallurgy which reached a high standard during the Gupta period.

(ii) The famous Iron Pillar at Mehrauli stands near the Qutub Minar bears witness to assert the high standard of metallurgical skills and metal casting of the artists of the Gupta Age.

Q. 12. State two distinctive features of the sculpture of that period.

Ans. (i) The art of sculpture reached the highest peak of perfection in the Gupta period.

(ii) Images of Buddha, Vishnu and Shiva more beautifully represented in sculpture and were known for their balance, proportion and close filling transparent garments.

Q. 13. State any two contributions of Varahmihira.

Ans. (i) Varahmihira authored two renowned books named Brihat-Sanhita and Panch-Siddhantika.

(ii) He even studied planetary movements under the influence of the greeds and gave proofs for his claim that the moon rotates around the earth which in turn rotates around the sun.

Q. 14. Write in brief about the books composed by Varahmihira.

Ans. (i) The first work composed by Varahmihira, the Panch-Siddhantika is a treatise on mathematical astronomy and it summarizes five earlier treatises namely the Surya Siddhanta, Romata Siddhanta, Paulisa Siddhanta, Vasishtha Siddhanta and Paitamaha Siddhanta.

(ii) The next one Brihat-Sanhita is an encyclopedia of science which dealt with astrology, planetary movements, eclipses, rainfall, clouds, architecture, growth of crops, manufacture of perfume, matrimony domestic relations, gems, pearls and rituals.

Q. 15. Mention one great work of each of the following:

(a) Shudraka (b) Harisena

(c) Bharavi (d) Subandhu

Ans. (a) Shudraka — Mrichchakatika

(b) Harisena — The poem inscribed on Allahabad pillar

(c) Bharavi — Kiratarjuniya

(d) Subandhu — Vasavadutta

Q. 16. Mention the features of seated Buddha at Sarnath.

Ans. (i) The figure of seated Buddha at Sarnath near Varanasi dating back to the 5th century.

(ii) The figure is shown sitting in a yogic position and preaching his first sermon to disciples.

Q. 17. Why is Samudragupta called the 'Napoleon of India'?

Ans. Samudragupta is called the Napoleon of India for his monumental achievements in a single life time and amazing military powers and his lifestyle.

Q. 18. Why is the Gupta period called the 'Golden Age' of Indian culture?

Ans. The Gupta period is called the Golden Age of India because there was an all round progress in arts, architecture, literature and science.

Q. 19. Why has the Gupta period been called the period of Hindu Renaissance?

Ans. The Gupta period has been called the period of Hindu Renaissance because of the revival of Brahmanism culture in India.

Q. 20. Why Kalidas is called the Shakespeare of India?

Ans. Kalidas was acclaimed as Shakespeare of India due to his master pieces of plays, poems, epics, etc.

Q. 21. Mention two ways in which the hinduism of the Gupta period differed from the Brahmanical religions of the vedic time.

Ans. (i) The old gods of vedic period like Surya, Indra, etc receded into the background and new gods such as Brahma, Vishnu and Mahesh come to the forefront.

(ii) The supreme position of Brahmanism replaced by the Bhakti cult.

Q. 22. Write two contribution of Aryabhatta in the field of science.   **[November, 2019]**

Ans. Two contributions of Aryabhatta in the field of Science are:

   (i) He worked out the exact value of π (pi), that is, 3.1416.

   (ii) He discovered a formula to find the area of a triangle.

Chapter 7. The Cholas

Q. 1. What is the other name of the Brihadeshwara temple? Mention one architectural feature of the temple.

Ans. Brihadeshwara temple is also known as Rajarajeshwara temple. The temple consists of the Nandi mandapa, a pillard portico and an assembly hall. They are all interconnected.

Q. 2. Name the important sources of the Chola period.

Ans. Important sources of Chola period are copper plate inscriptions and inscriptions of the pillars and walls of temples.

Q. 3. Name the Chola ruler who adopted the title 'Gangaikonda'. State the purpose of such a title.

   [February, 2020]

Ans. Rajendra-I adopted the title 'Gangaikonda'.

   (i) Rajendra-I annexed the whole of Sri Lanka. He then marched through the northern region till the Ganga Valley and defeated the Pala Kings of Bengal and Odisha.

   (ii) He took over Andaman and Nicobar Islands and the Malay Peninsula and Sumatra.

   (iii) He adopted the title 'Gangaikonda' and built a capital called Gangaikonda Cholapuram.

Q. 4. Mention the two types of soldiers of the Chola kingdom.

Ans. The soldiers of the Chola kingdom comprised of two types:

   (i) Kaikkolar : They formed the royal troops and received regular pay from the treasury.

   (ii) Nattupadai : They formed the militia men recruited for local defence.

Q. 5. State any two points to support that women in Chola society were given status and freedom.

Ans. Women in Chola society were given high status and freedom.

   (i) They were appointed as officers in the Chola Government.

   (ii) The women of the upper classes enjoyed the right to property. Some queens were associated with the administration of the kingdom and were patrons of temples.

Q. 6. How were the members of the village assembly elected during the Chola rule?

Ans. Villagers who owned the land were chosen for the council by vote. The method of election included the name slips of all candidates were put and mixed in a pot. A small boy pulled out the slips one by one. The village priest announced the results.

Q. 7. What is Gangaikondacholapuram famous for?

Ans. After conquering complete territory of Sri Lanka, Rajendra Chola assumed the title of Gangaikonda. He built a new capital named Gangaikondacholapuram.

Q. 8. Which poem describes the reign of Kulottunga, with the Kalinga war of Kulottunga Chola I as its theme? Who wrote this poem?

Ans. Kalingattuparani is a Tamil war poem which describes the reign of Kulottunga, with the Kalinga war of Kulottunga Chola I as its theme. This poem is written by the Chola court-poet Jayamkondar.

Q. 9. What names are given to the following territorial divisions of the Chola kingdom

   (a) Province and   (b) the District

Ans. (a) The Province was known as Mandalam.   (b) The district was known as Nadus.

Q. 10. Why did the Cholas build a strong naval fleet?

Ans. The Cholas built a strong naval fleet in order to keep a strong control over the trade activities of Arabian traders with the Indian merchants of the southern coastal region.

Q. 11. Mention any two notable inscriptions of Chola rulers. Which Chola king issued that inscription?

Ans. Two notable inscriptions of Chola rulers are:

   (i) The Thiruvalangadu grant of Rajendra Chola I   (ii) The Anbil plates of Sundaara Chola

Q. 12. What information do we get from the various inscriptions of the Chola period?

Ans. The inscriptions of the Chola period provide us with the following information:

   (i) Important achievements of the Chola kings   (ii) Chola administration

   (iii) Records of land revenue, grants, gifts and endowments made by the Chola rulers to the temples and brahmanas.

   (iv) Temples constructed by Chola rulers.

Q. 13. What were the military achievements of Rajendra Chola?

Ans. Military achievements of Rajendra Chola :

   (i) Rajendra Chola conquered territories up to the east coasts of India, through the kingdom of Orissa and defeated the ruler of Bengal.

   (ii) In the south he conquered Ceylon (Sri Lanka).

   (iii) He also invaded the territories of King Srivijaya in Malaysia.

   (iv) He raided the territories of Pandyas and Chera and seized precious stones.

Q. 14. How can we say that Rajendra Chola was a great builder?

Ans. Rajendra Chola was a great builder.

   (i) He founded a new capital city called Gangaikondacholapuram and built a Shiva temple similar to the Thanjavur Brihadeshwara temple built by his father Rajaraja Chola.

   (ii) He also built a Shiva temple on the banks of river Ganga.

   (iii) He expanded the Pathirakali Amman Temple and Koneswaram temple of Trincomalee.

Chapter 8. The Delhi Sultanate

Q. 1. Who was the Wazir in the administration of Delhi Sultanate?

Ans. Wazir or the Chief Minister was the highest officer in the administration of Delhi Sultanate. He was in-charge of the general administration of the empire, especially revenue and finance.

Q. 2. Mention any two literary sources of Delhi Sultanate.

Ans. Two literary sources of Delhi Sultanate are 'Tarikh-i-Firoz Shahi' written by Ziauddin Barani and 'Prithviraj Raso' written by Chand Bardai.

Q. 3. Which two court practices were introduced by Balban?

Ans. Balban introduces rigid court discipline and practices, such as sijda (prostration before the Sultan) and paibos (kissing the sultan's feet)

Q. 4. Name any two archaeological sources to reconstruct the history of Delhi Sultanate.

Ans. Two archaeological sources to reconstruct the history of Delhi Sultanate are:

   (a) Qutub Minar built by Iltutmish

   (b) Alai Darwaza of Ala-ud-din Khalji

Q. 5. State any two steps that Alauddin Khilji took to establish control over the markets.

[February, 2020]

Ans. Alauddin Khilji's market control and strategy was remarkable. He maintained a large army on a relatively small pay. Hence, he had to take measures to control the market prices. Two steps that he took to establish control over the market were:

   (i) He regulated the prices of foodgrains, sugar and cooking oil, cloth and horses, cattle, slaves and other commodities.

   (ii) The traders had to sell the goods at fixed rates.

Q. 6. Mention any two land revenue reforms introduced by Ala-ud-din Khalji?

Ans. Ala-ud-din Khalji introduced the following reforms in the land revenue system:

   (a) Total land was measured and then the share of the state was fixed.

   (b) Officials were appointed to collect the land revenue for the state.

Q. 7. What would have happened if Ala-ud-din Khalji had not been able to repel the Mongol attack?

Ans. The Delhi Sultanate rule would have come to an end if Ala-ud-din Khalji had not been able to repel the Mongol attack. Moreover, a lot of people would have been masacred and taken as slaves.

Q. 8. Why is Iltutmish considered as the real founder of the Delhi Sultanate?

Ans. Iltutmish is considered as the real founder of Delhi Sultanate due to the following reasons:

(i)   He made Delhi his capital in place of Lahore.

(ii) Iltutmish ensured the security of the Delhi Sultanate from internal dangers as also from foreign aggressions.He suppressed the rebellious governors and also saved Delhi Sultanate from the wrath of Chengiz Khan.

Q. 9. Who were iqtadaars? What was their role?

Ans. The practice of giving revenue grants from a territory was known as iqta system and the grantees were known as the iqtadaars. The role of the iqtadaars was to lead military campaigns and to maintain peace and order in their iqtas.

Q. 10. What kind of struggle did Razia have to face as a woman ruler?

Ans. Being a woman Razia had to face many challenges, especially strong opposition from the Chahalgani.

Q. 11. Write the main difference between the Slave dynasty and other dynasties of the Delhi Sultanate.

Ans. The rulers of the slave dynasty were once slaves of the Turkish rulers while rulers of other dynasties following the slave dynasty were not slaves and were free and independent rulers.

Q. 12. What was the impact of Timur's invasion on Delhi?

Ans. The Sultanate of Delhi which had already broken up before Timur's invasion, now shrank to the capital city and a few villages around it.

Q. 13. Which battle marked the advent of the Mughal Empire in India? When and between whom was this battle fought?

Ans. Battle of Panipat marked the advent of the Mughal Empire in India. This battle was fought in the year 1526 between Babur and Ibrahim Lodhi.

Q. 14. Describe the importance of inscriptions as a source of the sultanate period.

Ans. Inscriptions are an important source of the Sultanate period.

(i)   Inscription of this period have been found on coins, seals and on the walls of buildings such as mosques and tombs.

(ii) Some inscriptions were written either in Arabic or Persian while some are bilingual that is written both in Arabic and Persian. Sometimes inscriptions were written in Sanskrit and Urdu.

(iii) These inscriptions have dates in Hijri year.

(iv) They are valuable source to reconstruct the history of that period as they provide information about the social, economic, political and cultural life of the period.

Q. 15. Name the five major projects for which Muhammad bin Tughluq has been criticised.

Ans. Five major projects for which Muhammad bin Tughluq has been criticised were:

(i)   Transfer of the capital from Delhi to Daulatabad.

(ii) Introduction of token currency.

(iii) Planning an expedition for the conquest of Khurasan and Iraq.

(iv) Qarachil expedition aimed at Kullu-Kangra region of Himachal Pradesh.

(v) Increase of land Revenue in the doab region.

Q. 16. State briefly the political achievements of the following rulers.

(a) Qutbuddin Aibak   (b) Ala-ud-din Khalji

(c) Muhammad bin Tughluq

Ans. Below mentioned are the political achievements of

(a) **Qutbuddin Aibak :** Qutbuddin founded the slave dynasty or Mamluk dynasty and this new kingdom is known as the Delhi Sultanate. He ruled for a very brief period. During his rule he did not make any fresh conquests. Rather he devoted his attention to the establishment of law and order in the Empire. His generous nature earned him the title of 'Lakh-baksh' meaning giver of lakhs.

(b) **Ala-ud-din Khalji :** His reign is famous for a series of brilliant conquests leading to the expansion of Muslim arms to South India. He became the first Muslim ruler to successfully defeat and conquer Southern parts of India. He successfully tackled the Mongol menace.

(c) **Muhammad bin Tughluq :** He annexed several kingdoms around his territories. He defeated the Mongols, who attacked the Delhi Sultanate. He created central financial offices to keep check on the financial activity.

Q. 17. Discuss the revenue reforms introduced by Ala-ud-din Khalji.

Ans. Ala-ud-din Khalji is known for his revenue reforms. In order to get maximum revenue, Ala-ud-din Khalji introduced a number of important measures such as:

(i) All the land of the Empire was brought under the direct control of the Sultan.

(ii) He introduced the practice of measuring the cultivable land for determining land revenue and fixing the state share accordingly.

(iii) Biswa was the standard unit of measurement.

(iv) He also increased the land revenue from one-third to one-sixth.

(v) He demanded the revenue to be paid in cash and not in kind.

Q. 18. What steps were taken by Alauddin Khalji to control market?

Ans. Following steps were taken by Alauddin Khalji to control market:

(i) Alauddin set up three markets at Delhi-one for foodgrains, one for horses, slaves and cattle and the third one for costly articles such as imported cloth.

(ii) Prices were fixed and quite low.

(iii) A strict watch was kept over buying and selling, and anyone cheating on price or weight was severly punished.

(iv) Hoarding was prohibited.

Q. 19. How can we say that the Muhammad bin Tughlaq's decision to shift the capital was a bad move? Give reason to support your answer.

Ans. This experiment of shifting of capital from Delhi to Devagiri, by Muhammad bin Tughlaq was a bad move.

(i) First, Daulatabad was situated far from the north Indian kingdoms, and there was a possibility of revolt by the Hindu Rajputs at any time.

(ii) Secondly, shifting of the capital also exposed Delhi and other states of the Sultanate to attacks by the Mongols who frequently raided the northwestern frontiers of India.

Chapter 9. The Mughal Empire

Q. 1. What were the two phases of Aurangzeb's moves in the Deccan?

Ans. Aurangzeb's moves in the Deccan are divided into two phases.

(i) The first was the invasion of Bijapur and Golconda.

(ii) The other was the long-standing war with the Marathas that continued for four generations.

Q. 2. What reforms did Aurangzeb impose in the Deccan when he was the viceroy?

Ans. Aurangzeb imposed land settlement in the Deccan during his second term of viceroyalty. Todarmal's zabt system of survey and assessment was duly extended to the Deccan too. These measures led to an improvement in agriculture and an increase in the revenue every year.

Q. 3. Who were the nine gems of Akbar's court?

Ans. Nine gems of Akbar's court were Abul Fazl, Faizi, Raja Todarmal, Raja Man Singh, Abdul Rahim Khan-i-Khana, Fakir Azio-Din, Mulla do-Piyaza, Birbal and Tansen.

Q. 4. Mention any two important features of the religious policy of Akbar.

Ans. Two important features of Akbar's religious policy were:

Short Questions

    (i) He followed a liberal religious policy. Full religious freedom was allowed not only to the Hindus but also to the people of other religious faith.

    (ii) He built a building called Ibadat Khana where he held discussions with the religious leaders.

Q. 5. Mention any two measures taken by Aurangzeb which made him unpopular.

Ans. The following steps taken by Aurangzeb made him unpopular among the masses:

    (i) He reimposed the jiziya tax on non-Muslims.

    (ii) He banned the celebration of Hindu festivals.

    (iii) He ordered the destruction of Hindu temples and Sikh shrines.

Q. 6. Which law of succession did Mughal's follow? How was it different from the traditions that other communities follow?

Ans. The other communities followed the tradition of Primogeniture under which eldest son inherited all his parent's property and the right to rule, but Mughal's followed the Timurid custom of coparcenary whereby there was a joint heir to an undivided property.

Q. 7. How was the Rajput policy followed by Aurangzeb different from the one followed by his predecessors?

Ans. Aurangzeb reversed the policy which was enunciated by Akbar and pursued by Jahangir and Shah Jahan. His predecessors maintained good relations with the Rajputs. Aurangzeb attempted to destroy the power of the Rajputs and annex their kingdoms.

Q. 8. When was the second battle of Panipat fought? What was its significance?

Ans. Second battle of Panipat was fought in 1556 between Akbar and Hemu, a nephew of Sher Shah Suri. In this battle, the Afghan army was defeated. This battle ended the rule of Afghan dynasty in India and re-established the Mughal rule in India and made Akbar the ruler of India.

Q. 9. Highlight Sher Shah Suri's achievements as a ruler?

Ans. Sher Shah was one of the most capable rulers of the medieval Indian history. He defeated Humayun in 1540 and laid the foundation of the Sur dynasty. Some of the notable achievements of Sher Shah Suri as a ruler were introduction of land revenue system and restoring of peace and order.

Q. 10. Write a short note on any one military conquests of Aurangzeb.

Ans. Aurangzeb was an excellent military commander. One of his military campaign was against the Ahoms, rulers of present-day Assam. They were defeated in 1663 by his governor in Bengal, Mir Jumla. But due to floods and starvation, the Assam expedition proved to be failure.

Q. 11. Explain the terms zabt and zamindar.

Ans. Zabt was a land revenue system introduced by Raja Todar Mal. In this system the cultiviable land was first measured and the land revenue was fixed on the basis of the quality of land and the quantity of produce. Zamindars were the intermediaries who collected revenue on behalf of the government.

Q. 12. Explain the functions of a diwan under the Mughal Empire.

Ans. The functions of a Diwan under the Mughal Empire are as follows:

    (i) He looked after the departments of revenue, finance and expenditure.

    (ii) He audited accounts (revenue and expenditure) of all departments.

Q. 13. Mention any two principles of Din-i-Illahi.

Ans. Two principles of Din-i-Illahi were as follows:

    (i) God is one and Akbar is his representative on earth.

    (ii) The members of Din-i-Illahi were expected to be tolerant and respectful to other religions and avoid marrying old women and young girls.

Q. 14. Mention the position of the following :

    (a) Khan-i-Saman   (b) Wazir

    (c) Diwan   (d) Mir Bakshi

    (e) Chief Qazi

Ans. (a) Khan-i-Saman : Head of the Imperial Household department

(b) Wazir : Highest position below king   (c) Diwan : Exchequer

(d) Mir Bakshi : Account Officer   (e) Chief Qazi : Judicial Officer

Q. 15. What problems did Humayun face upon taking over the Mughal throne?

Ans. At the time Humayun took over the throne, Mughal rule in India was still in its early stages. He had the tough task of consolidating it in the face of resistance from other regional rulers, such as the Rajputs. Babur had not been able to establish a system of administration over his territories. So, this task had also fallen on Humayun's shoulders. In addition, at the time Humayun took over the throne, Mughal finances were in a bad shape. Besides, Humayun faced stiff opposition from his brothers. This ultimately weakened his power against his rivals.

Q. 16. What was the reason for the conflict between Khurram and Nur Jahan?

Ans. Reasons for the conflict between Khurram and Nur Jahan were:

(i) Nur Jahan practically became the real ruler of the Mughal empire during the later years of Jahangir's rule.

(ii) She got her close relatives appointed to high positions, issued royal orders, and had coins minted with her name.

(iii) This led to a conflict with prince Khurram, who was alarmed by her rise to power.

Q. 17. What were the political achievements of Akbar?

Ans. During the rule of Akbar, the Mughal empire tripled in size and wealth. Akbar created a powerful military system and instituted effective political and social reforms. Akbar's main achievements were:

(i) Political unification of the Subcontinent.

(ii) Mansabdari system and efficient land revenue administration.

(iii) Friendly alliances with Rajputs.

(iv) Racial and religious conciliation in the country through a new religion Din-i-Illahi.

Chapter 10. Emergence of Composite Culture

Q. 1. Who was Sant Jnaneswar? What was his famous work?

Ans. He founded the Bhakti movement in Maharashtra. He wrote Gyaneshwari, a commentary on the Bhagvadgita in Marathi.

Q. 2. What is the importance of Guru Granth Sahib in Sikhism?

Ans. Guru Granth Sahib is the sacred book of the Sikhs. It contains the sayings of all the ten Sikh Gurus as well as of some other saints belonging to religions such as Hinduism and Islam.

Q. 3. Who were Sufis?

Ans. Sufis were Muslim mystics.

(i) They rejected outward religiosity and emphasised love and devotion to God and compassion towards all fellow human beings.

(ii) They condemned the elaborate rituals and codes of behaviour demanded by Muslim religious scholars.

Q. 4. What is meant by composite culture?

Ans. The term Composite culture means 'culture drawn from various strands'. It is a fusion of many elements drawn from several different traditions such as Classical Hindu tradition and the Islamic and Christian thoughts and beliefs.

Q. 5. Mention the two main principles of Sufism.

Ans. the two main principles of Sufism are:

(a) God is the supreme reality. He should be worshipped through love and personal devotion.

(b) Brotherhood and equality of all human beings, irrespective of colour, caste, creed and religion.

Q. 6. Who was Mirabai? What are her devotional songs known as?

Ans. Mirabai was a Rajput princess married into the ruling family of Mewar. She was a devotee of Lord Krishna since childhood and continued to devote her full time to Lord's worship even after her marriage. Her devotional songs are known as bhajans.

Q. 7. Explain the significance of Bhakti movement on Indian culture.   **[February, 2020]**

Ans. The Bhakti movement had a significant impact on Indian culture:

(i) **Equality:** The Bhakti movement denounced the caste distinctions. It brought about great social changes as it set free the minds of the people from the domination of the priests by condemning rituals and sacrifices.

(ii) **Harmony:** This movement brought about harmony among the Hindus and Muslims and spread the message of religious tolerance. The saints and reformers gave the people a simple religion that could be followed without complex rituals. It required only devotion to god. Their messages attracted large number of people from both the communities. It brought peace and sanctity in the society.

(iii) **Development of language and literature:** Most of the saints of the Bhakti movement preached in language of the common man. This encouraged the development of many regional languages, such as Hindi, Bengali, Marathi, Gujarati, Maithili, etc. Literature of very high class developed but it was in a language, which was easily understood by all. Kabir, Guru Nanak, Surdas, Mirabai, Chaitanya wrote dohas, couplets, hymns, poetry, sang kirtans or devotional songs. There was emergence of musical instruments like Robab, Sitar and Tamboora.

Q. 8. What led to the rise of the Bhakti cult?

Ans. Extreme orthodoxy and increasing rigidity in the caste system in the Hindu society brought a revolutionary change in the beliefs of the Hindus. It led to the development of the Bhakti cult.

Q. 9. What do you understand by the term 'sufi'? Discuss the spread of the Sufi movement.

Ans. Sufis were Muslim mystics who rejected any display of religious beliefs, and elaborate rituals and rules of behaviour laid down in the Shariat. The Sufi movement flourished under the patronage of the Delhi Sultans under whose rule several Sufi orders came up all across India.

Q. 10. Define Chisti order.

Ans. The Chisti order was introduced in India by Khwaja Moinuddin Chisti. It began in Chisti, a small town near Herat, Afghanistan about 930 CE. The Chisti order is known for its emphasis on love, tolerance and openness.

Q. 11. How can we say that Sufism held the orthodox Muslim in restraint?

Ans. Sufism induced many Muslim rulers like Akbar, Jahangir and Shah Jahan to be tolerant to non-Muslims. Many Muslim rulers allowed religious freedom to their subjects. Alauddin Khalji and Firoz Tughluq also respected Hindu saints.

Q. 12. Mention some important principles of the Bhakti cult.

Ans. Some important principles of Bhakti cult are:

(i) Selfless love and single-minded devotion to one God, who could be formless (Nirguna) or with form (Saguna).

(ii) The followers of both Saguna and Nirguna Bhakti believed in the philosophy of Advaita (non-duality of God) illustrated in the Upanishads.

(iii) Rejection of rituals and superiority of Brahmanas.

(iv) Belief in equality of all humans.

(v) Belief in the virtues of kindness, and purity of heart and mind.

(vi) Extreme reverence for Gurus (spiritual teachers).

Q. 13. State any three contributions made by Sant Jnaneswar.

Ans. Sant Jnaneswar was a 13th century Maratha saint poet, philosopher and yogi.

(i) He rejected caste system and identified with the common people.

(ii) He chose to write and preach in Marathi and his ideas conveyed the message of the Bhakti movement.

(iii) He wrote a commentary on the Gita called Dhyaneshwari and an independent philosophical work called Amrutanubhava.

(iv) He popularised Yoga and believed in Vithala or Lord Vishnu.

Q. 14. How did Sufi saints play an important role in the society?

Ans. Role of Sufi saints in the society:

(i) The Chisti saints helped in creating a situation in which people belonging to different classes and religious communities could live in harmony.

(ii) The Khanqahs helped promote peace and harmony. The dargahs of sufi saints became pilgrim centres for people of all castes and religions.

(iii) These khanqahs played an economic role also.

(iv) Some of them undertook the cultivation of wastelands. The institution of khanqahs played an important role in the process of urbanisation.

Q. 15. How did the Bhakti cult influence the Indian society in the medieval period?

Ans. The influence of Bhakti cult on Indian society in the medieval period:

(i) The Bhakti cult emphasised on the importance of a guru to guide the devotee's life. Thus many people began to question the authority and domination of their religion by the religious authorities.

(ii) The Bhakti saints condemned idol worship and the existence of rituals in the Indian society.

(iii) Universal brotherhood and religious tolerance was taught by the Bhakti saints. As a result, an environment of mutual love and respect was created among different sections of society.

(iv) Since, the Bhakti saints preached their teachings in the local language. This led to the development of the local and the vernacular languages.

Q. 16. Name two ways in which Sufism contributed to the religious unity of India.

Ans. It played an important role in promoting feelings of tolerance among the Muslim rulers. Their emphasis on love resulted in tolerance of other religions. They held that all religions were equal and important. In this way Sufism contributed to the religious unity of India.

Q. 17. State any two factors which promoted a composite culture during the Mughal Age.

[November, 2019]

Ans. Two factors which promoted a composite culture during the Mughal Age were :

(i) Prolonged interaction between Hindu and Muslim populations resulted in the development of a new composite culture, called the Indo-Islamic culture.

(ii) The Mughals used artists and architects from Persia and Central Asia to design and decorate their palaces, mosques and mausoleums. They were influenced and adopted the various Indian architectural styles from different part ot India. Thus, there developed a fusion of India and other Islamic artistic traditions Known as Indo-Islamic art.

Q. 18. Write any two ways by which the Bhakti Movement impacted Indian society.

[November, 2019]

Ans. Two ways by which the Bhakti Movement impacted Indian society were :

(i) The message of religious tolerance of saints and reformers who followed the Bhakti Movement made a profound impression on several Muslim rulers.

(ii) They tried to evolve a new social order by denouncing caste distinctions.

Chapter 11. The Modern Age in Europe Renaissance

Q. 1. How was the fall of Constantinople a blessing in disguise for Europe?

Ans. Due to the fall of Constantinople the Greek scholars from the Byzantine Empire fled to the European countries for protection and patronage. Wherever they went they spread their progressive ideas. This spread of liberal ideas led to the beginning of a new intellectual movement, Renaissance.

Q. 2. In what ways did Crusades give impetus to original thinking?

Ans. The crusades brought Europe in close contact with the economically and culturally rich Islamic world. The progressive ideas of Aristotle and Plato from the East migrated to the Western European nations that stimulated the imagination of their people who started questioning the blind faith. In this way Crusades give impetus to original thinking.

Q. 3. Name any two paintings of Leonardo da Vinci.

Ans. The two paintings of Leonardo da Vinci are

    (i) Monalisa   (ii) The Last supper

Q. 4. Name any two works of Rafael.

Ans. Two works of Rafael are:

    (i) Sistine Madonna   (ii) Painted the Chigi Chapel

Q. 5. Point any two reasons behind the European nations taking upon geographical explorations.

Ans. Two reasons behind the European nations taking upon geographical explorations were:

    (i) After the capture of Constantinople by the Turks even the land-routes were cut off. Now it became essential for Europeans to find out new and safe routes to Asia, because European trade flourished with Asia.

    (ii) The growth of trade encouraged the traders to find new sources and markets for their products.

Q. 6. What do you understand by the term 'Renaissance'?

Ans. The word 'Renaissance is defined as a 'rebirth' or a 'reconstruction'. Historically speaking, 'Renaissance' indicates a phenomenal cultural and transitional movement, characterized by the resurgence of interest in the classical age of the Romans and the Greeks.

Q. 7. What is the main feature of humanism? Who is known as the father of humanism?

Ans. Humanism stressed on the individual skills. A person with many skills and interest has been referred to as the Renaissance man. Petrarch, a great scholar and writer, has been called 'the father of humanism'.

Q. 8. What was impact of Renaissance literature?

Ans. The Renaissance in Europe ushered in a new era in literature. It led to the enrichment of the certain languages. Due to Renaissance modern European languages replaced Latin as the language of poetry, drama and fiction. The Renaissance literature was marked by the adoption of humanist philosophy and the revival of classical antiquity.

Q. 9. Mention any two consequences of Renaissance.

Ans. Two consequences of Renaissance were:

    (i) Due to Renaissance human understanding of physical world completely changed.

    (ii) The willingness to question previously held truths and search for new answers resulted in a period of major scientific advancement that ultimately resulted in the Scientific Revolution.

Q. 10. Name the personalities who are famous as the:

    (a) Father of modern political philosophy

    (b) Father of humanism

Ans. (a) Niccolo Machiavelli is known as the father of modern political philosophy.

    (b) Francesco Petrarca is known as the father of humanism.

Q. 11. Before Renaissance, how did feudalism and the Church control the freedom to think? Explain in your own words.

Ans. During the middle Ages, religion played the most significant role in people's life. The church controlled education and knowledge made available by the church authorities had to be accepted without asking any questions. They could not challenge it. The feudal system was a chain of obligation and defence where the rulers granted lands to the nobles in lieu of tributes and military service. It was a system opposed to progress.

Q. 12. How did compass help the sailors in their exploration?

Ans. Compass helped the sailors in the following ways:

    (i) It helped the sailors in finding out their ways. The compass told sailors how many degrees in which direction they were going.

(ii) It made discovery a lot easier during the Age of Exploration.

(iii) It helped the Portuguese in their discovery of sea route to India.

Q. 13. Mention the discoveries of

    (a) Ferdinand Magellan   (b)   Bartholomew Diaz

    (c) Columbus

Ans. (a) Ferdinand Magellan attempting to sail around the world for Spain reached a vast ocean which he called the Pacific Ocean. He landed at the islands of the Phillippines.

    (b) Bartholomew Diaz was a Portuguese explorer. He reached the southernmost tip of Africa, which later came to be called the 'Cape of Good Hope'.

    (c) Columbus discovered a western sea route to the East Indies and discovered a new continent known as the Americas in 1492 CE.

Q. 14. Mention any three effects of geographical explorations in the Renaissance.

Ans. Geographical exploration holds a very important place in the history of Europe and even in the world history. It was due to these discoveries that the world became a smaller place.

    (i) After the capture of Constantinople by the Turks even the land-routes were cut off. Now it became essential for Europeans to find out new and safe routes to Asia, because European trade flourished with Asia.

    (ii) Many new sea routes were discovered. In 1492 Columbus reached the Caribbean. Vasco da Gama discovered India in 1498 and Magellan circumnavigated the earth.

    (iii) Due to these discoveries, contacts with the East developed and people become more adventurous and attitude of people broadened.

Q. 15. How did the decline of feudalism contribute to the rise of Renaissance?

Ans. In feudalism, the society functioned through the means of land tenure which bound everyone, right from the King to the smallest landowner through a series of defenses and obligations.

    (i) This feudal system greatly contributed to the rise of Renaissance.

    (ii) Feudal lords possessed huge estates and exploited the serfs, who were virtually slaves. Freedom or equality of rights was denied.

    (iii) Towards the 13th and 14th centuries, Feudalism declined. It gave impetus to free thinking.

    (iv) Free thinking paved the way for awakening and new learning. Consequently, new development came into being in the sphere of art, literature, science and philosophy and contributed to the rise of Renaissance.

Q. 16. Give an account of any three great works of Michelangelo in the field of art.

Ans. Michelangelo (1475-1564AD) was a great painter and sculptor. The Last Judgment and the Fall of Man are among the most beautiful frescos on the ceilings of the Sistine Chapel in Vatican. Some of his greatest works are:

    (i) **David :** This sculpture is about 13 feet tall, depicting self-confident affirmation of the beauty of the human form.

    (ii) **Pieta :** This statue presents a sitting Mary carrying Jesus body.

    (iii) **Descent from the Cross :** This statue had been placed at the tomb of Michelangelo, which depicts Virgin Mary mourning over the dead body of Christ.

Q. 17. Mention any two works of William Shakespeare.   **[February, 2020]**

Ans. William Shakespeare was a famous English poet and a dramatist of the 16th century. Two of his greatest works were a historical drama known as 'A Merchant of Venice' and a tragedy called 'Hamlet'.

Q. 18. Who was William Shakespeare?

Ans. William Shakespeare was an English poet, playwrighter and actor.

Q. 19. Why did Renaissance begin in Italy?

Ans. After the siege of Constantinople in 1453 by the Ottoman Turks, the Greek scholars fled to Italy with their books and manuscripts which then became the new seats of culture, there by laying the foundation of Renaissance.

Chapter 12. The Modern Age in Europe Reformation

Q. 1. Why did the kings in Europe support the movement against the church?

Ans. The Church interfered in the internal affairs of European Nations, which was disliked by both the king and the people. The monarchs of England, France, Spain and other nations supported any movement which would strengthen their hands and weaken the Church.

Q. 2. State two economic factors that led to Reformation.

Ans. Two economic factors that led to Reformation were:

(i) The Church levied a variety of taxes like tithe, Peter's Pence, etc. on the commoners while nobles were exempted from taxation. This angered the common people as they were overburdened with tax.

(ii) The church offices were openly sold to the highest bidder. This practice was called Simony.

Q. 3. In what way did the spirit of enquiry affect the Reformation?

Ans. Spirit of enquiry affected the Reformation in the following ways:

(i) People started questioning the authority of the Pope.

(ii) People developed a more secular outlook.

(iii) They began questioning the vast wealth of the Church.

Q. 4. Give two examples to show that the Church in the 16th century followed practices which led to corruption within its ranks.

Ans. Following examples show that the Church in the 16th century followed practices which led to corruption within its ranks:

(i) Some of the priests and leaders of the Church hierarchy were appointed through corrupt means.

(ii) The offices of the Church were sold by the Pope.

Q. 5. What is Diet of Worms? What did it decide about Luther?

Ans. Diet of worms was a council of high dignitaries and Princes of Holy Roman Empire. It ordered writings of Luther to be burned and banned in 1521.

Q. 6. Mention one contribution each of Ulrich Zwingli and John Calvin in the Protestant movement.

Ans. Ulrich Zwingli spread Lutheranism in Switzerland. John Calvin was against all kinds of luxury, feasting, dancing, sports and games and wanted utter simplicity in the religion.

Q. 7. Mention any two causes of Reformation.

Ans. Two important causes of the Reformation were:

(i) Reformation was mainly a revolt against the abuses and antagonisms of the church.

(ii) The common people were overburdened with tax and were hardly given anything in return for their money. This angered the people and they protested.

Q. 8. Who were the Lollards?

Ans. The Lollards were followers of John Wycliffe, an English priest and Oxford professor, who translated the Bible into vernacular English. The Lollards had profound disagreements with the Catholic Church. They were critical of the Pope and the hierarchical structure of Church authority.

Q. 9. What is meant by Sale of Indulgences?

Ans. Indulgences were a theological principle of forgiveness and punishment in the Catholic Church. By the late Middle Ages, many church officers and clerics used to sell Indulgences, offering pardon to those who paid money. This practice is said to be the Sale of Indulgences.

Q. 10. Why did Martin Luther object to the power of Pope?

Ans. Martin Luther observed that the practice of granting 'indulgences' to provide absolution to sinners became increasingly corrupt. He turned strongly against the Church and openly criticised the powers of papacy for selling indulgences.

Q. 11. What did Anabaptists profess about Christianity?

Ans. They promoted separation of Church and State. They denied the necessity of priests, denounced accumulation of wealth and distinctions of rank and advocated sharing of things in common by Christians.

Q. 12. What do you mean by Counter-Reformation?

Ans. In order to restore the reputation of the Catholic Church, a large number of dedicated Christians including some Popes had adopted certain reforms within the Church. It was known as Counter Reformation.

Q. 13. How did the rivalry between the Church and the royalty manifest itself in France and England?

Ans. The rivalry between the Church and the royalty manifested itself in the politics of France and England.

    (i) The French monarch, Philip IV had forced Pop Clement V to leave his Rome headquarters in 1309 and shift to Avignon in France. This was a result of the Pope's interference in the political affairs of the Crown.

    (ii) In England, King Henry VIII showed scant regard for the Pope. He set up an independent Church known as Anglican Church.

    (iii) In 1534 AD, he passed the Act of supremacy through Parliament. By this Act, he became the clergy and the Supreme Head of the Church of England.

Q. 14. Why did the Church order the expulsion of Professor John Wycliffe of the Oxford University?

Ans. John Wycliffe was an English priest and Oxford professor.

    (i) He severely criticised the worldliness of the Church and many of its questionable practices.

    (ii) He declared that the Pope was not Christ's representative on Earth but an anti-Christ.

    (iii) He proclaimed that the Holy Bible was the sole guide to salvation and the clergy should not be taken for its word blindly.

    (iv) As a result of this, the Church took offense and ordered his expulsion from the Oxford university.

Q. 15. State any two causes of the Reformation Movement during the 16th Century A.D.

[November, 2019]

Ans. The causes of Reformation are as follows:

    (i) **Lifestyle of Popes and the clergy:** The Popes and the Clegy led lives of luxury and immorality.

    (ii) **The priests were exploitative:** The priests charged high fees for conducting religious ceremonies. The offices of the Church were sold by the Pope. The priests could pronounce a marriage lawful or unlawful. They extracted money for each such transaction.

    (iii) **Sale of Indulgences:** Money was collected through the sale of letters which remitted punishment for sin. Those who had money would be made free from doing penance for sins by buying a Letter of Indulgence.

    (iv) **'Tithe', a tax for the support of the Church:** The people were required to pay 'tithe' (one-tenth of their income) to support churches and priests. Besides, the clergy collected another tax called ,Peter's pence' from the people. The burden fell mainly on the peasants and the middle class families.

    (v) **Raising funds to build St. Peter's Basilica:** Emissaries were sent to sell Indulgences and an agent was sent to Wittenberg with the mission of rainsing sums for the building.

    (vi) **Rulers' resentment at Pope's interference in administrative affairs:** As early as the 13th century, the rulers of Europe had quarrelled with the Pope over the Church property which could not be taxed. The rivalry ended in defeat of papacy. French king, Philip IV had forced Pope Clement V to leave his headquarters at Rome in 1309 and stay in Avignon in France, when the latter intergered in the former's political affairs.

Chapter 13. The Modern Age in Europe Industrial Revolution

Q. 1. How did the invention of the steam engine help the Industrial Revolution?

Ans. The discovery of steam as a power source ushered in the Industrial Revolution. Steam engine was used to run large factories. Steam was used to run locomotives which greatly helped in Industrial Revolution.

Q. 2. Define Industrial Revolution? **[February, 2020]**

Ans. The term 'Industrial Revolution' was first used by a French Socialist Blanqui in 1837. This term was later adopted by the British historian Arnold Toynbee. Industrial Revolution means a change in the method of production through the use of mechanical, chemical and electrical power.

Q. 3. State any two economic impacts of the industrial revolution.

Ans. Two economic impacts of the industrial revolution were as follows:

(i) Scientific innovations and technological improvements contributed to the advancement of agriculture, industry and trade and to the expansion of the economy.

(ii) With the increase of capital and the need for credit, banking developed not only in London but also in the countryside.

Q. 4. Why is the period of Industrial Revolution also known as the 'Age of Machines'?

Ans. The period of Industrial Revolution is also known as the Age of Machines as the invention of machines brought about a total change in manufacturing and production and revolutionised the Industrial system in England.

Q. 5. What were the negative effects of the Industrial Revolution?

Ans. The negative effects of the Industrial Revolution were as follows:

(a) Shifting of population from villages to cities.

(b) Large-scale unemployment.

(c) Exploitation of workers. A new form of imperialism called capital imperialism.

Q. 6. Give any two causes that led to the development of socialism.

Ans. A number of factors led to the development of Socialism. Two of the factors were:

(i) It developed as a reaction to the evils of Capitalism.

(ii) The British Government was forced by the strong Trade Union Movements to recognise the worker's rights.

Q. 7. The Industrial Revolution had a great impact on the introduction of the philosophy of socialism. How?

Ans. A great impact of the Industrial Revolution was the division of society into the working class and capitalists.

(i) Social evils sprang up, owing to the factory system and communism.

(ii) This led to the rise of Socialism which aimed at eliminating the capitalist class and substituting some form of working class and substituting some form of working class ownership and control of the means of production.

Q. 8. Why was the process of 'transition from small-scale production to large-scale production' given the name of Industrial Revolution?

Ans. (i) Prior to the Industrial Revolution, manufacturing was often done in Guild's home, using hand tools or basic machines for a limited group of consumers.

(ii) The industrial Revolution marked a shift to large-scale production of goods through powered, special-purpose machinery and technology for larger groups of clients.

(iii) This transition from hand production methods to machine production is termed as Industrial Revolution.

Q. 9. How was the Industrial Revolution responsible for dividing the society into two classes? Name the classes.

Ans. The Industrial Revolution polarised the society into two main groups – the haves and the have-nots.

    (i) A few individuals became capitalists, meaning the owners of the main means of production. The capitalists had power, wealth and prestige.

    (ii) On the other hand, another class of poor people emerged who had migrated to the cities in search of work.

    (iii) This class was of poor workers lived in slums or in inhuman living conditions.

Q. 10. In what ways did the use of steam engine and the invention of machinery help the Industrial Revolution?

Ans. Use of steam engine and the invention of machinery helped the Industrial Revolution in the following ways:

    (i) Invention of machinery such as spinning jenny and its application to the process of manufacture led to an increase in the volume of production.

    (ii) The discovery of steam as a source of power also contributed greatly towards ushering in the Industrial Revolution. James Watt's steam engine was used to power spinning mules and power looms in 1781 CE.

    (iii) Railway trains started running with the help of steam in AD 1830 greatly helping in Industrial Revolution.

Q. 11. In what way did industrial revolution break away social order and the family ?

Ans. Industrial Prevalution placed immence resources in the hands of the capitalists who therefore, gained in social status and also became very influential in politics and government. The spread of education made people less attached to traditional values and encouraged individualism which broke away families and resulted in an increase in family tensions.

●●

SECTION : A (CIVICS)

Chapter 1. Indian Constitution

Q. 1. With reference to the Preamble to the Constitution of India, answer the following:
    (a) What is meant by a sovereign state?
    (b) What is Preamble to Indian Constitution? State its purpose to the Constitution of India.
    (c) Why were the terms 'Socialist' and 'Secular' added in the Preamble by the 42nd amendment to the Constitution of India in 1976?

Ans. (a) By declaring India as a sovereign entity, Preamble entails complete political freedom.
       (i)   It implies that India is internally powerful and externally free. She is not a subject of any other country or state and is free from foreign interference.
      (ii) There is none within her to challenge her authority and it is free to choose her allies in war and peace alike.
    (iii) This suggests that sovereignty is one of the most important values of a state as it allows the state to frame her own social, economic and foreign policies and develop her resources the way she likes.

    (b) The Preamble is considered to be prelude to the Indian Constitution, as the terms 'Sovereign', 'Socialist', 'Secular', 'Democratic Republic' emphasise not only the nature of the Constitution but the nature of the Indian state. It describes the 'soul and spirit' of the Constitution of India. It is an integral part of the Constitution, containing the basic framework or structure of the Constitution. It serves the following purposes to the Constitution of India:
       (i)   It indicates the source from which the Constitution derives its authority; and
      (ii) It also states the objects, which the Constitution seeks to establish and promote.

    (c) (i)   The word 'Socialist' was included in the Preamble in 1976 for emphasising the need to strive for socialism. Socialism as seen by the Indian leaders means equitable distribution of National Income to all sections of the people for the well-being of one and all.
      (ii) The state is expected to prevent the concentration of wealth in a few hands and bring about economic and social equality.
    (iii) The word 'Secular' which means 'Not connected to any religion or faith' was also included in the constitution in 1976. Since India is home to most major religions in the world, therefore to keep the followers of all religions together secularism has been found to be a convenient formula.

Q. 2. With reference to the basic ideal of Constitution of India, write short notes on the following:
    (a) Equality   (b) Liberty
    (c) Fraternity

Ans. (a) **Equality:**
       (i)   The Indian Constitution guarantees its citizens, social, political and economic equality for the development of the best in them.
      (ii)   It also implies equal opportunity to all its citizens, in matters of public employment irrespective of caste, creed, colour or economic status.
    (iii) Every citizen of India is entitled to equality before law and equal protection of law.

(b) Liberty :
    (i)   The word 'Liberty' means freedom that has been ensured to every citizen through a set of Fundamental Rights by our Constitution.
    (ii) The freedom of thought and expression provides the citizen the right to think, write or speak freely on any subject, especially in the matter of 'faith and worship', provided the restrictions imposed on this right are abided by him or her.
    (iii) The makers of our Constitution believed that the idea of democracy was unattainable without the presence of certain minimal rights which are essential for a free and civilised existence.

(c) Fraternity:
    (i)   The word 'Fraternity' stands for the spirit of common brotherhood. The constitution promotes this feeling of fraternity by the system of single citizenship.
    (ii) The Preamble declares that fraternity has to assure two things the dignity of the individual as well as the unity and integrity of the nation.
    (iii) This is the foremost objective to achieve in a country like India, which is composed of diverse races, religions, languages and cultures.
    (iv) As a result, the word 'fraternity' was added to the Constitution in 1976, declaring that it is the duty of every citizen to promote harmony and the spirit of common brotherhood amongst all the people of India transcending religious, linguistic and regional or sectional diversities.

Q. 3. With reference to the constitution of India, answer the following questions:
  (a) What is the philosophy underlying the Constitution?
  (b) What is Universal Adult Franchise?
  (c) What are the salient features of the Constitution?

Ans. (a) The philosophy underlying the Constitution is as follows:
    (i)   The Constitution derives all its authority from the citizens of the country and the State is the creation of the people.
    (ii) The Constitution is binding upon all governments irrespective of which political party or Prime Minister is in charge.
    (iii) The Supreme Court has the sole authority to interpret the Constitution.

  (b) The Constitution gives all adult Indian citizens, who are above 18 years of age, the right to vote, irrespective of caste, sex, religion, social status, wealth and education. The right to vote is denied to those who are of unsound mental health or are insolvent. This right is called Universal Adult Franchise or Universal Adult Suffrage.

  (c) The salient features of the constitution are as follows:
    (i)   Indian Constitution is a written constitution. It is the longest Constitution in the world.
    (ii) The powers are divided between the Union or Central Government and the State governments.
    (iii) Our government ensures that every Indian citizen enjoys certain Fundamental Rights.
    (iv) The Constitution embodies the Directive Principles of State Policy, which are certain ideals, directives and goals which the government should strive to achieve.

Q. 4. With reference to the Preamble to the Constitution of India, answer the following:
  (a) How can we say that India is a socialist state?
  (b) What is socialism? What are its two basic aims?
  (c) When did India become a sovereign state? How does India's membership of the Common wealth not infringe upon the sovereign character of India?

Ans. (a) India is considered a socialist state because:
    (i)   The successive governments have launched programmes so as to raise the standard of living of the poor.
    (ii) Restrictions are imposed on private capital and foreign investment.

(iii) Government has imposed heavy taxes on people with higher income to reduce the difference in the level of income between rich and poor.

(b) The word 'Socialism' means equitable distribution of national income and opportunities among all sections of people for the wellbeing of one and all. The basic aims of socialism are as follows:

   (i) To replace competition for individual profit with co-operation and social responsibilities.

   (ii) To secure more equitable distribution of income and opportunity. In order to ensure a basic minimum for all, the Government of India has adopted various measures to raise the living standard of the weaker section of people.

(c) (i) India became a Sovereign republic on 26 January 1950. Our Constitution emphasises that India is a sovereign republic, yet it continues to be a member of the Common wealth of Nations without any domination of the British Crown.

   (ii) India's membership of the Common wealth Nations does not compromise her position as a sovereign republic.

   (iii) India chose to be a member of the Common wealth of Nations voluntarily without accepting any formal or informal domination of the British Crown.

   (iv) The Common wealth is an association of free and independent nations. The British Monarch is only a symbolic head of that Common wealth of Nations.

Q. 5. The Constitution of India was framed by the Constituent Assembly. In this context answer the following questions.

(a) What was the role of B.R. Ambedkar in framing the Constitution?

(b) What was the Constituent Assembly?

(c) How can we say that this body was the 'Mirror of the Nation'?

Ans. (a) B.R. Ambedkar was a renowned social reformer, politician and jurist.

   (i) On 29th August 1947, the Constituent Assembly set up a Drafting Committee to prepare a Draft Constitution for India.

   (ii) B.R. Ambedkar was appointed as the Chairman of the Drafting Committee. Ambedkar is called the Father of Indian Constitution.

   (iii) Under the Chairmanship of Dr B.R. Ambedkar, the Constitution was drafted and introduced in the Constituent Assembly, which later came into force on 26th January 1950.

(b) The Constituent Assembly was a body formed to frame the Constitution of India.

   (i) It was constituted in 1946 under the provisions of Cabinet Mission.

   (ii) The Cabinet Mission decided that the members of the Constituent Assembly were to be indirectly elected by the Provincial Assemblies, while the Princely states would have their own representation by way of nomination.

   (iii) The Constituent Assembly of undivided India comprised 389 members, out of which 296 were from British India and 93 from the Princely Indian states.

   (iv) After the partition of the country, the number was reduced to 299, with 90 members forming a separate body to frame the Constitution of Pakistan.

(c) The Constituent Assembly was the 'Mirror of the Nation' due to the following reasons:

   (i) After independence, the Constituent Assembly of India became a fully sovereign body.

   (ii) It reflected the diversity of caste, religion, race, language and culture of India.

   (iii) It included members from all sections of Indian society such as Hindus, Muslims, Sikhs, Parsis, Indian Christians, Anglo-Indians, Scheduled Castes, Scheduled Tribe and women.

Q. 6. Justice implies the administration of law in a reasonable and fair way without any privilege or prejudice. In this context explain

(a) Social Justice   (b) Political Justice

(c) Economic Justice

Ans. (a) Social Justice:

   (i)   Social justice avoids discrimination on the basis of religion, race, language, sex or caste.

   (ii) Each individual is given what is due to him, without privilege or prejudice.

   (iii) Though, the State might make provision for the advancement of educationally and socially backward classes of citizens.

(b) Political Justice:

   (i)   Political Justice consists of various things like free and fair elections, right to vote and equal access to public offices.

   (ii) All Indian citizens have the freedom to express their political views as long as such views do not go against the interest of the country.

   (iii) Every citizen of India can stand for election and hold office, except for those who are debarred on account of criminal offences.

(c) Economic Justice:

   (i)   Economic justice means that the citizens are given their due without discrimination on the basis of their economic standard or wealth.

   (ii) The Directive Principles of State Policy are directed towards giving the citizens adequate means of livelihood, including the right to work.

   (iii) The government ensures the economic justice is carried out by legislations on minimum wages, no pay differences between men and women, equal work-equal pay, etc.

Q. 7. India is a Secular Democratic Republic. In this context explain :

(a) Why India is considered a secular state?

(b) How does the Indian Constitution provide the basis of political democracy, social and economic democracy?

(c) Describe the essential features of a democratic state.

Ans. (a) (i)   India is called a secular state because there is no official religion and is not guided by any religion or religious considerations.

   (ii) No religion is given special rights or some other religion is deprived of certain rights.

   (iii) The citizens of the country have the freedom to profess, practise and propagate any religion of their choice. The government also cannot interfere in religious matters except if these matters can be damage to public.

(b) (i)   The Indian Constitution has provided the basis of political democracy by accepting the principles of adult suffrage, equality between citizens, freedom of speech and expression and the joint electorates.

   (ii) The political democracy in India takes the form of a representative or parliamentary type of democracy.

   (iii) The word 'Democratic' includes not only political democracy but also social and economic democracy. Social democracy implies equal social treatment to all without granting any one special privilege based on race, religion, caste or sex. The economic democracy denotes that the material resources of the country are used for selfish interests but for the common good.

(c) Essential features of a democratic state are as follows:

   (i)   In democracy people choose their rulers who make laws and frame policies of the government. Elected representatives are accountable to the people.

   (ii) Another important characteristic of democracy is that citizens enjoy freedoms of speech, expression, and information.

   (iii) Another characteristic of democracy is that it ensures rule of law. All the citizens are equal in the eyes of law and no one is above law.

   (iv) In a democratic state Judiciary is independent from any control of the executive or the legislature.

Chapter 2. Salient Features of the Constitution

Q. 1. What is the scope of Fundamental Rights?

Ans. Scope of Fundamental Rights is as follows:

(a) The Fundamental Rights are Universal *i.e.* they are guaranteed to every citizen of India irrespective of caste, colour, religion, gender or social status.

(b) The Fundamental Rights cannot be altered or removed by any simple process from the Constitution.

(c) The Fundamental rights are not absolute. They have certain restrictions imposed on them in the larger interests of the society.

(d) The Fundamental Rights can be taken away during an Emergency. When there is a war or an economic or political crisis, an Emergency can be declared by the President. During this time, one or more of the Fundamental Rights can be suspended until the condition normalises.

Q. 2. (a) Why was 26th January chosen as the date for the enforcement of the Indian Constitution ?

(b) Explain the meaning of 'Single Citizenship' and state the reason why it has been incorporated in the Indian Constitution.

(c) What is 'Welfare State' ?   **[February, 2020]**

Ans. (a) The Indian Constitution was enforced on 26 January for the following reasons :

(i) The Congress Session at Lahore on 29 December, 1929 has passed a resolution declaring complete independence as the goal of India. It was decided that 26th January should be observed as Purna Swaraj Day.

(ii) Complete Independence Day was celebrated for the first time on 26 January, 1930, This was observed till the achievement of Independence.

Therefore, 26 January was selected as the date for the commencement of the new Constitution.

(b) Single Citizenship means that the Indian Constitution recognizes all the people irrespective of states or territories in which they reside are the citizens of the country.

(i) Normally under a federal system there is dual citizenship. This means a person is a citizen of the State to which he/she belongs and that of the Nation, which includes all the States. Such a system is followed in America.

(ii) However, in India, every Indian is a citizen of India and has the same rights of citizenship, no matter in which State he/she resides.

(iii) Single Citizenship helps in promoting unity and integrity among the people of nation.

(c) The Constitution of India declares India a welfare state. A welfare state is a concept of government in which state plays a key role in the protection and promotion of economic and social well being of its citizens.

(i) It provides for its citizens a vast range of social services, such as medical care, education, financial aid during old age, sickness and unemployment.

(ii) Under Part IV of the Directive Principles of State Policy, the State is directed to ensure to the people employment, education and assistance in circumstances of old age, sickness and disablement.

(iii) The Constitution lays down in the Directive Principles of State Policy that 'the State shall strive to promote the welfare of the people'.

Q. 3. Describe briefly any four important economic rights enshrined in the Directive Principles of State Policy.

Ans. Four important economic rights enshrined in the Directive Principles of State Policy are as follows:

(i) adequate means of livelihood for all citizens irrespective of men and women equally.

(ii) equal distribution of wealth and resources among all classes.

(iii) equal pay for equal work for both men and women.

(iv) just and humane conditions of work, a decent standard of living , full employment, leisure and social and cultural opportunities.

Q. 4. State the utility of the Directive Principles with reference to the following points :
   (a) They have an educative value
   (b) They help to establish economic democracy
   (c) They provide an element of permanence in a democracy
   (d) They provide guidance in interpretation of law
Ans. (a) Directive Principles enlighten and educate the citizens about what they can expect from the politicians, whom they vote to power.
   (b) Directive Principles aim to create social and economic conditions under which the citizens can lead a good life. The state should ensure equal pay for equal work for men as well as women.
   (c) In a democracy, power changes hands very frequently. Whichever party is in power, it has to implement these directives.
   (d) Directive Principles of State Policy provides for guidance to interpretation of fundamental rights of a citizen.

Q. 5. What is the importance of Fundamental Rights?
Ans. Importance of Fundamental Rights is as follows:
   (a) They are essential for the harmonious growth of human personality.
   (b) They are a check on the arbitrary action of the Union and the State governments as well as of local bodies such as municipal corporations.
   (c) They are necessary for the stability of international peace and order.
   (d) They give self-confidence to citizens providing them equality of status and opportunity and protecting them from exploitation by an individual or State.

Q. 6. What are the principles laid down in Article 51 ?
Ans. Article 51 lays down the following principles :
   (i)   The state shall ensure to promote international peace and unity.
   (ii) The state shall maintain honourable relations between nations.
   (iii) It shall settle international disputes through arbitration.

Q. 7. With reference to the Right to Constitutional Remedies, answer the following questions:
   (a) What is the writ of Habeas Corpus and why is it important?
   (b) What is the purpose of writ of Quo Warranto?
   (c) What is the difference between a writ of certiorari and a writ of mandamus?
Ans. (a) **The writ of Habeas Corpus protects the safety of any person held in prison or taken into custody.**
   (i)   This writ can be issued where a person is illegally held even by a private individual.
   (ii) By issuing this writ, the court can order the detaining authority to bring the detained person to the court to explain why such a prisoner is being held.
   (iii) This writ also acts as a deterrent to unlawful imprisonment of people under trial.
         The writ of Habeas Corpus is reckoned as "the popular and effective writ, as far as illegal confinement is concerned".
   (b) **Purpose of writ of Quo Warranto:**
   (i)   The writ of Quo Warranto is generally issued against a person who has illegally or forcefully occupied a public office.
   (ii) It also questions the bona fide of the person holding such an office.
   (iii) If a person illegally occupies a post, this writ is generally issued against that person.
   (c)

S.No.	Writ of Certiorari	Writ of Mandamus
(i)	The word 'certiorari' means 'to be fully informed'.	The Latin word 'mandamus' means 'we command'.

(ii)	By this writ, the lower court has to hand over all the relevant records of a case to the higher court.	This writ is issued when a petition is filed against any public official or unit who is not performing its duty.

Q. 8. With reference to the Fundamental duties, answer the following questions:

    (a)   What are the Fundamental Duties? Why were these duties incorporated in our Constitution?

    (b)   Discuss the importance of Fundamental Duties.

    (c)   Mention any four Fundamental Duties.

Ans. (a) The Fundamental Duties are defined as the moral obligations of all citizens to help promote a spirit of patriotism and to uphold the unity of India. The Fundamental Duties were inserted in article 51A of Part IV of the Constitution, by the 42nd Amendment Act, 1976. Every right has a corresponding duty and like rights, duties may be both moral and legal. The incorporation of fundamental duties in the constitution was thus an attempt to balance the individual's civic freedom with civic obligations and thus to fill a serious gap in the constitution.

    (b) **Importance of Fundamental Duties:**

        (i)   The Fundamental duties have been enlisted in the Constitution to make the citizens aware of their economic and social obligations.

        (ii)   These duties warn the citizens of our country to respect the National anthem and National Flag as it stirs up patriotism and strengthens national harmony.

        (iii)   It also intends to uphold the right of equality among all individuals, to disown violence, to offer compulsory education and to protect the environment and public property.

    (c) **Four Fundamental duties are:**

        (i)   To abide by the Constitution and respect its ideals and institutions, the National flag and the National Anthem.

        (ii)   To safeguard public property and to abjure violence.

        (iii)   To promote harmony and spirit of common brotherhood amongst all the people of India transcending religious, linguistic and regional or sectional diversities, to renounce practices derogatory to the dignity of women.

        (iv)   To provide opportunities for education to his child or, as the case may be, ward between the age of 6 and 14 years.

Q. 9. With reference to the salient features of the Indian Constitution answer the following questions:

    (a)   Define the term 'Fundamental Duties'. What is the importance of fundamental duties?

    (b)   What do we mean by Freedom of Conscience?

    (c)   Give any two differences between the Directive Principles of State Policy and the Fundamental Rights.

Ans. (a) The Fundamental Duties' are defined as the moral obligations of all citizens to help promote a spirit of patriotism and to uphold the unity of India.

        Importance of Fundamental Duties:

        (i)   The Fundamental duties have been enlisted in the Constitution to make the citizens aware of their economic and social obligations.

        (ii)   These duties warn the citizens of our country to respect the National anthem and National Flag as it stirs up patriotism and strengthens national harmony.

        (iii)   It also intends to uphold the right of equality among all individuals, to disown violence, to offer compulsory education and to protect the environment and public property.

    (b) Article 25 guarantees freedom of conscience and the right to practice, profess and propagate any religion to every individual. However, the state may impose restrictions on the freedom of conscience and the free profession and propagation of religion in the interest of health, morality and public order. Thus, no one can be allowed to hurt the religious feelings of any class of Indian citizens. Religious practices like sacrificing animals or human beings for offering to gods and goddesses or to some supernatural forces are not permissible.

(c)

S.No.	Directive Principles	Fundamental Rights
(i)	They are contained in Part-IV (Article 36 to 51) of the Constitution.	They are contained in Part-III (Article 12 to 35) of the Constitution.
(ii)	They are aimed at securing welfare, social and economic freedoms by appropriate State action.	These are primarily aimed at assuring political freedom to the citizens by protecting them against excessive State action.

Q. 10. The Constitution of India guarantees equality of all persons before the law. In this context explain the following rights guaranteed under the Right to Equality:

(a) Prohibition of Discrimination

(b) Abolition of Untouchability

(c) Equality of Opportunity in matters of Public Employment

Ans. (a) **Prohibition of Discrimination:**

    (i) Article 15 ensures social equality by prohibiting discrimination against any citizen on the basis of race, religion, sex, place of birth, creed or caste.

    (ii) No citizen shall be denied access to public places, wells, tanks, shops, hotels, etc.

    (iii) However, the state can make special provisions or concessions for women and children and socially backward classes of citizens.

(b) **Abolition of Untouchability:**

    (i) Practicing untouchability in any form is a punishable offence by Article 17 which declares that 'untouchability is abolished and its practice in any form is forbidden'.

    (ii) This provision is an effort to uplift the social status of millions of people who had been looked down upon and kept at a distance because of their caste or the nature of their profession.

    (iii) The untouchability Offences Act of 1955 provided penalities for preventing a person from entering a place of public worship or taking water from public well or tap. This Act was renamed as 'the Protection of Civil Rights Act' in 1976.

(c) **Equality of Opportunity in matters of Public Employment:**

    (i) Article 16 states that there shall be equal opportunity for citizens 'in matters relating to employment or appointment to any office under the State'.

    (ii) The State cannot discriminate against anyone in matter of public employment.

    (iii) All citizens can apply and become employees of the State based on the merits and qualifications.

    (iv) However, there is a special provision for the reservation of posts for citizens belonging to scheduled Castes (SCs), scheduled Tribes (STs) and Other Backward Classes (OBCs).

Q. 11. Articles 19-22 deal with the citizen's basic right to freedom in a democracy. In this context answer the following questions:

(a) What are the six fundamental rights mentioned under the Indian Constitution?

(b) How are the rights of a person in respect of conviction for offences protected?

(c) How are the rights of a person arrested under ordinary circumstances protected?

Ans. (a) The Constitution provides for six Fundamental Rights. These are as follows:

    (i) Right to Equality   (ii) Right to Freedom

    (iii) Right Against Exploitation   (iv) Right to Freedom of Religion

    (v) Cultural and Education Rights   (vi) Right to Constitutional Remedies

(b) Article 20 provides protection to individuals who are punished or accused of an offence. The three such protections are:

    (i) No individual shall be prosecuted and punished for the same offence more than once.

(ii) No individual can be convicted for an act that was not an offence at the time of its commission. Moreover, no one should get a greater penalty than what is actually prescribed under the law.

(iii) No individual can be forced to give witness against his or her own self.

(c) Article 22 states the Rights that are conferred by the Constitution upon a person arrested under ordinary circumstances. They are as follows:

   (i) Whenever a person is arrested, he or she should be informed, as soon as possible, of the grounds for arrest.

   (ii) He/She should be allowed to consult and to be defended by legal practitioner of his/her choice.

   (iii) The individual must be produced before the nearest magistrate within twenty-four hours of the arrest.

   (iv) Without the orders of the magistrate, he/she cannot be detained in custody beyond the said period.

Q. 12. The incorporation of fundamental duties in the Constitution was an attempt to balance the individual's civic freedom with civic obligations. In this context answer the following questions:

(a) What is a citizen's duty towards self?

(b) Explain a citizen's duty towards the state.

(c) Mention any four fundamental duties of a citizen towards the Nation.

Ans. (a) The Constitution declares that it shall be the duty of every citizen

   (i) To develop scientific temper, humanism and the spirit of inquiry and reform.

   (ii) To strive towards excellence in all spheres of individual and collective activity, so that the nation constantly rises to higher levels of endeavor and achievement.

   (iii) To be dutiful towards his state and country.

(b) Among various duties towards the state, the foremost duty of every citizen is

   (i) To abide by the Constitution and respect its ideals and institutions, the National flag and the National Anthem.

   (ii) To uphold and protect the sovereignty, unity and integrity of India.

   (iii) To safeguard public property and to abjure violence.

(c) The duty of a citizen towards the Nation is

   (i) To defend the country and render national service when called upon so.

   (ii) To value and preserve the rich heritage of our composite culture.

   (iii) To promote harmony and spirit of common brotherhood amongst all the people of India transcending religious, linguistic and regional or sectional diversities, to renounce practices derogatory to the dignity of women.

   (iv) To cherish and follow the noble ideas which inspired our national struggle for freedom.

Chapter 3. Elections

Q. 1. Discuss the role of the Election Commission in providing for free and fair election.

Ans. Following measures are taken by the Election Commission to ensure free and fair elections:

   (i) **Scrutiny of nomination papers :** It is the duty of the returning officer to scrutinize the nomination papers and accept or reject the nomination papers as the case may be.

   (ii) **Checking undue interference of the Party-in-power :** Election Commission ensures that the party in power does in no way take an advantage over other parties or individuals.

   (iii) **Checking Election Expenses incurred by the candidate :** The Election Commission scrutinises the election expenses incurred by a candidate during the election process. The nomination of a candidate is declared invalid if he/she is found to transgress or make illegal use of this expenditure limit set by the Commission.

   (iv) **Supervising the Election machinery :** The Election Commission supervises the election machinery throughout the country so as to ensure that elections are held in free and fair manner.

Q. 2. What do you understand by the term 'General' and 'Mid-term' elections?

Ans. General Elections:

    (i)   These are the regular elections, conducted after the completion of a period of five years of the Lok Sabha and State Assemblies.

    (ii) The First General Election in India based on Adult Franchise was held in 1952.

    Mid-Term Election:

    (i)   These type of elections are held to bring a new house to power, when the full term of five years of State Assemblies or Lok Sabha has not been completed

    (ii) And the house has to be dissolved.

Q. 3. Who issues voters photo identity card? What is the importance of issuing it?

Ans. Importance of Voter's Identity Cards:

    (i)   A voter's identity card, also known as Electors Photo Identity Card (EPIC) is a photo identity card, which is issued by the Election Commission of India.

    (ii) The photo identity card is given to all the citizens of India who are entitled to vote.

    (iii) To improve the accuracy of the electoral rolls and prevent electoral frauds, the Election Commission ordered the making of photo identity cards for all voters in the country in August, 1993.

    (iv) More than 450 million identity cards have been issued till date.

Q. 4. (a) State the meaning of 'Mid-term Election'.

    (b) Explain what is meant by Indirect elections.

    (c) What do you understand by the term 'By-elections'?   **[February, 2020]**

Ans. (a) If the Lok Sabha or any of the State Assembly dissolves before the completion of its full term of five years, an election needs to be held to constitute a new house. This is known as mid-term elections. A mid-term election is held to form a new house.

    (b) (i)   In indirect election, the voter does not elect the candidate directly from their representatives to the legislatures or Head of the State.

         (ii) The voters elect an intermediate body, which in turn elects the representatives or the President.

         (iii) The President and Vice-President of India, Members of Rajya Sabha and State Legislative Councils are elected through indirect elections.

    (c) By-elections is known as by-polls in India.

         (i)   By-election is held to choose a member of the Lok Sabha or a member of the State Legislature who has resigned suddenly or died while in office.

         (ii) Sometimes there needs to be a by-election if a seat becomes vacant due to a member becoming disqualified under certain circumstances.

         (iii) The elected member holds the post only for the unexpired term of the House.

Q. 5. What are the disadvantages of the direct elections?

Ans. Disadvantages of direct elections are as follows:

    (i)   The voters may develop partial attitude towards the wrong candidates based on caste, religion or emotions.

    (ii) The accurate public opinion that is expressed through the voting ballots may get disfigured as all voters do not vote, out of indifference or due to corrupt practices like threats, rigging or booth capture.

    (iii) A huge amount of time, energy and money is involved in direct elections.

    (iv) Moreover, election campaigns may result in disputes, tension and even killing.

Q. 6. With reference to Elections in India, answer the following questions:

    (a) Why elections are an important event in India?

    (b) What is the importance of Universal Adult Franchise in Indian democracy?

    (c) What do we mean by the term 'General Elections'?

Ans. (a) Elections in India are events involving political mobilisation and organisational complexity on a huge scale. They are important because:

(i)   During the election time, the electorate or the common mass becomes educated and aware of the ideologies of different political parties.

(ii)   This is the time when the leaders arouse interest of the people in public affairs like economic, political and social problems affecting the entire nation.

(iii)   By contesting elections either as members of a political party or as an independent candidate, people get a chance to participate in government formation and enact laws and execute policies for the good of the people and their country.

(b)   India is the world's largest democracy where people under the system of Universal Adult Franchise vote to elect a representative government.

(i)   The system of Universal Adult Franchise helps all the citizens to get involved in the governance of their state.

(ii)   Every individual irrespective of their caste, colour, religion, gender, or status has the right to vote and each vote has equal value *i.e.,* "one vote one value".

(iii)   This enables them to elect their representatives for the purpose of administering and protecting the interests of the people.

(c)   General Elections:

(i)   These are the regular elections, conducted once in 5 years to elect 543 members of the Lok Sabha (Lower House)

(ii)   The First General Election in India based on Adult Franchise was held in 1952 wherein the adult citizens of the country elected their representatives to the first Lok Sabha and State Assemblies.

(iii)   Candidates who win the Lok Sabha elections are called 'Members of Parliament' and hold their seats for five years or until the body is dissolved by the President on the advice of the council of Ministers.

(iv)   A party needs 272 MPs to hold a claim to form the Central Government. Leader of the party/alliance takes oath as the Prime Minister.

Q. 7. With reference to the kinds of elections in India, explain:

(a)   Direct Election   (b) Indirect Election

(c)   Advantages of Direct Election

Ans. (a)   **Direct Elections :**

(i)   The voters directly choose their representative to the legislatures through voting.

(ii)   Members of the Lok Sabha, Vidhan Sabha or Legislative Assemblies, local bodies like Municipal Corporation. Municipalities and Grampanchayat are directly elected.

(iii)   There is a large body of voters called the electorate.

(iv)   The age and qualifications of the voters are established and regulated by law for the officials of the State.

(b)   **Indirect Elections :**

(i)   Representatives are indirectly elected by the people through an intermediary group who further elect the representatives.

(ii)   Members of Rajya Sabha, Vidhan Parishad, Zila Parishad, President and Vice President are indirectly elected.

(iii)   There is a very small voting body generally called Electoral College.

(iv)   The elected representatives are not based on qualifications and treated equally.

(c)   **Advantages of Direct elections:**

(i)   It stimulates the interest of the masses in various affairs related to public welfare and the nation.

(ii)   The elected representatives are accountable to the voters for their actions.

(iii)   Depending upon their judgment, the voters can select as well as reject representatives.

Q. 8. With reference to the election procedure, answer the following questions
   (a) Discuss the scrutiny of Expenses during elections.
   (b) Who does the scrutiny of nomination papers and how?
   (c) What is an electoral roll? What steps have been taken to improve the accuracy of the electoral rolls?

Ans. (a) The Election Commission scrutinises the election expenses incurred by a candidate during the election process.
   (i)   The nomination of a candidate is declared invalid if he/she is found to transgress or make illegal use of his expenditure limit set by the commission.
   (ii) The monitoring of election Expenditure follows a coordinated mechanism.
   (iii) There are several aspects of monitoring Election expenditure.
   (iv) The management of Expenditure overseers and Assistant Expenditure overseers, Video Surveillance Teams, Media Certification and Monitoring Committee and Video viewing Team are needed for the scrutiny.

   (b) Scrutiny of nomination papers:
   (i)   It is the duty of the Returning Officer to scrutinise the nomination papers of each candidate thoroughly. This responsibility cannot be passed down to the Assistant Returning Officer by the returning officer.
   (ii) The nomination of any candidate with incomplete and invalid papers is rejected by the Commission.
   (iii) The candidates have to be genuine, qualified and fulfilling all criteria like election symbol, deposit money, election gent, etc.

   (c) The electoral roll is a list of all people in the constituency who are registered to vote in elections. To improve the accuracy of the electoral rolls and prevent electoral frauds, the Election Commission
   (i)   Adds the names of those who have turned 18 or have moved into a constituency and to remove the names of those who have died or moved out of a constituency.
   (ii) Issues photo identity cards for all voters. This photo identity card is given to all the citizens of India who are entitled to vote.

Q. 9. With reference to the functions of the Election Commission, answer the following questions:
   (a) What is the role of Election Commission in free and fair elections in India?
   (b) What are the Election Commission's rules governing election symbols?
   (c) How are Election Commissioners elected? What is their tenure?

Ans. (a) The role of Election Commission in free and fair elections in India is as follows:
   (i)   The commission is responsible to prepare electoral rolls and get them revised before every election so as to add the names of new voters and remove the name of those who have either died or moved out of constituency.
   (ii) To improve the accuracy of the electoral rolls and prevent electoral frauds, the Election Commission issues photo identity card to all citizens who are entitled to vote.
   (iii) The Commission can also cancel polls in case of large scale rigging, irregularities or violence during the election process.

   (b) The Election Commission's rules governing election symbols are as follows:
   (i)   The Commission has stipulated that all National and State level parties can have a reserved symbol for all the candidates nominated by them. Thus, the BJP's 'lotus' symbol will not be allotted to any other party or individual, even if the BJP does not have a candidate in a particular constituency or state.
   (ii) The independent candidates can select any symbol out of a list of 'Free Symbols'.
   (iii) The purpose behind allotting symbols is that illiterate masses cannot read the names of the candidates of the parties. It is easy for them to identify the symbols for electing candidates of their choice.

   (c) Appointment and Tenure of Election Commissioners:
- (i) The President appoints the Chief Election Commissioner and Election Commissioners.
- (ii) They have tenure of six years or up to the age of 65 years, whichever is earlier.
- (iii) They do not hold any office of profit after retirement.
- (iv) Through impeachment by the Parliament, the Chief Election Commissioner can be removed from the office of the Election Commission. Other Election Commissioners can be removed by the President at the behest of the Chief Election Commissioner.

Q. 10. Every election has rules about who can compete to be elected and how those individuals are selected. In this context answer the following:

(a) Mention any three differences between secret ballot and open ballot.

(b) Under what circumstances is a repoll ordered?

(c) What is Election Petition? Explain the process of filling an election petition.

Ans. (a)

S.No.	Secret Ballot	Open Ballot
(i)	A secret ballot system is a voting method in which all votes are cast in secret.	An open ballot system is a voting method in which voters vote openly.
(ii)	In this system nobady to know to whom the vote is being cast.	In this system the voter's choice is not anonymous.
(iii)	Voter cannot be influenced by intimidation, blackmailing and potential vote buying.	There are great chances of influencing the voter by intimidation, blackmailing and potential vote buying.

(b) Under following circumstances, the Election Commission orders repoll in a constituency:
- (i) In case of booth capturing.
- (ii) In case ballot papers or boxes are destroyed.
- (iii) Election Commission can suspend polling when it fears a threat to voter's security or other genuine reasons. In this situation the Election Commission orders a repoll which takes place within two or three days after the first polling.

(c) An election petition refers to the procedure for challenging the result of a Parliamentary election. If the defeated candidate has any doubt regarding unjust elections, he can file a petition in a court of law especially in High Court. He may be declared winner on the basis of merits of case; however, litigations have always a final choice to appeal to the Supreme Court.

Q. 11. As a democratic country, India is built on the foundation of election. In this context, answer the following questions:

(a) Under what circumstances can a 'By-Election' be held?

(b) State any four functions and powers of the Election Commission.

(c) Mention any three points of difference between 'Direct' and 'Indirect' elections.

Ans. (a) By-Elections, known as special elections in the USA and by-polls in India, are used to fill the elected offices that have turned vacant or empty due to the death or sudden resignation of any member of the Central legislative Assembly or the State Legislative Assembly before the full-term expires. The newly elected member holds office only till the term of the existing government is not complete. By-elections may also be conducted to fill up the vacant seat of a candidate who has been disqualified under parliamentary law for some reason or the other.

(b) Some of the important functions and powers of Election Commission are as follows:
- (i) To superintendence, direction and control of elections.
- (ii) To conduct elections and to look after all the problems connected with such elections.
- (iii) To prepare electoral rolls and get them revised before every election.
- (iv) To improve the accuracy of the electoral rolls and prevent electoral frauds.

(c)

S.No.	Direct Elections	Indirect Elections
(i)	Representatives are directly chosen by the people through voting.	Representatives are indirectly elected by the people through an intermediary group who further elect the representatives.
(ii)	Members of the Lok Sabha, Vidhan Sabha or Legislative Assemblies, local bodies like Municipal Corporation, Municipalities and Gram Panchayats are directly elected.	Members of Rajya Sabha, Vidhan Parishad, Zila Parishad, President and Vice President are indirectly elected.
(iii)	There is a very large body of voters called the electorate.	There is a very small voting body generally called Electoral College.

Q. 12. It is said that elections are the barometer of democracy. In this context answer the following:
   (a) What is the need for elections in India?
   (b) Suggest three ways to curb the rigging and violence in elections?
   (c) How can we say that elections are barometer of Democracy?

Ans. (a) Elections are needed in India for the following reasons:
    (i)   These elections give an opportunity to the voters to indirectly participate in the administration of the country.
    (ii) It is the best way by which the representatives of the people can be chosen and sent to legislature.
    (iii) By contesting elections either as members of a political party or as an independent candidate, people get a chance to participate in government formation and enact laws and execute policies for the good of the people and their country.

  (b) Three ways to curb the rigging and violence in elections are as follows:
    (i)   People with criminal record should not be allowed to contest elections.
    (ii) Elections should be considered invalid in those constituencies, where unfair means are used.
    (iii) In case of rigging and booth-capturing, severe penalities should be inflicted on the accused.

  (c) Elections are barometer of Democracy because :
    (i)   They are the indicator of the efficiency of our democracy.
    (ii) Elections at regular interval are a striking aspect of democratic polity.
    (iii) If there are no elections people would not be able to choose their leaders.
    (iv) Elections display sovereignty and integrity of all the citizens of the nation.

Q. 13. (a) What type of elections are direct and what type are indirect in a Parliamentary Democracy?
   (b) Explain the following terms:
   (i) By-Election
   (ii) Mid-Term Election
   (c) State the Composition of the Election Commission.   **[November, 2019]**

Ans. (a) (i) In direct election, people actully vote for the persons to represent them in Parliament or State Assembly or a local body.
    (ii) Members of the Lok Sabha in India are directly elected by all the people who have the right to vote. Similarly, members of the State Assembly are directly elected by the people of the State concerned. Members of the local bodies, such as Gram Panchayat and Municipal Corporation, etc., are also directly elected by the voters.
    (iii) In indirect election, the voters do not directly elect their representatives to the legislatures or Head of State (the President), but elect an intermediate body which finally proceeds to elect the representatives or the President. The members of the

Rajya Sabha, the members of The State Legislative Council, the President of India, and the Vice-President of India are elected indirectly.

(b) (i) **By-Election :** By-election is held to choose a member of the Lok Sabha or that of State Legislature to replace a previus member who has resigned suddenly or died.

(ii) **Mid-Term Election :** The Lok Sabha or the State Assembly may be dissolved before its term is over because of no-confidence motion. As a result, a midterm poll is required to constitute a new House.

(c) (i) The Election Commission is headed by the Chief Election Commissioner. He is assisted by three election commissioners.

(ii) The Regional Commissioners are responsible for the functioning of the Election Commission in the States.

(iii) The Constitution of India states that the President of India or the governors of States should make available staff to help during elections. Then requirement could be for security personnel or administrative staff.

(iv) The Election Commissioners are assisted by a Deputy Election Commissioner and a Secretary. Nirvachan Sadan in New Delhi is the office of Election Commission.

Chapter 4. Rural Local Self-Government

Q. 1. Mention the main judicial functions of the Panchayats.

Ans. The judicial functions of the Gram Panchayat include:

(i) Hearing minor social and civil cases, such as marriage dispute, divorces, etc.

(ii) Hearing criminal cases such as assault, theft, etc.

(iii) Giving verdicts on the cases which cannot be challenged.

(iv) Imposing fines as mutually decided by the members of the Panchayat.

Q. 2. Explain briefly the discretionary functions performed by the Gram Panchayat.

Ans. If Gram Panchayat has extra resources, it may undertake on its own discretion some of the following functions:

(i) Planting of trees on both sides of roads.

(ii) Promoting cooperative farming.

(iii) Running of community centres.

(iv) Constructing and maintaining dharamshalas and public ghats.

(v) Promoting social and moral welfare of the people.

(vi) Helping villagers during famine and flood.

Q. 3. Explain briefly the judicial functions performed by the Gram Panchayat.

Ans. Judicial Functions performed by the Gram Panchayat are:

(i) In some states there are separate judicial Panchayats called the Nyaya Panchayats. In some states Gram Panchayat performs the judicial functions.

(ii) It is responsible for meeting out justice to the villagers in a speedy and economical manner.

(iii) They deal with petty civil cases dealing with minor offences like petty thefts, assaults, cheating, trespassing, and illegal occupation of common places.

(iv) They cannot award a sentence of imprisonment.

Q. 4. With reference to local self-governing bodies answer the following questions:

(a) What is the composition of the Gram Panchayat?

(b) What are the basic functions of Zila Parishad catering to the Public?

(c) State functions of the Panchayat Samiti related to Supervision and delegation.

Ans. (a) (i) Gram Panchayat is a body elected by the members of the Gram Sabha for a period of five years. The number of members in a Gram Panchayat may vary Depending on the size of the village.

    (ii)   Sometimes two or more small villages form a gram panchayat. The Gram Panchayat is headed by a Sarpanch while other members are known as panchas.

    (iii) In some states the Sarpanch is elected directly by the members of the Gram Sabha whereas in others, the members of the Gram Panchayat elect the Sarpanch indirectly.

(b) Zila Parishad is a recurring functioning body that carries out its functions mostly through different Standing Committees. Some of the basic functions of Zila Parishad catering to the Public are as follows:

    (i)   Building and conserving public roads, parks, culverts and bridges.

    (ii) Introducing and applying new programmes related to agriculture.

    (iii) Development of water, land and human resources of a district.

    (iv) Setting up of libraries, dispensaries and educational institutions.

    (v)   Providing help in situations of drought, distress of any kind and scarcity.

    (vi) Upholding the welfare of the weaker sections of the society.   **(Any four)**

(c) Functions of the Panchayat Samiti related to Supervision and Delegation are as follows:

    (i)   The duty of coordinating and supervising the works of Gram Panchayat rests with the Panchayat Samiti.

    (ii) The Samiti scrutinizes the budget of the Panchayats and proposes necessary changes in it.

    (iii) Through scheme like Integrated Rural Development Programme (IRDP), Sampoorna Gramin Rozgar Yojana, Indira AwasYojna, the Panchayat Samiti works to improve the quality of life in the rural areas.

    (iv) Additionally, the Panchayat Samitis act as the link between the Zila Parishad and the Gram Panchayat.

Q. 5. With reference to the functions of the Local Self-Government, explain:

    (a) Functions of the Zila Parishad related to Coordination and Supervision.

    (b) Functions of the Gram Panchayat related to the Regulation and General administration.

    (c) Functions of the Gram Panchayat related to Social and Economic measures.

Ans. (a) The functions of the Zila Parishad related to Coordination and Supervision are as follows:

    (i)   The work of the gram Panchayats and Panchayat Samitis are supervised by the Zila Parishad.

    (ii) It is also responsible for probing and approving the accounts of the Samitis in states like Assam, Punjab and Bihar.

    (iii) It co-ordinates the developmental plans prepared by the Panchayat Samitis in the District.

(b) The functions of the Gram Panchayat related to the Regulation and General administration are as follows:

    (i)   Registering marriages, births and deaths.

    (ii) Maintenance of burial grounds for the cremation rites.

    (iii) Upkeep of watch and ward services like chowkidars, etc.

    (iv) Extending help to the government in preserving law and order.

    (v)   Collecting and maintaining of records and statistics of the villages' purchases, sales, land grants, etc.

(c) Functions of the Gram Panchayat related to Social and Economic measures are as follows:

    (i)   Building libraries, guest houses, marriage halls, etc.

    (ii) Planting trees, gardens, constructing parks and playgrounds for entertainment and leisure.

    (iii) Arranging fairs and exhibitions in the village.

    (iv) Setting up of fair price shops and societies for cooperative credit.

Q. 6. With reference to local self-governing bodies discuss:

(a) The composition of the Panchayat Samiti

(b) The functions of Gram Panchayat with respect to civic facilities and welfare

(c) What are the functions of the Panchayat Samiti with regard to:

    (i) Land reforms   (ii) Cooperative societies

    (iii) Higher educational institutions

Ans. (a) The members of the Panchayat Samiti are:

    (i) Presidents or Sarpanchas of all the Panchayats within the specified area.

    (ii) Members of the Legislative Assembly (MLAs), Legislative Council (MLCs) and Parliament (MPs) belonging to that area.

    (iii) Chairman of the Nagar Panchayats or the town area Committees of that area.

    (iv) The Block Development Officers of an area are also members of the Panchayat Samitis aong with the voted members of the Zila Parishad of that block.

    (v) The representatives of women, Co-operative Societies, Scheduled Castes and Scheduled Tribes.

(b) Functions of Gram Panchayat with respect to civic facilities and welfare are as follows :

    (i) Providing safe drinking water that includes measures like building and maintaining wells, tanks and drains for the public.

    (ii) Health Care Facilities like setting up of health centres and dispensaries by the Panchayat.

    (iii) Maintenance and construction of roads, good drainage, street lights, culverts, footpaths, bridges and car tracks.

    (iv) To look after the well-being of expecting mothers and their children.

    (v) Introducing welfare programmes for youth, children and women.

(c) Following are the functions of the Panchayat Samiti with regard to

    (i) **Land reforms:** The Samiti acquires the surplus land in the block and then distributes it among the landless farmers in the area.

    (ii) **Cooperative societies:** The Samiti establishes cooperative societies which provide financial assistance to small farmers. The Cooperative societies are responsible for providing improved quality of agricultural equipment, undertaking small irrigation schemes, providing chemical fertilizers, improved seeds and distributing pesticides to small farmers.

    (iii) **Higher Education Institutions:** Samiti is also responsible for setting up Higher Secondary Schools or colleges for higher education for the use of many villages in the area.

Q. 7. The beneficial aspect of Self-Government is that it offers the opportunity to the public to govern, which is the true essence of Democracy. In this context, answer the following questions:

(a) What is Local Self-Government?

(b) Differentiate between Local Government and Local Self-Government.

(c) What is the importance of Local Self-Government?

Ans. (a) Local Self-Government means a system of management of local affairs by the people of locality and their elected representatives.

    (i) It manages the affairs at the grassroot level through the local representatives of that area.

    (ii) It forms an integral part of the three-tier system of the Indian government.

    (iii) It looks after the needs and issues of people of a village, a town, a district or a city.

(b)

S.No.	Local Self-Government	Local Government
(i)	Local Self-Government means "an elected body that enjoys a certain extent of autonomy and serves as a government unit for local affairs."	Local Government means, "Administration of a locality by officials appointed by the government".
(ii)	Local Self-Government is managed by locally elected representatives who take care of the issues of a locality and provide the people with basic amenities.	Local government is the public administration of towns, cities, countries and districts.

(c) Importance of Local Self-Government:

   (i) Local people can effectively manage the local affairs related to their areas like water supply, sanitation, education, electricity and other public works.

   (ii) The beneficial aspect of self-government is that it offers the public the opportunity to govern themselves.

   (iii) The local institutions act as training grounds to prepare its members to manage State or National affairs in later years.

   (iv) The local institutions are capable of relieving the workload of State as well as Central Government by taking over some of their duties.

Q. 8. Local self-government can be stated as an institution managed by locally elected representatives. In this context , answer the following questions:

(a) What are the criteria for becoming the member of the Gram Panchayat?

(b) What are the sources of income of Panchayat Samiti?

(c) How can we say that local self-government is extremely economical system? **(Any there)**

Ans. (a) In order to become the members of the Gram Panchayat, the following criteria have to be fulfilled by the aspiring members:

   (i) As per the Act, a candidate has to attain the prescribed age.

   (ii) The name of the candidates must be registered as voters in the particular Panchayat area.

   (iii) The candidates must be mentally sound.

   (iv) The State Legislatures must not have disqualified the candidates under any law.

   (v) The candidate should not hold any office of profit under the government.

(b) The income of the Panchayat Samiti comes from three sources:

   (i) Taxes levied upon land and water usage, professional taxes, liquor taxes and others.

   (ii) Income generating programmes.

   (iii) Grants-in-aid and loans from the State Government and the local Zila Parishad and voluntary contributions.

(c) (i) The local bodies are generally less expensive to run than the expenses incurred by the officials of State administrations to manage a locality.

   (ii) These local institutions foster the idea of voluntary services and self-help that helps in saving substantial State funds.

   (iii) These saved funds are then used for constructive work of the State itself.

   (iv) Many honorary members join these local institutions that work without the involvement of money so that it doesn't create any economic burden on the people for their wages.

Q. 9. Panchayati Raj is a three-tier system. There is a Panchayat for each village. In this context, explain:

(a) The three-tier institutions of the Panchayati Raj System.

(b) Difference between traditional panchayats and modern panchayats.

(c) Achievements of Panchayati Raj System.

Ans. (a) The three-tier system in the Panchayati Raj comprises:
   (i) At the village level, there are three bodies- Gram Sabha, the Gram Panchayat and Nyaya Panchayat.
   (ii) At the block level, there are Panchayat Samitis that fall in the middle level.
   (iii) At the district level, Zila Parishads are set up.
   (b)

S.No.	Traditional Panchayats	Modern Panchayats
(i)	These panchayats comprised of five members.	Number of members is not fixed in modern panchayats.
(ii)	Elderly members used to become the members of the panchayat.	Persons are elected through adult franchise.
(iii)	Seats were not reserved for SCs, STs and women.	Seats are reserved for SCs, STs and women.

   (c) **Achievements of Panchayati Raj System :**
   (i) Panchayati Raj System ensures effective coordination between Government Programmes and those of Voluntary agencies.
   (ii) It has brought political awakening in the rural parts of India.
   (iii) It is successful in improving the conditions of villages in India, by taking up various welfare activities.
   (iv) It has increased representation of men and women from backward classes as well.

Chapter 5. Urban Local Self Government

Q. 1. State one optional function of a Municipal Corporation with respect to each of the following:
   (a) Transport facilities   (b) Cultural activities
   (c) Recreational facilities   (d) Welfare activities
Ans. One optional function of a Municipal Corporation with respect to each of the following is as follows:
   (a) **Transport facilities :** The Corporation arranges bus service for the people of the city.
   (b) **Cultural activities :** Beside setting up museums, libraries and reading rooms, the Corporation also organises dramas and kavi sammelans.
   (c) **Recreational facilities :** The Corporation looks after the maintenance of public parks, setting up of gymnasiums and up keeping of playgrounds.
   (d) **Welfare activities :** The Corporation establishes and maintains homes for children and the aged, orphanages, night-shelters and rest-houses.
Q. 2. With reference to local self-governing bodies answer the following questions:
   (a) What are the powers and functions of the President of a Municipal Committee?
   (b) Mention the various functions performed by the Chief Executive Officer and other officers of Municipal Committee.
   (c) Functions of the Municipal Corporation with respect to Public works.
Ans. (a) The Chairman or the President is considered as the presiding officer who enjoys the below mentioned powers and functions:
   (i) He/She presides over all the meetings of the Board and regulates how business is to be conducted in these meetings.
   (ii) Acts as the communicating link between the government and the Municipal Board over various matters.
   (iii) Acts as the custodian to all the documents and records of the Municipality.
   (b) Functions performed by the Chief Executive Officer and other officers of Municipal Committee are as follows:
   (i) He/She looks after Municipal Office and allocates work among all the Municipal Officers.

(ii) The employees of the Municipal Committee have to secure his approval while getting leave sanctioned.

(iii) Preparing estimates of the Municipality budget each year.

(iv) Responsible for issuing licenses and agreements for different jobs that feature under the rule of Municipal Board.

(v) Participating in every meeting of the Municipal Board or any of its committees. In these meetings, he/she hold the position of a Secretary.

(c) The functions of the Municipal Corporation with respect to public works are as follows:

(i) Providing buildings, roads, bus-shelters and public urinals for the convenience of people.

(ii) Preserving and giving names to various public streets and roads.

(iii) Setting of rules with regard to the building of hotels, restaurant and shopping centres.

Q. 3. With reference to the functions of the Local Self-Government, explain:

(a) Optional and discretionary functions of the Municipal Corporation

(b) The functions of the Mayor

(c) Functions of a Municipal Commissioner

Ans. (a) **Optional or discretionary functions of Municipal Corporation are:**

(i) The Corporation can arrange for a bus service for transportation of people across the city.

(ii) Providing facilities like public housing via organisations that handle housing related issues like housing boards, etc.

(iii) Some cultural activities of the Municipal Corporation include funding of museums, libraries, theatres, public parks, etc. The Corporation also sets up picnic resorts and Akharas.

(b) **The Mayor performs various functions, which are as follows:**

(i) Presiding over the meetings of the Corporation and regulating the conduct of business.

(ii) Maintaining discipline and decorum at the meetings.

(iii) Fixing the agenda of discussion for the meetings of the Corporation.

(iv) Receiving foreign guests visiting the city.

(v) Securing reports of the different programmes and projects from the Municipal Commissioner.

(vi) Acting as the link of communication between the Corporation and the Union or the State Government.

(c) **The functions of a Municipal Commissioner are:**

(i) Controlling and administering the Corporation and giving guidelines to every officer of the Corporation.

(ii) Implementing the rules, policies and decisions of the Corporation.

(iii) Preparing the budget and making estimations that are to be presented before the General Council and similar related financial functions.

(iv) Putting the various projects and programmes that have been laid out by the General Council into operation.

Q. 4. A Municipal Corporation is set up in cities which have large population. In this context discuss:

(a) Compulsory or Obligatory functions of a Municipal Corporation.

(b) Sources of income.

(c) The election and composition of the General Council of the Municipal Corporation.

Ans. (a) The Obligatory functions of a Municipal Corporation are as follows:

(i) **Providing electricity, water supply and sewage disposal:** The Corporation performs basic public services like providing safe drinking water, building new water works and maintaining the existing ones, proper supply of electricity and sewage disposal on a daily basis.

(ii) **Services rendered to Health and Sanitation:** It is the duty of the corporation to maintain hospitals, centres of welfare, maternity homes and dispensaries. It is the duty of the Municipal Corporation to organise vaccinations and inoculation camps for eradication of infectious diseases.

(iii) **Provision related to education and sports:** The Corporation is responsible for setting up schools up to primary and secondary levels, along with centres for educating adults, setting up libraries, museums, and night schools. The Corporation ensures that children below the age of 14 go to schools.

(b) Three sources of income of a Municipal Corporation are:

(i) Grant-in-aid from state government

(ii) Education cess, Entertainment tax, octroi duties

(iii) Taxes on water, houses, markets, etc.

(c) Election and composition of the General Council of the Municipal Corporation:

(i) The General Council is composed of members known as Municipal Councillors, who are elected directly based on Universal Adult Franchise via secret ballot.

(ii) Depending on the population of the city, the state government determines the number of Seats in the General Council.

(iii) Besides elected members, there are some chosen Alderman in the Council who are generally renowned and important personalities of the city and are nominated by the Governor.

(iv) With respect to the population, a proportion of the seats are also reserved for the SCs and STs and a specific one-third proportion of the total number of seats are reserved for women.

Q. 5. Municipal Corporation is the term used for describing the local governing body in countries, cities, towns, townships, and villages. In this context, answer the following questions:

(a) Where would you find the Municipal Corporation, Municipalities and Nagar Panchayats?

(b) What is the eligibility for contesting for Municipal elections?

(c) Distinguish between the obligatory and discretionary functions of a Municipal Corporation.

Ans. (a) (i) **Municipal Corporation:** In order to have a Municipal Corporation as the local self-governing unit, a city must have a population of at least one lakh and preferably more than that.

(ii) **Municipal Committee:** In cities and towns that have a smaller population ranging 20,000 to 300,000 a Municipal Committee is constituted.

(iii) **Nagar Panchayats:** An urban centre with more than 11,000 and less than 25,000 populations is classified as Nagar Panchayat is constituted.

(b) In order to become a candidate for contesting Municipal elections, a person needs to be:

(i) A registered voter in the area of the Municipal Corporation.

(ii) At least 21 years of age and not more than 25 years as prescribed under the State Corporation act.

(iii) Not hold any office of profit under State Government or any of the local bodies of the State Government.

(iv) Prior to filing of his nomination papers, he is expected to resign his current post.

(c)

S.No.	Obligatory Functions	Discretionary Functions
(i)	The Municipal Corporation performs basic public services like providing for safe drinking water, electricity and sewage disposal.	The Corporation can arrange for a bus service for transportation of people across the city.
(ii)	It provides services rendered to health and sanitation.	Providing facilities like public housing via organisations that handle housing related issues like housing boards.
(iii)	The Corporation is responsible for setting up schools up to primary and secondary levels, along with centres for educating adults, setting up libraries, museums and night schools.	The Corporation organises exhibitions, functions, fairs or melas and wrestling events and similar recreational facilities for the entertainment of the citizens.

SECTION : B (HISTORY)

Chapter 1. The Harappan Civilisation

Q. 1. With reference to the Indus Valley Civilisation answer the following questions:
    (a) Throw a light on the origin of this civilisation.
    (b) Write in brief the extent of this civilisation.
    (c) What were the probable cause for decay and decline of this civilisation.
Ans. (a) (i) Some historians believe that the Harappan civilisation was only an extension of the village Mehgarh (6000 BC) where its oldest remains have been founded.
      (ii) Others believe that prior to Harappa, village culture developed in the remote areas of India at popular sites in Punjab, Haryana, Rajasthan, Baluchistan and Sindh.
      (iii) Besides Mehgarh, other important sites of this culture are Gomal Valley Jabalpur (Punjab), Amri and Koldji (Sind), Kalibangan (Rajasthan) and Banwali (Haryana).
    (b) (i) The influence of the Indus Valley Civilisation extended to the Punjab, Sind, North-West Frontier Province, Baluchistan, Rajasthan, Gujarat, Uttar Pradesh and some parts of South India.
      (ii) It was spread over an area of about 1600 kilometres from West to East and 1100 Kilometres from North to South.
      (iii) Latest excavations in Gujarat and recent researches have shown that this civilisation spread over 1,300,000 square kilometres.
    (c) Some of the major reasons for the decline of this civilisation are as follows:
      (i) Excessive use of natural resources and vegetation might have had an adverse impact on fertile area of the Indus region and turned it into barren land thus depopulated the cities.
      (ii) The land might have been destroyed due to contnuous heavy floods which led to the break down of the civilisation.
      (iii) Some historians like Mortimer Wheeler believe that probably the Aryans's invasions brought destruction to the Harappan civilisation.
      (iv) Earthquakes and epidemics might have altered the course of Indus River, causing huge damage to the cities.

Q. 2. The Indus Valley Civilisation comprised all the elements of an urban civilisation.
    In the light of this statement, answer the following questions:
    (a) State the basic typology of urban settlements.
    (b) Write any three important characteristics of the drainage system.
    (c) Describe the building of Harappan cities.

Ans. (a) Basic typology of Harappan settlements can be describe as follows:

    (i) The early settlements of Mohen-jo-daro, Harappa and Kalibangan had the twin mounds, enclosed separately.

    (ii) Lothal had a single enclosed complex that housed public buildings and other residential forms.

    (iii) Most of the sites shared similar features such as burnt-brick houses, drains and granaries.

  (b) (i) The drainage system made of burnt brick was the most extensively used structure in the Harappan cities.

    (ii) The floors of kitchen and bathrooms were water tight and slightly slanted towards corner, to allow water to drain out into the drains constructed alongside.

    (iii) The house drains were joined to the underground sewers in the streets that were equipped with the brick-lined drainage channel.

    (iv) These channels carried wastes to the large wells located outside the city.

  (c) (i) The double or triple-storied buildings in the Harappan cities were made of baked bricks.

    (ii) Houses were constructed in a sequence and most of them had a well-architectured bathrooms.

    (iii) There was a proper drainage system in every house and even in public areas.

Q. 3. With reference to town planning in the Indus Valley Civilisation, write short notes on the following :

  (a) Division of the town   (b) Roads and streets

  (c) Residential buildings

Ans. (a) (i) The ruins indicate that most of the city had two divisions : a raised area called the 'Citadel' and the 'Lower Town'.

    (ii) Public buildings such as assembly hall, the granaries and the workshops were located on the 'Citadel' while the residential buildings were housed in the 'Lower Town'.

    (iii) The whole city was intersected by streets into rectangular and square blocks. Each block was further sub-divided into number of lanes.

  (b) (i) All the roads and streets were straight and intersected at right angles.

    (ii) The fire-burnt bricks were used to pave the streets.

    (iii) The corners of the streets were rounded to make the movement of heavy carts easy.

  (c) (i) The double or triple storied houses were constructed on raised platforms to protect the buildings from floods.

    (ii) These buildings had enough-sized rooms, bathrooms, solid staircases and water wells.

    (iii) The rooms were placed around on open courtyard while the kitchen was positioned at the corner of the courtyard.

Q. 4. Religion played an important role in the life of the people during the Harappan civilisation. In this context explain how each one of the following gives evidence to the existence of religion among the people:

  (a) Worship of Mother Goddess   (b) Worship of Lord Shiva

  (c) Worship of trees and animals.

Ans. (a) (i) A large number of semi-nude terracotta figures have been excavated which identify some female energy of Shakti or Mother Goddess who is the source of all creation.

    (ii) She is wearing several ornaments and a fan shaped head-dress.

    (iii) It is concluded from the smoke stained figures that people worshipped her by offering burnt incense before her.

  (b) (i) The Pashupati seal signify the belief of Harappan people in Lord Shiva.

    (ii) In this seal the three-faced male god is shown seated in a yogic posture, surrounded by a rhino and a buffalo on the right and an elephant and a tiger on the left.

Long Questions

    (iii) A large number of conical or cylindrical stones have been discovered which show that the people worshipped linga, the symbol of Lord Shiva.

(c) (i) A large number of seals with pipal trees engraved on them were discovered which suggests that this tree was considered sacred.

    (ii) One of the seals shows a god standing between the branches of a Pipal trees and being worshipped by a devotee on his Knees.

    (iii) Besides trees, the worship of mythical animals is evident from the existence of a human figure with a bull's horns, hoofs and a tail.

Q. 5. With reference to the economic life of the Harappan civilisation, discuss the followings :

    (a) Agriculture   (b) Trade and Commerce

    (c) Transport.

Ans. (a) (i) Agriculture was the main occupation of the Indus Valley people.

    (ii) The excavation of a wooden plough and granaries indicates that the Harappans produced surplus food grains.

    (iii) Traces of canal found at shortaghai (Afghanistan) and water reservior at Dholavira (Gujarat) indicate the availability of irrigation facilities.

(b) (i) The trade was done in the form of Barter system.

    (ii) Internal trade was thriving in metullary, tools and weapons, rice, ornaments and shell works.

    (iii) Besides internal trade, international trade had also flourished by both land and sea.

(c) (i) A number of seals with pictures of ships embedded on them indicate the use of ships in the Harappan civilisation.

    (ii) People also used boats and bullock carts.

    (iii) Skeleton remains of camels excavated at Kalibangan site reveals that camel was also an important mode of transport.

Q. 6. The Harappan civilization was a highly developed urbanised civilisation that revealed the architectural skills of the people. In this context answer the following questions:

(a) State three examples as evidence to prove that the Harappan town planning was urbanised and developed.

(b) Explain the significance of the Great Bath.

(c) State the importance of Harappan trade relations with other civilizations.

[November, 2019]

Ans. (a) The ruins of the sites reveal that the Harappan people were primarily urban and their cities were designed skilfully.

    (i) Streets divided the entire city into square or rectangular blocks, each of which was further divided by a number of lanes. The main streets were wide and straight and intersected each other at right angles. Fire-burnt bricks were used for paving the streets. The street corners were rounded off for easy movement of heavy carts. Houses were not allowed to encroach on the streets.

    (ii) One of the unique features of the city was its elaborate drainage system. A brick-lined drainage channel flowed alongside every street. The drains of the house were connected to the underground main drains. There were manholes at regular intervals for proper inspection and cleaning. People paid attention to sanitation and health.

    (iii) The city was divided into two parts—the raised area called the citadel and the lower town called the residential area. The citadel was constructed on a mud brick platform. The important buildings, such as the Great Bath, the granary and the assembly hall were located on the citadel. The lower town had the residential buildings. The houses were built on a raised platform for protection against floods.

(b) The most imposing structure that was unearthed at Mohen-jo-daro was the Great Bath.

    (i) The Great Bath was a large rectangular tank in a courtyard, surrounded by corridor on all four sides. There were rooms on three sides, in one of which was a large well.

(ii) There were two flights of steps on the north and the south leading into the tank, which was made watertight by setting bricks on edge and using a mortar of gypsum. Water from the tank flowed into a huge drain.

(iii) Across a lane to the north lay a smaller building with eight bathrooms, four on each side of the corridor. Drains from each bathroom connected to a drain that ran along the corridor.

(iv) It was situated on the citadel or the upper town, which suggests it must have been used for some kind of ritual bath.

(c) (i) The Harappans had commercial relations with southern and eastern India, Kashmir and countries of Central Asia.

(ii) They imported various metals, precious stones and other articles. It is believed that they imported gold from Karnataka, copper from Rajasthan and precious stones from Afghanistan and Iran.

(iii) There is evidence that Harappans used sets of cubical stone weights in the far-flung areas. Evidence reveals that trade was carried with Egypt and Crete. Objects of Sumerian origin have been found at the Indus cities.

(iv) Trade was carried on both by land and sea routes. The representation of a mastless ship on a Seal reflects the popularity of sea routes.

Q. 7. State the reasons why seals are very important for historians.

Ans. The seals are considered very important for historians because:

(i) These are the authentic sources of information about the culture and civilisation of the Harappan people.

(ii) The figures engraved on the seals provided information about the physical features, ornament dresses and hairstyles of the Harappan people.

(iii) These also explain the religious belief of the Indus people.

(iv) These also offer ideas about the commercial activities of the people.

Q. 8. The Harappan civilisation reveals the architectural skills of the people. Discuss the significant features of their civilisation with reference to:

(a) the dwelling houses, (b) the Assembly hall.

Ans. (a) The significant features of the Harappan civilisation with reference to the dwelling houses :

(i) The dwelling houses were situated on either side of the streets.

(ii) They were made of burnt bricks of higher quality.

(iii) Rooms were built around an open courtyard.

(iv) The houses had wells and bathrooms and were provided with covered drains connected to street drains. The bathroom was placed on the street side with the corner sloping floor for draining off water.

(b) (i) The Assembly Hall was an important feature of Mohenjo-Daro and its 24 square metres pillared hall.

(ii) It had five rows of pillars, with four pillars in each row.

(iii) Kiln baked bricks were used to construct these pillars.

(iv) It is said that it also housed the Municipal Office which had the charge of town planning and sanitation.

Q. 9. How can you say that Harappan people had knowledge of trade?

Ans. The following points suggest that Harappan people had knowledge of trade.

(i) The people of the Indus Valley had commercial contact with Southern and Eastern India, Kashmir and with other countries of Asia.

(ii) They used weights and measures in their business transactions.

(iii) They imported various metals, precious stones and other articles.

(iv) Bullock carts with or without the roof were the chief means of conveyance.

(v) The representation of a mastless ship on a seal suggests the popularity of the sea-routes.

Long Questions

(vi) Harappan seals were founded at Bahrain and Mesopotamian cities. This concluded their extensive overseas trade.

(vii) Lapis Lazuli (a bright blue stone used in ornaments) was imported from Central Asia, gold from Karnataka and possibly copper and tin from Mesopotamia. **(Any four)**

Q. 10. Was the Harappan Civilisation confined to the valley of the Indus river and its tributaries extended far beyond that area?

Ans. The Harappa Civilisation was extended far beyond the area of Indus river and tributaries bed besides. Harappan and Mohen-jo-daro, many other sites were discovered such as :

(i) Chanhundaro in Sindh

(ii) Lothal in Gujarat

(iii) Kalibangan in Hanumangarh district of Rajasthan

(iv) Ropar at the foot of the Simla hills and Suktagendor on the coast of Baluchistan.

(v) Alamgirpur in UP and Banawali in Hissar district of Haryana

Q. 11. What were the religious beliefs of the Indus Valley people? Explain.

Ans. The following were the religious beliefs of the Indus Valley people:

(i) They believed in polytheism (the belief that there is more the one god).

(ii) They also believed in image worship as the figure of a male dieties and figurine of Mother Goddess were found.

(iii) Priests were held in great esteem.

(iv) They had faith in the doctrine of animism (the belief that plants, objects and natural things have a living soul).

(v) The pipal tree was regarded as sacred.

(vi) The pigeon was the only bird worshipped.

(vii) Discovery of fire altars at Kalibangan and some other Harappan sites suggests that fire sacrifices were also performed.

(viii) Use of incense was common. **(Any four)**

Chapter 2. The Vedic Period

Q. 1. The advent of the Aryans in India is an important event in History. Keeping this in view, write briefly on the following:

(a) The most probable place of their origin.

(b) Their early settlement in India.

(c) Three features of political life of the Aryans during the early Vedic Period.

Ans. (a) (i) It is usually believed that the original home of the Aryans was central Asia.

   (ii) Some others believed that they came from southern Russia (near the caspian sea) or in South-East Europe (in Austria and Hungary).

   (iii) The most approved view of Prof. Max Muller, the German scholar was that the original home of Aryans was somewhere near the Caspian Sea. From there two groups of Aryans are said to have come to Persia and India.

(b) (i) First of all the Aryans settled in the areas of North-Western Province in Pakistan and then Punjab.

   (ii) They pushed their way along the river Ganga and Yamuna from Sapta Sindhu region.

   (iii) Gradually they occupied the whole of northern India from the Himalayas to the Vindhyas.

(c) (i) In the Early Vedic Period, the king was not an autocrat.

   (ii) He was assisted by several ministers particularly the commander-in-chief and Purohit.

   (iii) The king was a hereditary successor but in case the king proved to be cruel, people had the right to replace him by another chosen king.

Q. 2. Rigveda is believed to be the oldest source of religion in the Early Vedic Period. In this concern, write briefly on the following:

(a) The Aryans belief in monotheism.

(b) Religious sacrifices done by Aryans.

(c) Advent of ritualism in the later part of the Vedic period.

Ans. (a) (i)   Some of the hymns or mantras exhibit the idea that God is one but he is called by many names such as Indra, Mitra, Agni, etc.

(ii)   All these gods represent various phenomena of nature and were the manifestations of one Supreme God who is the Creater; Preserver and Destroyer of the universe.

(iii) They called Him as Ishwar, Bhrama or Vishnu.

(b) (i)   Sacrifices had an important place in both the early and later Vedic rituals.

(ii)   Small sacrifices were performed by every household as a daily ritual but bigger sacrifices were performed by learned Brahmins on a grand scale for only some occassions.

(iii) These sacrifices were offered to please the gods who in turn would bless their people with peace and prosperity.

(c) (i)   In the later Vedic Period the powerful priestly class or Brahmins transformed the simple vedic religion into a complicated ritualism with many superstitions.

(ii)   The emphasis was given more on rituals than on religious chanting of the sacred hymns of the Vedas.

(iii) Complicated mantras were composed to make sacrifices more effective.

Q. 3. (a) Explain briefly the importance of Epics in the Vedic period.

(b) Differentiate between the Early Vedic Age and the Later Vedic Age with reference to its Economy. **[February, 2020]**

Ans. (a) Most of our knowledge about the later Vedic period comes from the Vedic literature produced during this period. Two of the well-known epics are the Ramayana and the Mahabharata. The importances of these epics in the Vedic period are:

(i)   They are remarkable for their philosophical and literary value.

(ii)   They are the main source of information about the social, political and cultural, army and military situation of the later Vedic period.

(iii) These epics reflect the principles, values and ideals of a family life of the Aryans.

(iv) The Bhagavad Gita, which is a part of the Mahabharat, is the most sacred text for the people of India.

(b) The differences between the Early Vedic Age and the Later Vedic Age with reference to economy are as follows:

S.No.	Early Vedic Age	Later Vedic Age
(i)	Aryans were primarily agriculturists and practiced cultivation of land.	Agriculture became a dominant economic activity. The Aryans grew rice, wheat, millet and sugarcane.
(ii)	Progress was made in arts and crafts. There were weavers, potters, carpenters, jewellers, iron and goldsmiths, metal workers, etc.	People began using iron on a large scale. Leather work developed. Making of jewellery progressed. Chariot-making developed.
(iii)	Trade and commerce was carried out by the Aryans through barter system,	Barter system continued. Guilds were organized to look after the various trading communities.

Q. 4. With reference to social life in the Vedic period, answer the following questions briefly:

(a) What do you understand by the term Ashrams? How many stages were there in the journey of a man's life?

(b) How do you describe the Caste system in both the Early and Later Vedic Period?

(c) How did gurukulas impart education in the vedic period?

Ans. (a) (i) The term ashrama describes a stage in the long journey of a man's life about 100 years.

      (ii) The first stage was the Brahmacharya from birth to 25 years of age in which man acquired knowledge by leading the life of a student.

      (iii) After the gurukulas the man entered the second stage *i.e.,* grihastha ashram till the age of 50 in which he was supposed to marry and lead a family life.

      (iv) After 50, man entered vanaprastha ashram till the age of 75 during which he was supposed to break the family ties and serve community.

      (v) This stage was followed by vanaprastha, a renounced life in the forest.

(b) (i) The society in the vedic period was divided into 4 vernas or classes on the basis of occupation of the people rather their birth.

      (ii) Members of priestly class were called brahmin, those of the warrier called kshatriya; agriculturists and traders were vaishyas and the menials were shudras.

      (iii) Change of varna was common by choosing any occupation or through inter caste marriages.

(c) (i) During the brahmacharya, a man was supposed to be studying in the gurukulas where students possessed a literature handed down by word of mouth.

      (ii) The word gurukula means a family of the teacher in which students lived as the family members of teacher.

      (iv) Education was free but students from affordable families paid gurudakshina after completion of their studies.

Q. 5. With reference to the Ramayana and the Mahabharata, answer the following questions:

(a) Name the authors of these epics.

(b) What is the historical importance of these epics?

(c) Which battle is known as Mahabharata?

Ans. (a) (i) Ramayana is believed to have been written by Rishi Valmiki in Sanskrit language.

      (ii) Mahabharata was originally composed by Rishi Ved Vyas.

(b) (i) These epics serve as the primary source of information about the political institutions and the cultural and social organisations of the Epic Age.

      (ii) These epics revealed the high ideals of the family life of Aryans.

      (iii) They provide informations about various Aryan kingdoms, their armies and weapons.

(c) The battle tought between 'kurus' or 'Kauravas' and 'Pandus' or 'Pandavas' along the battlefield of 'Kurushetra' is known as 'Mahabharata'.

Q. 6. With reference to the Caste System, state the answers of the following questions:

(a) Give any three merits of the caste system.

(b) What are the disadvantages of the caste system?

(c) How did the caste system become rigid in the later Vedic Period?

Ans. (a) (i) The caste system developed brotherhood among members of the same caste.

      (ii) Caste system ensured continuity of occupation to reduced unemployment and thus brought about perfection of several arts and crafts.

      (iii) Marriages within the caste reduces maladjustment in family life.

(b) (i) Caste system gave rise to untouchability and against the feeling of common brotherhood.

      (ii) It suppressed an individual's talent and became an obstacle for his personal advancement.

      (iii) Multiple caste system had replaced the simple system of the Varnas.

(c) (i) In the Later Vedic Period the Brahmins and Kshatriyas became powerful and the Vaishyas had to pay tributes.

   (ii) Shudras became miserable and were treated as untouchables.

   (iii) Transformation of one caste to another had become difficult.

   (iv) Inter Caste marriages had ceased to exist.

Chapter 3. Jainism And Buddhism

Q. 1. The supremacy of Brahmanical society led to the emergence of two new sects of religion. Jainism and Buddhism. In this context explain the following:

   (a) Dominant Brahmanical society   (b) Rigid Caste System

   (c) Rigid and Expensive Ritualism.

Ans. (a) (i) The Brahmins considered themselves to be supreme and they started to dominate and claims certain privileges.

       (ii) They had become corrupt, naughty and demanded respect.

       (iii) The common people could not reconcile to this attitude of the priests and were unhappy.

    (b) (i) In the 6th century BC the Varna system had become rigid and exploitative for the lower classes.

       (ii) Shudras were ill-treated and were harrassed through many ways.

       (iii) Both Buddhism and Jainism rejected caste distinctions and encouraged equality among each other.

    (c) (i) In the Later Vedic Period, Hindu religion had become too ritualistic and complex which failed to satisfy the spiritual needs of common people.

       (ii) The universal truth and purity of heart vanished from hinduism which led the people to crave for a simple religion.

       (iii) The ceremonial rituals and sacrifices had become so complex and expensive that the common man was left at the mercy of the priests. It gave rise to faiths that were not expensive and could be understood by all.

Q. 2. With reference to Jainism Explain the followings:

   (a) Doctrine of Jainism   (b) Spread of Jainism

   (c) Unpopularity of Jainism

Ans. (a) (i) The most renowned doctrine of Jainism was ahinsa or non-injury to any living being, even a tiny insect.

       (ii) All living beings from the tiny insect to the highest form of life, should be shown compassion.

       (iii) Jains believed in penance and to die of starvation regarded as a virtue.

    (b) (i) Jainism spread around Kosala, Magadha, Mithila, Champa and Several other parts of the country due to royal patronage.

       (ii) Mahavira travelled on foot for thirty years preaching his religion and doing penance.

       (iii) He founded monastries headed by learned sages.

    (c) (i) Too severe a penance and rigid fasts could not be undertaken easily by common man.

       (ii) Yet the Jainism preached equality of men, it could not eradicate the low and high positions in society.

       (iii) It accepted the doctrine of karma and its influence on rebirth in a higher or lower sections of society according to one's deeds in one's previous life.

Q. 3. With reference to Buddhism explain the following terms:

   (a) The Four Noble truths   (b) Eightfold Path of Buddhism

   (c) The Tripitaka

Ans. (a) The four Noble truths are as follows:

       (i) The world is full of sufferings.

       (ii) Suffering is caused by human desire.

(iii) The renunciation of desires is the path of salvation.

(iv) Salvation can be attained by following the Eight-Fold Path.

(b) (i) The Eight Fold Path of Buddhism:

    (i) Right belief   (ii) Right thought

    (iii) Right speech   (iv) Right action

    (v) Right means of livelihood   (vi) Right meditation

    (vii) Right effort   (viii) Right memory

(c) The Buddhist sacred literature is known as the Tripitaka or the three baskets.

    (i) The first basket or part is called the vinayapitaka which contains rules and the guidance for Buddhist monks for the management of the monasteries.

    (ii) The second part sutrapitaka has the collection of the lectures and discourse of Buddha.

    (iii) The third part abhidhammapitaka has the explanation of the philosophical principles of the Buddhist religion.

Q. 4. In context to Buddhism explain the following:

(a) Karma   (b) Dharma

(c) Sangha

Ans. (a) **Karma:**

    (i) Buddhism authorised the laws of karma.

    (ii) It believed that man is the maker of his own destiny.

    (iii) If man does good deeds in his life, he will be reborn to a higher life and attains salvation whereas evil deeds will be surely punished.

(b) **Dharma:**

    (i) As per Buddhist Philosophy, the whole universe was controlled by dharma a universal law.

    (ii) Buddha was silent about the presence of God , though he never denied it formally.

(c) **The Sangha:**

    (i) The Sangha is a part of the three fold refuge a basic creed of Buddhism.

    (ii) Every man and woman above the age of 15 years may join the Sangha.

    (iii) The Sangha is composed of four groups: monks, nuns, laymen and laywomen.

Q. 5. With reference to Jainism answer the following:

Questions :

(a) Name the two sects of Jainism.

(b) Name any three rulers who patronised the Jainism.

(c) Explain any two beliefs of Jainism.

Ans. (a) The two sects of Jainism are:

    (i) Digambaras, the sky-clad, and   (ii) Swetambaras, the white-clad

(b) (i) Bimbsara   (ii) Chandragupta Maurya

    (iii) Bhadrabahu.

(c) (i) Refusing the Sacrifices and rituals : Mahavira did not believe in sacrifices and rituals, which involved violence, killing and meaningless ceremonies.

    (ii) Ahimsa : Lord Mahavira opposed the three kinds of violence:

        (1) Physical violence inflicting physical pain, injury or killing.

        (2) Verbal violence causing pain by harsh languages.

        (3) Mental violence by thinking ailing about people.

Q.6. India saw the rise of two great religions-Jainism and Buddhism in the Sixth Century B.C. In this context explain the following: **[November, 2019]**

(a) State three causes for the rise of Jainism and Buddhism.

(b) Write any three reasons for decline of Jainism.

(c) State any four teachings of Gautama Buddha.

Ans. Besides, intellectual unrest, and social and economic inequalities during the 6th and 5th centuries, people yearned for a different kind of society and a different system of religion. The causes for the rise of Jainism and Buddhism were:

(i) **Ritualistic Vedic religion:** As simple religion of early Aryans became meaningless rituals and complicated ceremonies, and costly for ordinary people to perform, people became discontended with the religious beliefs and practices of that age.

(ii) **Killing of animals to perform sacrifices:** As the yajnas became expensive and demanded a large number of animals to be sacrificed for the ceremonies, people started resenting such meaningless expenditure and sacrifices.

(iii) **Supremacy of the priestly class:** With the introduction of elaborate rites and rituals, the priests gained supreme power in the society. They dominated the life of a man from birth to death. People turned against the priests who made religion complicated, expensive and burdensome.

(iv) **The caste system:** The caste system became rigid. It was decided according to birth and not profession. People of lower castes were ill-treated by people of higher caste. Untouchability came into practice. The reformers and intellectuals resented these discriminations. The Buddhist Sangha was therefore, open to all.

(v) **Difficult Vedic language:** Vedic literature had been written in Sanskrit, which was beyond the comprehension of the common people. Many could not understand the Vedic mantras recited by the Brahmin priests.

(vi) **Efforts of religious reformers:** The unrest against the evils that had crept into the Vedic religion and society led to the rise of a number of intcllectuals and reformers. They questioned the purpose of meaningless rituals and supremacy of the priestly class. The simple life and teachings of the Mahavira and Buddha attracted many who longed to be liberated from the oppression of the Brahmanical order.   **(Mention any three causes)**

(b) The loss of royal patronage hampered the growth of Jainism. Other factors that led to the decline of Jainism were as follows :

(i) Common people found it difficult to follow the severe penance and austerity advocated by Mahavira. Many hesitated to embrace Jainism because of the rigid principles.

(ii) After Mahavira's nirvana, Jainism was divided into two sects—the Swetambaras and the Digambaras. This division made it impossible to continue any concrete religious or social work among the people.

(iii) The revival of Brahmanism was a great setback to Jainism.

(c) The teachings of Gautama Buddha are emphasised in The Four Noble Truths and The Eight-Fold Path.

The Four Noble Truths were:

(i) The world is full of sorrow and suffering.

(ii) The main cause of suffering is man's desire for sensual pleasures and earthly possession.

(iii) Suffering can be removed by getting rid of desires, that is, renunciation.

(iv) One can overcome desires by following the Eight-Fold Path that includes right faith, right aspiration, right action, right living, right speech, right effort, right meditation, and right contemplation.

Chapter 4. The Mauryan Empire

Q. 1. With reference to sources, highlight the political history under the Mauryas during the Age of:

(a) Chandragupta Maurya

(b) Bindusara

(c) Ashoka

Ans. (a) (i) Chandragupta Maurya founded the Mauryan Empire after defeating the Dhanananda, the last Nanda ruler, with the help of Kautilya.

      (ii) He liberated Punjab and North west by defeating Seleucus Nicator in 305 BC.

      (iii) The empire of Chandragupta stretched up to Kandhar and Kabul in the North-West to Mysore in the sourth and from Western Saurashtra to the Eastern region of Bengal.

   (b) (i) Chandragupta's son Bindusara succeeded to the throne in 300 BC and continued to rule for 27 years till 273 BC.

      (ii) He is known to have maintained pleasant relations with the Greeke.

   (c) (i) Ashoka was the most popular Mauryan Cmperor, who ruled from 269 BC to 232 BC.

      (ii) Kalinga war was the first recorded event of the reign of Ashoka after eight years of his coronation.

      (iii) He became a Buddhist in the 9th year of his coronation.

      (iv) He issued 16 Major and 15 Minor Rock Edicts in India alongwith 7 pillar edicts.

Q. 2. Explain the importance of Ashoka's Edicts as sources of information with special reference to the followings:

   (a) Ashoka's conversion to Buddhism   (b) Ashoka's Dhamma

   (c) Ashoka's characteristics.

Ans. (a) (i) The minor Rock Edict I mentioning Ashoka's conversion to Buddhist faith since 259 BC.

      (ii) As per the Sri Lankan chronicle Mahavamsa, Ashoka was converted to Buddhism by Nigrodha, a seven year old boy monk.

      (iii) Later he came in contact with Mogaliputta Tissa, who headed the third Buddhist council called by Ashoka in 500 BC.

   (b) (i) Rock Edict XIII declared that the Kalinga war filled the heart of Ashoka with guilt and regret after which his main objective was to promote Dhamma.

      (ii) Ashoka's Dhamma was free from the intolerant sectorianism.

      (iii) His Dhamma is a "Moral Law" that deals with ideas such as virtue, justice, morality and law and duty.

   (c) (i) The Rock Edicts XII and XIII mention non-violence, truthfulness, obedience, respect and the transformation of Ashoka after the conquest of Kalinga.

      (ii) The Barabar cave Inscription prescribes the religious tolerance of Ashoka.

      (iii) The Queen's Edict describes the sacred donations of Ashoka's wife to Buddhist Sangha.

Q. 3. "A centralized form of government was first introduced during the Mauryan Empire". Explain the statement with reference to the followings:

   (a) Military Administration   (b) Judicial Administration

   (c) The benefits of the Pan-Indian character of the Mauryan Empire.

Ans. (a) (i) The king was the supreme authority of the armed forces.

      (ii) Historical records evident that Mauryan army was consisted of 9000 war-elephants, 30,000 cavalry, 6,00,000 infantry and 1000 chariots alongwith fleet of ships.

      (iii) A military committee of 30 members controlled the entire army.

   (b) (i) During the Mauryan Period, criminal laws were very strict and death penalty was the final punishment for serious offenders of law.

      (ii) Those who were involved in lighter crimes were punished by shaving of the head of the criminal to humiliate him or cutting his nose off.

      (iii) The king was the supreme judge and having power to enact new laws and amend the existing one.

   (c) (i) The Mauryan empire presage the end of single small states.

      (ii) It aided in establishing links with foreign countries with the help of trade.

      (iii) India became a strong country under the Mauryan Empire.

Q. 4. With reference to the provincial administration answer the following questions:

(a) Write the functions of major officials at the district level.

(b) How did cities and capitals administer during the Mauryan Empire?

(c) Write in brief the village administration under the Mauryan Empire.

Ans. (a) (i) There were four major officials appointed for looking after the district administration who were Pradeshikas, Mahamatras, Yuktas, Rajukas.

(ii) The Pradeshikas were responsible for visiting the entire district to observe everything.

(iii) The Yuktas were in charge of accounting, collection of revenue and secretarial work.

(iv) Rajukas were responsible for examine and evaluating the land.

(v) Mahamatras or governors acted as in charges of the provinces.

(b) (i) All the major cities and capitals of the various provinces had a separate local administrative system with main administrative system.

(ii) The city superintendent or the Nagaraka was in-charge of maintenance of public roads and building and all other works which are done by modern municipalities.

(iii) The Nagarakas also worked as census officers as they were maintaining the birth and death records.

(c) (i) The village was the smallest unit of Mauryan administration which is an autonomous body.

(ii) The head of a village was called Gramika who was assisted by Gramvriddhas or village elders.

(iii) The Gramika was elected by the people.

Q. 5. (a) State any three features of Ashoka's Dhamma.

(b) Explain any four features of the central government under the Mauryan administration.

Ans. (a) After Kalinga War, Ashoka's outlook towards life changed completely. He wanted all the people to live happily and peacefully. This was called Dhamma, which is the Pali word for Dharma. This aimed at improving the lives of the people. Three features of Ashoka's Dhamma were:

(i) People should follow Ahimsa or the path of non-violence. No creatures should be hurt.

(ii) People must respect and be tolerant towards all religion.

(iii) A person should speak the truth at all times.

(b) Ashoka's inscriptions and Kautilya's Arthashastra throws light on the Mauryan administration:

(i) The king was the supreme head of the State and had executive, judicial and military powers. He had the authority to enact laws. It was the responsibility of the king to give close attention to people's welfare, social order and military action.

(ii) The king had council of ministers to advise the king, check his powers; and in the task of choosing Governors, Army generals, Treasurer of the State, Chief magistrates and other high officials.

(iii) The Mauryan State had a network of spies to keep the emperor informed about the opponents and their activities. They also reported to the king about their own army, the state and conduct of his officers.

(iv) The Mauryan Empire earned revenue from land, including mines and forests, from various manufactured goods, tolls paid for using bridges and roads, fines and license fees. The tax varied from one-third to one-sixth of the produce and could be paid either in cash or in kind. Considerable amount of money was spend on public works, especially in the construction of roads, wells and rest houses.

(v) The system of justice was strong and efficient with punishments of different degrees for different crimes.

Q. 6. With reference to the Ashoka's Dhamma answer the following questions:

(a) Write briefly about the principles of Dhamma.

(b) What was the contribution of Ashoka in spreading Dhamma?

(c) What were the impacts of Dhamma on the imperial policy of Ashoka?

Ans. (a) According to the Rock Edict XIII, the fundamental principles of Dhamma are as follows :

    (i) Susrusa: Obedience towards elders and parents.

    (ii) Anarhan to Bhutaanaam: Abstain from killing of living beings.

    (iii) Avihimsa Bhutaanaam: Non violence and no harming of all living creatures.

    (iv) Apichiti: Respect towards teachers.

    (v) Bhava-shuddhi: Purification of heart.

    (vi) Satyam: Truthfulness.

    (vii) Danam: Being liberal towards all.

    (viii) Sampratipatti: Appropriate treatment of ascetics, tolerance towards other religions.

    (ix) Dhamma-Rati: Remaining attached to morality.

    (x) Apa-vyayata apa-bhandatacha: Practising saving and spending moderately.

(b) Ashoka adopted the following measures to spread his Dhamma:

    (i) Ashoka inscribed the principles of Dhamma on the rock edicts that can be found at various significant places.

    (ii) He used pali, the common man's language to carry his message to all corners of his empire.

    (iii) He appointed Dhamma Mahamatras to promote Dhamma and take care of the happiness and welfare of the entire population.

(c) Impact of Dhamma on the Imperial policy of Ashoka:

    (i) People started leading a moral life under the influence of Dhamma.

    (ii) The continuous wars and conquest came to an end because of the Dhamma policy.

    (iii) People started following Ahimsa which ultimately led to the near end of crimes.

Chapter 5. The Sangam Age

Q. 1. With the reference of the Sangam literature write the importance of the following:

(a) Poems   (b) Grammar

(c) Epics

Ans. (a) (i) The Sangam literature ranging from 300 BC to AD 300 was composed by about 473 poets.

    (ii) All these poems deal with every aspect of Tamil life during the period more than 1000 years.

    (iii) After studying these poems, we get to know about love, war, governance and joys of the Tamil people.

(b) (i) The grammatical works such as 'Talkappiyam' give the inflection and syntax of words and sentences.

    (ii) These also provide classifications of habitats, animals, plants and human beings.

    (iii) Besides, human emotions and interaction are also discussed in these grammatical works.

(c) (i) Poems connected by goodness of content that forms a unity having elements of poetry, music and drama are considered as 'kavya' or 'epic' in Tamil.

    (ii) The five well known epics of the Tamil literature are Silappadikaram, Manimegalai, Civaka, Cintamani, Valayapathi and Kundlakesi.

    (iii) These epics give an important information about the Buddhist, the Jains and the common Tamil people.

Q. 2. How are the following archaeological sources helpful to us in forming an idea of the ancient Tamil society and culture?

    (a) Megaliths   (b) Herostones

    (c) Inscriptions

Ans. (a) (i) The graves of earliest people were encircled by huge piece of stone thus are called megaliths.

        (ii) These graves contained skeletons of the people with the objects like pottery and iron objects such as arrow heads, spearheads, hoes and sickles.

        (iii) Some of these graves have inscriptions engraved on them.

    (b) (i) The herostones were raised to honour the heroes who sacrificed their lives to the cause of security of the village.

        (ii) Most of the herostones have inscriptions on them, in which names of the heroes with their families and locality have been mentioned.

        (iii) This kind of practice of erecting herostone continued from 400 BC even upto the 1600.

    (c) (i) About thousands of inscriptions have been found inscribed on stones and copper plates.

        (ii) Most of these inscriptions belong to the Cholas, Chera and Pandya rulers.

        (iii) These inscriptions provide a lot of information about the Tamil people of the Sangam Age.

Q. 3. With reference to the Sangam Age answer the following questions:

    (a) Write in brief the meaning of Tamil Sangams.

    (b) What was the Sangam Age?

    (c) What were the three Sangams that existed in ancient Tamil Nadu?

Ans. (a) (i) The word Sangams refer to assembly of Tamil poets and scholars, a literary academy.

        (ii) It was established by the pandya rulers.

    (b) (i) The age of Sangam is the age to which sangam literature belonged.

        (ii) Historically the sangam literature is accepted as having existed in the third Sangam Age.

    (c) (i) As per Tamil traditions, three Sangams existed in the ancient Tamil Nadu, popularly known as Munchchangam.

        (ii) It is believed that the first Sangam or Talai Sangam held at Madurai was attended by Gods and legendry sages. However, no literary work of this assembly is available.

        (iii) The middle or Idai Sangam was held at Kapadapuram, but all literary work except, Tolkappiyam have destroyed.

        (iv) The third or Kadai Sangam held at the modern city of Madurai was attended by a large number of poets who produced voluminous literature.

Q. 4. With reference to the Sangam Age answer the following questions:

    (a) What was the position of women in the Sangam Age?

    (b) Write in brief the economy of the Sangam Age.

    (c) How did Sangam Age decline ?

Ans. (a) (i) The women enjoyed a respectable position in society but gender bias prevailed.

        (ii) Chastity was the important virtue of Tamil women.

        (iii) Women were allowed to choose their life partners.

        (iv) However, the condition of widows was miserable.

        (v) The sati system was also practiced in the higher classes of society.

    (b) (i) Agriculture and handicraft were the important occupations in the Sangam Age.

        (ii) The occupation of Tamil people differ as per the land features. For instance, Neydal people were mainly did fishing and salt manufacturing while Palai people were mainly robbers.

    (iii) The handicraft works included weaving, spinning, metal works, carpentay, making ornaments using beads, stones and ivory.

    (iv) Uraiyur and Madurai were the important centres for cotton industry.

(c) (i) The Sangam age witnessed its decline till the end of the 3rd century AD.

    (ii) The Tamil region was occupied by Kalabhras.

    (iii) Tamil culture was declining due to flourishing of Jainism and Buddhism.

    (iv) The Pallavas in northern Tamil Nadu and Pandyas in Southern Tamil Nadu drove the Kalabhras out of the country and established their own rule.

Chapter 6. The Age of Guptas

Q. 1. With reference to the Golden period of Gupta Age answer the following questions:

    (a) Name the first Chinese Buddhist who visited India during the reign of Chandragupta II.

    (b) Name the account he left India. Mention its characteristics also.

    (c) Mention any four features of his travelogue.

Ans. (a) Fa Hien was the first Chinese Buddhist pilgrim who visited India in AD 3rd during the reign of Chandragupta II.

    (b) (i) Fa Hien has left behind a vivid account called smritis which is the chief source of knowledge about the people during Gupta Age.

    (ii) Fa Hien observed that India under Gupta rulers was peaceful and flourishing.

    (iii) The people during the Golden Age were law-abiding, honest and free from pointless restrictions.

    (iv) There was no severe punishment and offences of any kind were ordinarily punished by charging fines and death sentence was completely unknown to people.

    (c) (i) In his travelogue, Fo-kwo-ki (The travels of Fa Hien), Fa Hien described Pataliputra to be a prosperous city that had many charitable institutions.

    (ii) He praised the people as well as the king of the city as a multitude of religions like Vaishnavism, Shaktism, Shaivism, Jainism and Buddhism all co-existed harmoniously in the society.

    (iii) As per Fa Hien there was no toll-tax or land-tax but agriculturists had to pay a part of their produce as tax to the ruler.

    (iv) On the whole, the kingdom was most satisfactory both culturally and economically.

Q. 2. The Gupta Age was the Golden Age of India. In this context discuss:

    (a) Architecture   (b) Science

    (c) Medicine

Ans. (a) (i) With the revival of Hinduism, changes were seen in the architecture during Gupta Age.

    (ii) Instead of cave temples, structural temples were built for the convenience of idol worship.

    (iii) The artists initiated use of permanent materials like brick and stone in place of perishable materials like bamboo, wood, etc.

    (iv) The interiors of these temples were plain and the most holy place Sanctum or shrine was provided with a flat roof to worshippers.

    (b) (i) The study of all branches of science, particularly astronomy, mathematics, medicine and metallurgy flourished under the Guptas.

    (ii) Aryabhatta and Varahamihira were the major astronomers and mathematicians of that period.

    (iii) The use of the zero figure and the decimal system of counting were evolved in India only during the Gupta period.

    (c) (i) Sushruta, Dhanvantari and Charaka were the most distinguished physicians of the Gupta period.

       (ii) Charak Samhita, Sushruta Samhita and Astanga Sangraha were important works on Ayurveda.

      (iii) There was usage of mercury and iron in medicine which indicates that the people of that era had knowledge of chemistry and they even practiced it.

      (iv) Hastyayurveda or the veterinary science also developed by Palakapya during this period.

Q. 3. With reference to the architectural sources of the Gupta period, write short notes on:

    (a) The Brick temple at Bhitargaon   (b) The standing Buddha of Mathura

    (c) Rock-cut architecture

Ans. (a) (i) The Brick temple at Bhitargaon was constructed in the 5th century AD.

       (ii) The temple has a pyramid for its roof and the exterior walls have been adorned with various figures and statues.

      (iii) A Shiva Linga has been placed inside the Garbhagriha.

      (iv) The main architectural feature of this temple is an arch, which is a curved structure laying support to the weight of the roof.

    (b) (i) The standing Buddha of Mathura is a 217 cm high Buddha sculpture made of red sandstone dates back to the 5th century.

       (ii) Here Buddha wears a robe, which is held in his left hand and the robe folds and drapes all around him.

    (c) (i) The most remarkable specimens of rock-cut architecture under the Gupta rulers are found in Ajanta, Ellora, Aurangabad (Hyderabad) and Bagh (Central India).

       (ii) Brahmanical rock-cut shrines are lesser in number than those of the Buddhists but were not rare.

      (iii) The stupas, Chaityas and Viharas of the Ajanta and Ellora caves were rock-cut temples that were carved out of the cave rocks.

Q. 4. Samudragupta had a strong reputation of being the greatest vanquisher and king. In context to this answer the following questions:

    (a) Explain the personal achievements of Samudragupta.

    (b) Describe his military conquests.

    (c) Write in brief the religious works and faiths of Samudragupta.

Ans. (a) (i) Harisena the court poet of Samudragupta described him as kaviraja (king of poets).

       (ii) Samudragupta was not just a powerful ruler but also a patron of arts.

      (iii) He was a great musician, scholar and poet.

      (iv) His court was full of literary figures and great scholars from various places.

    (b) (i) According to the Allahabad inscriptions composed by Harisena, Samudragupta defeated nine rulers of Northern India and wrested control of the western parts of Uttar Pradesh and present day Delhi.

       (ii) After that, he conquered the eastern part of India by defeating the kingdom of Nepal, Assam and Bengal and made them to pay him tribute.

      (iii) Next, he marched towards the southern kingdoms and defeated 12 rulers among which the regions of Andhra, Orissa and Tamil Nadu were included.

      (iv) In the inscription, he was described as the hero of 100 battles.

    (c) (i) Samudragupta performed the horse sacrifice or Ashvamedha Yajna.

       (ii) He issued gold and silver coins of eight different varieties with the legend 'Restorer of the Ashvamedha'.

      (iii) He was a follower of Brahmanism and believed in sacrifices of the Vedic religion.

      (iv) He allowed the king of ceylon to build a Buddhist monastery at Bodhgaya which revealed that he had respect towards all other religious faiths.

Q. 5. With reference to the Gupta administration answer the following questions:

(a) What was the role of kings during Gupta period?

(b) Explain the cabinet of Ministers under Gupta rulers.

(c) Explain provincial administration under Gupta rulers.

Ans. (a) (i) The Gupta kings assumed titles like Maharaja dhiraja, Parambhattarika, Vikramaditya, Samrat and Chakravartin.

(ii) The king had supreme power and was assisted by mantri or sachiva in his civil administration.

(iii) All the officials were appointed by the king in the home provinces and possibly paid in cash.

(b) (i) The senapati was appointed as commander-in-chief of the army.

(ii) The king was assisted by officials called 'kumarmatyas' for provincial administration who were the most important officers in the Gupta bureaucracy.

(iii) Another important official mentioned in the Gupta inscriptions was the minister for foreign affairs called Sandhibigrahika.

(c) (i) The Gupta empire was divided into several provinces called Bhuktis or Desas.

(ii) The provincial governors were called Uparika, Maharaja or Pradeshikas who generally belonged to the royal family.

(iii) A Bhukti was divided into districts called Vishayas ruled by Vishwapatis.

(iv) A district is divided into villages leaded by Gramika.

(v) Other important district level officials were prathamkayastha who wrote letters, pushtapal, the record keeper and Nagarshreshti, the chief Banker.

Q. 6. With reference to Harshacharita answer the following questions:

(a) Who wrote Harshacharita ? In which language was it written?

(b) Under whose patronage was this book is written?

(c) On what topic was this book written?

(d) Why is this book important today?

Ans. (a) (i) Harshacharita was written by Banabhatta.

(ii) It was written in Sanskrit.

(b) This book was written under the patronage of Harshavardhana, the last Hindu emperor who embraced Buddhism.

(c) The book reveals the history of Harshvardhan's family till the rescue of Rajyashri who was getting ready to immolate herself.

(d) It is very important today because it throws light on social, political, religious and economic conditions of the period.

Chapter 7. The Cholas

Q. 1. With reference to the Chola administration, explain:

(a) The three types of village assemblies.   (b) Functioning of Central government.

(c) Taxes imposed by Cholas.

Ans. (a) In many villages, the villagers themselves carried out the administration. The villages had three types of village assemblies:

(i) **Ur:** It was the common type of village assembly of normal villages, where the land was held by people of all classes, who were, therefore, members of this local assembly.

(ii) **Sabha:** The Sabha was an exclusively Brahmin assembly of the brahmadeya villages, where all the land belonged to the Brahmins.

(iii) **Nagaram:** The nagaram was an assembly of the merchants and belonged to localities where traders and merchants were in dominant position.

In these assemblies, the life and work of the village was discussed.

(b) Chola administration was highly efficient and organised, with the King as the pivot of administration and all authority resting in his hands.

    (i) The king discharged his responsibilities and duties with the advice and help of his Council of Ministers.

    (ii) A large number of officials operated the administrative system. Princes were actively employed in war and peace and were associated with the ruling sovereigns.

    (iii) The Central government looked after matters like internal peace and order, external defence, cultural progress and promotion of general prosperity of the empire.

(c) Different taxes were imposed by the Chola rulers :

    (i) The revenue of the Chola kingdom came from the produce of the land and taxes on land. The land revenue was fixed at one-third of the gross produce for wet land and one-sixth for dry land.

    (ii) The officials collected the taxes on land from the village councils.

    (iii) Other important sources of income were the taxes on trade, handlooms, mines, water courses and the customs.

    (iv) While a fraction of the revenue was set aside for the king, the rest was used on public works like building of tanks and roads, paying for the navy and army, on salaries of officials and on building of towns and temples.

Q. 2. With reference to the conquests of Rajaraja I and Rajendra I, answer the following questions:

    (a) Who defeated the Chalukyas of Vengi and extended his empire up to Kalinga?

    (b) Who defeated the kings of Bengal?

    (c) Who invaded the territories of King Srivijaya in Malaysia? Who developed a huge naval fleet in order to control the flourishing South-East Asian trade?

Ans. (a) Rajaraja I defeated the Chalukyas of Vengi and extended his empire up to Kalinga.

    (b) Rajendra Chola I defeated the kings of Bengal.

    (c) Rajendra Chola I invaded the territories of King Srivijaya in Malaysia. Rajaraja I developed a huge naval fleet in order to control the flourishing South-East Asian trade.

Q. 3. With reference to the South Indian temples, explain

    (a) State any three typical features of Chola temples.

    (b) Mention any three architectural features of Brihadishwara temple.

    (c) Why were the temples during Chola period centre of social activity?

Ans. (a) **Typical features of Chola temples:**

Majority of the Chola temples were built in Dravidian style. The Chola temples in the early period were simple structures but later, the temples became grander and bigger in size.

    (i) The main shrine of the temple was called garbhagriha, where the images of gods and goddesses were kept and the gateway was known as gopuram.

    (ii) In front of the main shrine was the audience hall or the mandapa where people gathered for prayers.

    (iii) The main features of the Chola temples are the spacious courtyards, interconnected pillared halls, magnificent sculptures and the massive towers or vimanas.

(b) The Brihadishwara or Rajarajeshwara temple at Thanjavur is the best example of Chola architecture.

    (i) It was built in AD 1000 by the Chola king, Rajaraja I. It was completed in AD 1035 and is dedicated to Lord Shiva.

    (ii) The entire temple structure is made of granite. It consists of an inter-connected Nandi mandapa, a pillared portico and an assembly hall.

    (iii) The 57 metres high tower or vimana comprises thirteen storeys and its top is crowned with an 8.6 metres high single block of stone that weighs 80 tonnes.

    (iv) The temple's interior walls are decorated with magnificent sculptures and elaborate paintings.

(c) According to the Chola inscriptions, the temples were the centres of social activity.

   (i) The temples during the Chola period were considered the biggest employers after the State as they provided work and means of livelihood to a huge number of people.

   (ii) The temples looked after the welfare of its workers by providing food, housing facilities and clothing to them.

   (iii) They established hospitals for taking care of the disabled and sick employees.

   (iv) Since there were no separate schools, the priests of the temple were the local teachers and the schools were held in the courtyards of the temples.

Q. 4. The most glorious epoch of the Cholas began with the accession of Rajaraja I Chola. In this context answer the following questions:

(a) What was the period of rule of Rajaraja I? What was the extent of his empire?

(b) Describe his activities as a ruler and great builder.

(c) Mention any four important conquests of Rajaraja I Chola.

Ans. (a) Rajaraja I was originally regarded as Arumolivarman, the son of Prantaka II. He ruled from AD 985-1014. He was also known as Rajaraja Chola. He was a brilliant commander. Chola Empire under Rajaraja I extended over the whole of present Tamil Nadu, Coorg, Andhra Pradesh, parts of Karnataka and northern part of Ceylon.

(b) Rajaraja I was an efficient administrator, a great builder and a great patron of arts and literature. He made excellent arrangements for the administration of his vast dominions. He constructed the famous Brihadeshwara temple at Thanjavur. Though he was a staunch follower of Lord Shiva, he ensured religious tolerance and patronised all religions alike. This is evident from the fact that he granted a village at Nagapatam in the Malay Peninsula to Buddhist Vihara. According to historical records, Rajaraja I initiated the process of prefacing the inscriptions of the reign with a set account of events.

(c) During the reign of Rajaraja I, the Cholas rose to a position of supremacy in southern India.

   (i) He conquered the Malabar coast from the Cheras in order to control Arab trade.

   (ii) He conquered some territories of Mysore and Travancore, Coorg and Vengi region in Andhra.

   (iii) He carried out raids into the territories of Western Chalukyas.

   (iv) Though he took out a naval expedition and attacked both the Maldives Islands and Sri Lanka, he was unsuccessful in controlling them. Later, he invaded Sri Lanka and annexed its northern part and towards the end of his rule, he conquered Maldives.

Chapter 8. The Delhi Sultanate

Q. 1. Give an account of the reign of Slave Sultans.

Ans. Slave dynasty was founded by Qutbud-Din Aibak in 1206.

   (i) He initially ruled from Lahore and later shifted to Delhi. His reign was short lived as he died in 1210. He was succeeded by Iltutmish.

   (ii) Iltutmish organised a group of forty nobles –Turkaan-e-Chahalgani to administer his kingdom. He also established a mint and introduced silver coins known as tanka. He was succeeded by his daughter Razia Sultan.

   (iii) Razia Sultan faced many challenges for being a woman ruler.

   (iv) Balban was the next famous Slave ruler. He took various harsh and strict measures to suppress internal and external revolts. He established an efficient spy system and gave severe punishments for petty crimes. He broke the power of the Chahalgani nobles.

   (v) He was succeeded by weak and incompetent rulers.

Q. 2. How did languages develop in the Delhi Sultanate period?

Ans. Persian was the court language of the Delhi Sultanate. So, it was important for both Hindus and Muslims to be well versed in it.

(i)   Both the communities contributed to the growth of Persian literature.

(ii) Amir Khusrau wrote in Persian and also composed lyrics in the local dialects of northern India.

(iii) His use of Persian and Khariboli in the same poem are some of his many lyrical experiments.

(iv) Many Sanskrit books were translated into regional languages.

(v) During the Sultanate period Urdu came to be known as a language.

(vi) It was a simple language, comprehensible by both Turks and Indians.

Q. 3. Feroz Shah Tughluq was a peace-loving monarch. Justify this statement with examples.

Ans. Feroz Shah Tughlaq was a peace loving king. He brought general peace and prosperity in the kingdom by adopting following measures.

(i)   He abolished many taxes.

(ii) He opened hospitals called dar-ul-shafa.

(iii) He opened a department, Diwan-e-Bandagan, to look after the slaves.

(iv) He was one of the first conservationists of India.

(v) He restored a water tank at HauzKhas in Delhi which was built for the city of Siri. He got several canals built.

Q. 4. Evaluate the economic policies framed by Alauddin Khalji.

Ans. Alauddin introduced certain economic reforms to collect more revenue for the upkeep of the army.

(i)   Such economic reforms made Alauddin's market system very efficient and ensured uninterrupted supply of goods in the market even in times of crisis.

(ii) With these economic policies Alauddin was able to recruit soldiers at low salaries and to enable them to maintain a higher cost of living.

(iii) The prices of commodities were low and the soldiers could provide themselves well even with the limited salaries paid to them.

(iv) A large amount of taxes could be collected and used to support the large army.

(v) This helped Alauddin to defeat the Mongols and keep them away from Delhi and India.

Q. 5. Taxation in the Doab region led to discontentment among the poor peasants during the rule of Muhammad bin Tughlaq. Discuss.

Ans. (i) Muhammad bin Tughlaq increased land revenue from 10 to 30 per cent and, further, ghari or house taxes and charahi or pasture taxes were added to it. So, the peasants were overtaxed.

(ii) The religious tax of Jiziya was also levied on non-Muslim peasants.

(iii) As a result of such harsh taxation, the rich peasants rebelled and the poor peasants were ruined totally.

(iv) Moreover, rains failed and famine occurred, and taxes were not relaxed, which continued for years.

(v) Thousands of people died and others left the region. This sowed seeds of discontent among the peasants of the Doab region.

Q. 6. With reference to the Ala-ud-din Khalji, discuss the following:

(a) What steps were taken by Ala-ud-din Khalji against the nobility? Mention any three.

(b) Compare and contrast the reforms undertaken by Muhammad bin Tughlaq and Ala-ud-din Khalji.

(c) Mention any four Military reforms introduced by Ala-ud-din Khalji.

Ans. (a) Owing to the rebellions caused by nobles, Ala-ud-din Khalji took some steps in handling the nobility. These steps were:

(i)   The nobles were required to take permission from the Sultan before forming matrimonial alliances or even hold parties or festivities.

(ii) Gambling, use of intoxicants and wine were forbidden. Severe punishments were inflicted on the gamblers.

(iii) An efficient spy system was established in order to gain intelligence on the activities of the nobles.

(iv) Soldiers were paid in cash.

(b)

S.No.	Muhammad bin Tughlaq	Alauddin Khalji
(i)	He was a keen administrator but most of his administrative innovations brought suffering to his subjects.	He was a good administrator and believed in the theory of sultan being the all-powerful entity.
(ii)	He faced many rebellions from his nobles in his reign of 26 years.	He did not allow his nobles to keep personal armies and thus was able to control internal rebellions.
(ii)	Reforms like increase in taxation in Doab region, shifting his capital from Delhi to Daulatabad and experimenting with currency, introduced by Muhammad bin Tughlaq failed badly.	Economic reforms and land revenue reforms introduced by him were very efficient.

(c) Military reforms introduced by Ala-ud-din Khalji are:

(i) He was the first ruler of Delhi who laid the foundation of a permanent standing army.

(ii) He imported high quality horses and started the system of branding horses (dagh) so that the soldiers could not replace them with inferior quality horses.

(iii) He also introduced the practice of recording hulia, giving a kind of identity card to every soldier.

(iv) He himself approved all recruitments to the army and soldiers were paid cash salaries from the royal treasury.

Q. 7. During the Sultanate period political, legal and military authority was vested in the Sultan. In this context discuss:

(a) Central administration of Delhi Sultanate.

(b) Provincial administration of Delhi Sultanate.

(c) Highlight the important features of local administration during the Sultanate period.

Ans. (a) The Central administration of the Delhi Sultanate followed a very systematic and well planned administration procedure which was run by different ministers who had specific work assigned to them.

(i) The Sultan was the head of the state and enjoyed unlimited powers in every sphere of state activity. The Wazir was the Prime Minister of the state and headed the financial department. Though the Sultan depended greatly on the advice and efficiency of the Wazir, the Sultan always took the final decisions.

(ii) Diwan –i-ariz was the controller-general of the military department.

(iii) The Sultan also appointed people to sensitive posts and kept an eye on the expenditure and revenue. The chief judge was the 'Qazi' who advised the Sultan on religious and civil matters.

(b) The Delhi Sultanate was further divided into smaller provinces for it was convenient for the ministers to help them in the administration. They were called iqtas.

(i) These iqtas were assigned to the various nobles, officers and soldiers for the purpose of easy and flawless administration and revenue collection. They were called iqtadars.

(ii) The iqtadars not only had to maintain themselves and their families out of this grant but also some soldiers used by the Sultan during the times of war.

(iii) Muhammad Ghori was the first to introduce the iqta system in India, but it was Iltutmish who gave it an institutional form.

(iv) The iqtadari system witnessed numerous changes during the Sultanate period. Initially, iqta was a revenue-yielding piece of land which was assigned in lieu of salary. However, during Feroz Shah Tughluq's reign, in the year 1351 AD it became hereditary.

(c) (i) In the Sultanate period the provinces were divided into smaller units of administration called shiqs. Each shiq was placed under the control of a Shiqdar.

(ii) Each shiq was divided into a number of parganas or districts in order to facilitate local administration.

(iii) The village was the smallest unit of administration. The official who worked at the village level were the 'muqaddams' or the village headman.

(iv) Each village had a 'mushrif' or village accountant and 'patwari' or record keeper.

(v) Disputes in a village were settled by its own Panchayat.

Chapter 9. The Mughal Empire

Q. 1. Explain the political conquests of Babur.

Ans. Political conquests of Babur :

(i) **The First Battle of Panipat (1526 CE):** The forces of Ibrahim Lodi and Babur met in Panipat in AD 1526. Babur crushed Ibrahim Lodi in this battle. This conquest brought Delhi and Agra under Babur's control.

(ii) **The Battle of Khanua (1527 CE):** This battle was fought between Babur and Rana of Mewar, popularly known as Rana Sanga. Although Rana Sanga and his forces fought bravely, they were defeated.

(iii) **The Battle of Chanderi (1528 CE):** After Khanua, Babur attacked Chanderi in Malwa, which was another Rajput stronghold, and managed to capture its fort.

(iv) **Battle of Ghaghar (1529 CE):** In 1529 CE, Babur defeated the Afghan chiefs under Mahmud Lodhi in the battle of Ghaghar. All these conquests consolidated Babur's hold on India.

Q. 2. Give a brief description of Ain-i-Akbari.

Ans. Ain-i-Akbari was written by Abu'l Fazl. He was a historian in Akbar's court. It was completed in 1598. It is an extraordinary document of its time due to the following reasons:

(i) The Ain is made up of five books. The first of which describes the royal household.

(ii) The second book gives details about the civil and military services and the servants of the Emperor.

(iii) The third book gives details about the administration of the empire that consists of a set of laws for the executive and judicial departments.

(iv) The fourth book provides information about science, literature, social customs and Hindu philosophy at that time.

(v) The fifth and the final book recounts the wise sayings of Akbar.

Q. 3. Some steps taken by Aurangzeb affected the Mughal Empire adversely. Do you agree with this statement? Explain with examples.

Ans. Some steps taken by Aurangzeb affected the Mughal Empire adversely, for example:

(i) He re-imposed the Jaziya and the pilgrimage tax on non-Muslims. As a result he lost the goodwill of vast majority of non-Muslim subjects.

(ii) He caused a serious rift in the Mughal-Rajput alliance by the annexation of Marwar in 1679 CE.

(iii) By an edict issued in April 1665 CE, Muslim merchants were charged only 2 per cent custom duty, whereas it was 5 per cent for Hindu traders.

(iv) In 1667 CE, this duty was totally withdrawn for the Muslim merchants.

(v) In 1668 CE, the observance of Hindu festivals was completely prohibited.

Q. 4. What were the causes of the decline of the Mughal Empire?

Ans. The Mughal Empire began to show signs of disintegration. Some of the factors responsible for the decline are as follows:

(i) Lack of worthy and competent successors to Aurangzeb. They were weak and lacked commitment to rule the empire strongly.

Long Questions

(ii) The absence of a definite law of succession led to bitterness, bloodshed and loss of money and prestige in the Mughal Empire and eventually its downfall.

(iii) Aurangzeb's long wars in the Deccan depleted the military and financial resources of the empire.

(iv) The raids by Nadir Shah and repeated invasions of Ahmad Shah Abdali resulted in further weakening of the empire.

Q. 5. Explain the following features of the Mughal administration.

    (a) The office of the Emperor   (b) Revenue administration

    (c) Judicial administration   (d) Military administration

Ans. (a) **The office of the Emperor:**

    (i) The Mughal Emperor was an absolute ruler. All the executive, legislative and judicial powers were vested in him. He was the seat of executive authority. He was considered as the fountain head of justice.

    (ii) He had several officials who helped him in administration, such as prime minister, finance minister, minister of war, etc.

    (iii) A qazi served as the head of the judicial system. The king was the ultimate authority to resolve matters if there was a disagreement among the officers.

  (b) **Revenue administration:**

    (i) Land revenue was the main source of income of the government.

    (ii) Raja Todar Mal devised a system in which all the cultivable land was first measured.

    (iii) The land revenue was fixed on the basis of the quality of land and the quantity of produce.

    (iv) The peasants had to pay land revenue mostly in cash.

    (v) Land revenue was generally one-third of the produce.

    (vi) During drought or famine, land revenue was reduced or even waived off.

    (vii) Land revenue was collected by revenue officers known as Amirs.

  (c) **Judicial Administration:**

    (i) The chief qazi was the head of the judicial department.

    (ii) Cases of Hindus were decided by Hindu judges according to the Hindu laws and customs.

    (iii) Cases affecting the Muslims were decided by the chief qazi, provincial qazis and muftis according to the Islamic law.

  (d) **Military Administration:**

    (i) The Mughals did not have a large standing army. They depended upon the hereditary chiefs and the mansabdars for the supply of men and horses.

    (ii) The mansabdars had to maintain a specified number of cavalrymen known as sawar.

    (iii) They did not pay the troops, but received their salaries from the Emperor.

    (iv) The mansabdars were given land or jagir from which they collected revenue in lieu of salary.

    (v) Periodic inspections of troops were conducted by the king.

    (vi) This system worked efficiently during the times of Akbar.

Q. 6. What do you think were the reasons for the success of the Mughal Empire?

Ans. Following reasons were responsible for the expansion of the Mughal Empire:

    (i) The Mughals had strong and large army which helped them to expand their empire in India.

    (ii) All the Early Mughal rulers were great military commanders and carried out various military expeditions in India.

    (iii) The Mughals adopted the policies of conciliation, alliances and conquests so as to firmly establish and strengthen their control over India.

(iv) The political system in the Mughal Empire was very well organised.

(v) Another important reason for the success of Mughal Empire in India was the pattern of administration. The great Mughal ruler, Akbar, started a centralized government and ruled over his empire with the help of ministers who looked after different departments.

Q. 7. With reference to the Mughal architecture, answer the following questions:

(a) Mention any three architectural features of Red Fort.

(b) Mention any three architectural features of Jama Masjid, Delhi.

(c) Why is Taj Mahal one of the supreme accomplishments of Mughal Empire?

Ans. (a) **Architectural features of Red Fort**

    (i)   It is a huge structure made of red sandstone and marble.

    (ii) The fort is in the shape of parallelogram with massive walls around it.

    (iii) It has two main Gateways of which the Lahori Gate was used for ceremonial purposes and other Gateway for private use.

(b) **Architectural features of Jama Masjid, Delhi**

    (i)   The mosque is built on a high platform with three domes of white marble decorated with stripes of black colour.

    (ii) The mosque has three great gates, four towers and two 40-metre tall minarets constructed of strips of red sandstone and smooth white marble.

    (iii) The face of the massive prayer hall consists of eleven arches. This is the most spectacular feature of this magnificent construction.

(c) Construction of Taj Mahal began in 1634 AD and continued for almost 22 years. Because of its exceptional qualities, the Taj Mahal is considered to be one of the wonders of the world.

    (i)   It is made of pure white marble.

    (ii) The bulbous dome in the centre has the appearance of an inverted lotus. There are four smaller domes at the four corners of the building.

    (iii) The four minarets at each corner of the terrace are decorated with beautiful cupolas and pinnacles.

    (iv) The outer walls and the interior walls of tomb are richly decorated with flawless sculptures and inlaid design of flowers and calligraphy called 'Pietradura'. It is highly remarkable in the field of architectural work and designing monuments.

Q. 8. The Rajput policy of Akbar was a milestone in his achievements. In light of this statement, answer the following:

(a) What were the chief obligations of the Rajput states to Akbar?

(b) When did Akbar fight the Battle of Haldighati and with whom?

(c) What was the result of Akbar's Rajput Policy?

Ans. (a) Three obligations of the Rajput states to Akbar were as follows:

    (i)   Regular payment of tribute

    (ii) Maintenance of contingents for the imperial army

    (iii) Circulation of Mughal coin in their territories.

(b) Akbar fought the Battle of Haldighati on June 18, 1576 CE. This battle was fought between cavalry and archers supporting the Rana of Mewar, Maharana Pratap, and the Mughal emperor Akbar's forces, led by Man Singh I of Amber. This battle was won by the Mughal army.

(c) Akbar laid the foundation for smooth relations between the Mughals and the Rajputs. He entered into matrimonial alliances and appointed Rajputs on high posts in his court. Defeated Rajput rulers were asked to administer their region on behalf of the Mughals. By end of 1570, every Rajput kingdom except Mewar came under Mughal Empire. All these conquests were done without resorting to arms, which marks the success of Akbar's conciliatory policy. Since the Rajputs were given equal status in the Mughal government, the centuries-old rivalry between Mughals and Rajputs was put to an end.

Q. 9. Akbar is regarded as the true founder of the Mughal empire in India. In this context, discuss:

    (a) Mansabdari system   (b) Administrative system

    (c) Religious policy

Ans. (a) Mansabdari system introduced by Akbar was a unique feature of the administrative system of the Mughal Empire. This system was made up of a group of Mansabdars, who were the officials of the Mughal Empire.

    (i) These officers were given specific rank or mansab either in the bureaucracy, military hierarchy or the nobility.

    (ii) The lowest rank was 10 while the highest was 5000 and these ranks had two divisions.

    (iii) First was Zat, which indicated the status of a person and how much he is to be paid.

    (iv) While the other, Sawar stands for the designated amount of cavalrymen, he had to maintain. For every 10 cavalrymen, 20 horses were to be kept.

    (b) The Mughal State was centralised autocracy. In other words the King's powers were unlimited. Akbar organised his Empire with admirable skill and expedition. He bequeathed to his successors the legacy of a well-organized administrative structure.

    (i) He divided the Empire into 12 Subas. These were again sub-divided into Sarkars, followed by further subdivisions known as Parganas or Mahals.

    (ii) The Wazir was the highest position below the king, but the finance department was in the hands of the Diwan.

    (iii) Mir Bkshi headed the military department while Mir Saman was incharge of royal household, Qazi was the head of the Judiciary and Sadar was in charge of helpful and religious matters.

    (c) Akbar was especially known for his numerous liberal religious policies which brought harmony and religious tolerance among his subjects.

    (i) He removed Jaziya, a tax paid only by non-Muslims.

    (ii) He also prohibited the conversion of war prisoners to Islam without their consent.

    (iii) He eradicated the pilgrim tax which non-Muslims had to pay for bathing in Banaras, Prayag and other holy places.

    (iv) He built a Hall of Worship called Ibadat Khana at Fatehpur Sikri, where he invited selected theologians and mystics to foster philosophical discussions.

    (v) Akbar came up with a new religion called Din-i-illahi. Through this religion he propagated notions of divine monotheism or oneness of God.

Q. 10. What is Abul Fazl famous for?

Ans. Abul Fazl was a great scholar as well as the leading historian of the Mughal age. He is famous for his historical works Ain-I-Akbari and Akbarnamah. Written in elegant Persian, Ain-i-Akbari gives information about the army and the legal and revenue system of Akbar's administration. We know from Abul Fazl that Akbar had a commanding personality. Abul Fazl writes of 'Admiralty Department', whose light functions were to build boats for river transport and to recruit skilled Seamen. Abul Fazl throws light in the leading artists and painters of the Akbar's reign.

Akbarnamah is a primary source to have an idea about Akbar's life, the royal household and the royal court in the sixteenth century.

Akbarnamah also contains a number of paintings illustrating events of those days.

Q. 11. Give an account of Akbar's conquests from 1561 to 1586 in northern India.

Ans. (i) In 1561, Akbar conquered Malwa and besieged the strategic fort of Chuanar.

    (ii) In 1562, he conquered the fortress of Merta in Marwar.

    (iii) In 1570, all prominent princes of Rajasthan, except the Rana of Mewar had submitted to Akbar.

    (iv) In1568, he seiged the fort of Chittor.

(v)   In 1572, he conquered Gujarat.

(vi)   In 1572, he seized Surat.

(vii)   In 1574-75, he conquered Bihar and Bengal.

(viii)   In 1576, he won the battle of Haldighati but Mewar was not subjugated till the death of Rana Pratap.

(ix)   In 1586, Kabul was annexed.

Q. 12. In the context of Mughal administration, discuss the following:

(a) Land revenue system   (b) Law and justice

Ans. (a) Mughal land revenue system owned its success to Akbar who in 1580 instituted a new system called dehsala system with the help of Raja Todarmal. Under this, the average produce of different crops and their average prices prevailing over the last ten years were calculated and one-third of the average produce was fixed as the State's shares.

A uniform system of land measurement was followed to calculate the land tax.

But this revenue system could not remain as efficient as it should have been when the administrative machinery got out of the control during Aurangzeb's reign.

(b) Law and justice were supervised by the judicial officer known as Chief Qazi.

(i)   Chief Qazi was helped by Muftis and Mir-adls.

(ii)   Muftis interpreted the muslim law and acted as advocates.

(iii) Mir-adls announced judgements.

(iv) Fines were charged and severe punishments were given.

(v)   Capital punishments could only be given with the consent of the Emperor.

Q. 13. How could Akbar extend his empire and strengthen Mughal dynasty in India?

Ans. Under the guidence of Bairam Khan, during the early years of his reign, Akbar faced the challenge of the Afghans. After defeating them he made fresh conquests to build a large empire with a strong government.

(a) His conquest in the South resulted in the annexation of territories of Bundelkhand, Malwa and Gondwanna to the Mughal empire.

(b) In the Deccan, the ruler of Khandesh submitted to him voluntarily.

(c) Except Rana Pratap, majority of the Rajput rulers submitted voluntarily and were rewarded. The Rajput Kingdoms of Gwalior, Ranthambore and Kalinjar which had resisted him were annexed.

(d) His other conquests in western, northern and north-western India included Gujarat, Sindh, Baluchistan, Kashmir and Kabul.

(e) In the east, Bihar and Bengal were annexed.

(f) By 1595, Akbar had become the undisputed emperor of the territory extending from Hindukush in the west to the river Brahmaputra in the east and from Himalayas in the north to the river Godavari in the south.

(g) Assam, Orissa, the greater part of the Ceccan and the far south remained out of his empire.

Chapter 10. Emergence of Composite Culture

Q. 1. Mention the teachings of Guru Nanak Dev.

Ans. Teachings of Guru Nanak are:

(i)   He preached that God was non-incarnate and formless (nirankar), eternal (akal) and ineffable (alakh).

(ii)   He insisted that caste, creed or gender were irrelevant for attaining liberation. He believed that a person need not renounce the world to find God.

(iii) He stressed on his followers living a family life and working for a living. He also believed that true salvation lay in living an active life and contributing to society.

(iv) He emphasised nam, dan, and isnan, or worship, welfare, and purity of behaviour.

(v) He preached three principles of naamjapo (meditating on God's name), kirtkaro (earning an honest livelihood), and vandchakko (sharing earnings with others).

Q. 2. Mention the teachings of Sant Kabir.

Ans. Teachings of Kabir are:

(i) Kabir was highly critical of all conventional religious beliefs and rituals prescribed by Brahmanas and Islamic clerics.

(ii) He also rejected differences amongst people based on caste.

(iii) Kabir believed that god was formless and one could unite with god if one followed the path of Bhakti.

(iv) He also spoke of the importance of a Guru in following the path of Bhakti.

(v) He also wanted to unite Hindus and Muslims.

Q. 3. With reference to Christianity, discuss:

(a) The role of Christian missionaries promoting language and literature in India.

(b) The role of St. Francis Xavier in spreading Christianity in India.

(c) Relation of Mughal emperors with Jesuits.

Ans. (a) **The Christian missionaries influenced the Indian society in the following manner:**

(i) The missionaries brought out grammars and dictionaries of the Indian languages. St. Francis Xavier learnt the language of Malabar and brought out a manual of grammar and a vocabulary which helped the Jesuits and other missionaries to learn the language of the people of Malabar.

(ii) The Missionaries taught Western music in Church schools in India. Apart from music, they also taught dance and instrumental music.

(iii) The Missionaries and the Church also patronised the arts of painting, carving and sculpture in India. These paintings influenced the Mughals. Portuguese, English and Mughal records show the interest of Akbar and Jahangir in Christian works of arts.

(b) **Main role played by St. Francis Xavier in spreading Christianity in India was:**

(i) He went street to street to spread the message of Jesus Christ, asking people to attend his meetings and listen to his sermons.

(ii) He raised money for the construction of nearly 40 churches along the Eastern coast. The most important among the churches was the St Stephen's church in Kombuthurai.

(iii) He prepared a summary of principles of Christian church in the form of question and answers, and also baptised the inhabitants of 30 villages.

(c) **Relation of Mughal emperors with Jesuits:**

(i) We find the first mention of contact of Mughals with Christianity when Jesuit Fathers from Goa and its neighbourhood came to meet Akbar after the siege of Surat.

(ii) Akbar was very friendly with the missionaries but had no intention of converting into Christianity. He commissioned Father Jerome Xavier to translate the Life of Christ into Persian as the Dastan-i-Masia which was completed in 1602.

(iii) Jahangir was more supportive to Christianity than his father. However, he too was not interested in converting to Christianity.

(iv) The next two Mughal emperors Shah Jahan and Aurangzeb, particularly the latter, were much less supportive of the Jesuits.

Q. 4. In the context of composite culture, explain the role played by the following:

(a) Ajmer Sharif Dargah

(b) Historic merit of St Francis Church, Kochi　　　(c) Nizam-ud-din Auliya's main beliefs

Ans. (a) (i) Ajmer Sharif or Ajmer Dargah is the shrine built over the grave of the Sufi Saint Hazrat Khwaza Muinuddin Chisti, which is located in Ajmer, Rajasthan.

(ii) Khwaza Muinuddin Chisti was revered by people belonging to all religious groups because of his message of peace, selfless service, helping the poor and the needy and fellow feeling.

(iii) Even today people flock to his Dargah especially during the Urs or his death anniversary because they believe that praying to him will take away all harmful things.

(b) The Church of St. Francis of Assissi in Fort Kochi is another monument to build the composite culture of India.

    (i) It was built by the Portuguese and once housed the remains of Vasco da Gama, which was later removed to Lisbon.

    (ii) There are many types of services — the baptism, marriages, etc. — that the Church provided and their record could be found in Church's Register from 1751 to 1804. For more than 40 years it was maintained in the handwriting of the Minister of the Church, Predikant Comelies.

    (iii) There is in its premises a Cenotaph, a monument or a War Memorial in memory of the residents of Cochin who fell during the First World War.

(c) Main beliefs of Nizam-ud-din Auliya were:

    (i) He preached that love of God implied love of humanity.

    (ii) He believed that one could embrace God within this life by Talab (deep desire for Union with God) and Fana (destruction of ego).

    (iii) He believed in unity and equality and shunned differences based on religion, social and economic status.

    (iv) He preached 'be generous to the needy, the poor, the exploited and the oppressed.

Q. 5. Sufism was a liberal reform movement within Islam that started in Persia and Arabia as an endeavor to bridge the differences between the Shia and Sunni sect of Islam. In this context, explain:

(a) Main doctrines of Sufism

(b) Impact of Sufism on the Indian society

(c) Chisti Silsilah and its famous sufi saints

Ans. (a) **The main doctrines of Sufism were:**

    (i) Fundamental unity and respect for all religions.

    (ii) God is the supreme reality. He should be worshipped through love and personal devotion.

    (iii) Meditation and chanting of God's name (zikr) are very important. Follow a guru or pir who would show the correct path.

(b) **Impact of Sufism on the society was as follows:**

    (i) It promoted the feelings of universal brotherhood among Hindus and Muslims.

    (ii) It played an important role in promoting feelings of tolerance among the Muslim rulers. Irrespective of religion, people began to understand and appreciate the faith of other people.

    (iii) A number of Sufi principles had similarity with those of the Bhakti cult. Hence, it led to the popularity of the Bhakti Movement.

(c) **Chisti Silsilah or Order:** This order was founded by Khwaja Muin-ud-din Chisti. In 1161 AD he came to India with Mahmud of Ghazni and founded this order.

    (i) He advised his followers to live in peace and harmony with one another and to respect all religions.

    (ii) His dargah or tomb at Ajmer is considered as an important pilgrimage centre and is visited by thousands of Muslims and devotees every year.

    (iii) An annual festival known as Urs is also held at this place.

    (iv) Other popular Sufi saints of the Chisti Silsilah were Sheikh Qutub-ud-din Bakhtiyar Kaki and his disciple Sheikh Farid or Baba Farid of Multan, Sheikh Salim Chisti of Sikri, Farid-ud-din Ganj-i-Shakar and perhaps the greatest Sufi saint, Hazrat Nizam-ud-din Auliya.

Q. 6. Medieval period saw the emergence of two great religious movements-the Bhakti Movement and the Sufi Movement. In this context explain:

(a) The reasons responsible for the rise of Sufi and Bhakti movements

(c) Summarise the teachings of Sufism with reference to God

(b) Similarities between the Sufi and Bhakti saints

Ans. (a) Reasons responsible for the rise of Sufi and Bhakti movements:

    (i) The Bhakti Movement originated in India as a reaction against the caste system and ritualism. It was started by the Vaishnava and Saiva saints of south India.

    (ii) Sufism in the medieval period developed within the fold of Islam. It was started as an endeavor to bridge the differences between the Sunni and Shia sects of Islam.

    (iii) Sufi movement in India was the result of the Hindu influence on Islam. Sufism was a Muslim movement whose followers seek to find divine truth and love through direct encounter with God.

(b) Teachings of Sufism with reference to God are:

    (i) There is only one God and all human beings are his children.

    (ii) Since all men are the children of one God, they are all equal. Therefore it condemned all distinction based on colour, caste, creed and religion.

    (iii) Individual souls are manifestations of the Supreme Soul and they finally merge into it.

(c) Some of the similarities between Sufi and Bhakti saints are as follows:

    (i) Both emphasised on salvation through love and devotion to the supreme God.

    (ii) Both criticised social barriers of caste, class, religion and challenged orthodoxy.

    (iii) Both condemned rituals and idol worship.

    (iv) Both emphasised on the importance of teacher to guide the devotee's life.

Q. 7. In the context of Indo-Islamic culture, answer the following questions:

(a) What is meant by Indo-Islamic culture?

(b) What led to the fusion of Indian and Islamic elements in art and architecture?

Ans. (a) Indo-Islamic culture is a composite culture. It was the synthesis of Islamic and non-Islamic cultural traditions that evolved as a result of a prolonged interaction between a migrant Muslim population and Hindu population.

(b) The Mughals used to invite artisans, artists and architects from Persia and Central Asia to design and decorate their palaces, mosques and mausoleums. Such artists worked along with Indian artists. The result was a fusion of Indian and Islamic artistic traditions which is known as Indo-Islamic art. The royal patronage proved helpful in the growth and development of Persian literature of great merit, consisting of poetry, prose, historical work and translations.

Q. 8. In the context of literary sources which give us a glimpse of the composite culture that emerged during the medieval period, briefly explain the following:

(a) Bijak   (b) Guru Granth Sahib

Ans. (a) Bijak is the best known for the compilation of the compositions of Kabir and as such is the holy scripture for the followers of the Kabirpanthi sect.

The term Bijak is derived from Bija meaning a document containing sacred texts.

It is divided into different sections, such as the following

    (i) Ramaini   (ii) Vipramatisi

    (iii) Kahara   (iv) Basant

Dohas of Kabir are full of ideas and vivid images. These are popular even today among the Hindus and Muslisms.

(b) Guru Granth Sahib is the central religious scripture of Sikhism, regarded by Sikhs as the final, sovereign and eternal living Guru.

Guru Granth Sahib is written in Gurumukhi script and has 1430 pages each containing the shabad (hymn) of the Gurus.

It can be cetegorized into two sections.

(i) Introductory section consisting of Mul Mantar, Japji and Sohila, composed by Guru Nanak.

(ii) Compositions of Sikh Gurus.

- The fifth Guru Arjan Dev compiled the Adi Granth which is a vast collection of the sermons and hymns of the five Sikh Gurus-Guru Nanak, Guru Angad, Guru Amardas, Guru Ramdas and Guru Arjan Dev.
- The ninth Guru, Guru Tegh Bahadur, composed many devotional songs which were added by his son.
- The tenth Guru, Guru Gobind Singh, announced the end of personal guruship and named Adi Granth as Guru Granth Sahib.
- The Granth is revered as eternal gurbani and the spiritual authority in Sikhism.

Chapter 11. The Modern Age in Europe Renaissance

Q. 1. State the theory followed by the painters.

Ans. The Renaissance artists considered the world as a place of beauty and for them the purpose of art was to provide pleasure to the eyes. Therefore, great attention was paid to the physical aspects of human existence by the artists. In order to show that perfection can be human they painted human figures as more beautiful than any other object in nature. The Renaissance painters looked upon art as an imitation of life. They closely observed nature and man.

Q. 2. How did encouragement given to art and learning led to the advent of Renaissance?

Ans. (i) The encouragement given to art and learning by popes, emperors, kings, princes and rich merchants of Europe were responsible for promoting the spirit of Renaissance.

(ii) Various Cathedral schools along with several universities were established at Paris, Oxford, Padua, Bologna, Cambridge, Montpellier, Naples and Salamanca which took the responsibility of disseminating information and developing eagerness towards learning and thinking.

(iii) Some families in Italy supported traditions in fostering art and learning.

(iv) They established schools and gave financial support to universities and to scholars, painters, musicians, sculptors, architects and scientists.

Q. 3. How did the progress in Science pave the way for the Renaissance?

Ans. Skills related to thinking and scientific understanding and a spirit of enquiry was fostered by the progress that was seen in Science during that time.

(i) New ideas came into existence with proof like the earth revolves around the Sun was proven by Copernicus.

(ii) Roger Bacon could plan the use of flying machines and horseless carriages while Galileo became famous for inventing the telescope.

(iii) With these innovations in town, people could open up their mental outlook and bring an end to age-old traditions and beliefs.

Q. 4. What changes occurred in the field of sculpture during Renaissance period?

Ans. In the middle Ages sculptures were used to promote religion.

(i) During Renaissance period development of free standing sculptures earned the respect of separate artworks.

(ii) The knowledge of human anatomy and celebrations of the beauty of mankind also inspired the sculptors to create works.

(iii) During this phase many renowned sculptors created new themes, motifs and techniques.

(iv) Out of these, octagonal dome of Florentine Cathedrals, resurgence of classical columnar system and a spatial integrity in all public and private structures came into being.

Q. 5. With reference to Modern Age in Europe, answer the following questions:

(a) Mention any three factors that led to the advent of Renaissance.

(b) Summarise the contribution made by Nicolaus Copernicus in the field of Science.

(c) How did Renaissance lead to the rise of monarchical form of governments in Europe?

Ans. (a) Three factors that led to the advent of Renaissance were:

(i) **Capture of Constantinople:** The fall of Constantinople compelled the Arab, Roman and Greek scholars to flee to Italy as its city states were then experiencing a flourishing age reminiscent of classical Greece. These scholars and learned men took their precious books and manuscripts with them to the Italian cities which then became the new seats of culture, thereby laying the foundations of Renaissance.

(ii) **The invention of Printing Press:** With the invention of printing press books were made available on varied subjects at low prices to the masses. Superstition and blind faith was loosened and people developed self-confidence which brought a new awakening in the European continent.

(iii) **Geographical discoveries:** During 15th century many new sea routes were discovered. Due to these discoveries, contacts with the East developed and people become more adventurous and attitude of people broadened.

(b) Nicolaus Copernicus was a Polish astronomer and mathematician who fulfilled the Renaissance ideals.

(i) He questioned the theories of Aristotle and Ptolemy.

(ii) He is best known as the first astronomer to propose a heliocentric system that the planets orbit around the Sun rather than the Earth.

(iii) He proposed that Earth is a planet which, besides revolving around the Sun annually also rotates once daily on its own axis. Copernicus's theory had important consequences for later thinkers of the scientific revolution, including Galileo, Kepler, Descartes and Newton.

(c) Renaissance lead to the rise of monarchical form of governments in Europe:

(i) During Renaissance, many European monarchs challenged the powers of the Papacy.

(ii) The decline of the authority of the Church and the feudal system strengthened the desire of the people to have peace, security and political stability.

(iii) Thus, they readily provided support to the kings and enhanced the powers of monarchs.

(iv) Monarchs in France, England, and Spain responded to the chaotic situation in Europe and consolidated their power.

Thus, we can say that Renaissance provided great impetus to the evolution of strong monarchical system of Government in Europe.

Q. 6. (a) How did the capture of Constantinople lead to the Renaissance?

(b) How did the Printing Press bring about a new awakening in Europe?

(c) Explain any two contributions of Copernicus that challenged the belief in the field of Science. **[February, 2020]**

Ans. (a) Constantinople, the capital of Byzantine Empire was the centre of Greek and Roman cultures. The libraries had valuable manuscripts of famous Greek and Roman writers.

(i) When the Ottoman Turks captured Constantinople in 1453, many Greek writers, scholars and students fled to various parts of Europe from this place with priceless manuscripts.

(ii) They were welcome in Italy, especially Rome and the interest in Greek learning was revived.

(iii) Some academies and schools were founded for encouraging Greek studies.

This led to the decline of feudalism and helped in growth of Renaissance.

(b) The invention of the printing press by Gutenberg in Germany in the 15th century was one of the major reasons for bringing a new awakening in Europe:

   (i) It helped in the printing of books in large numbers and at cheaper cost.

   (ii) The Holy Bible and other religious and classics books were widely printed and made available all over Europe.

   (iii) This helped in spreading knowledge, influenced people's attitude towards life and society.

  (c) Two contributions of Copernicus that challenged the belief in the field of Science are:

   (i) For centuries it was believed that the Sun and all the heavenly bodies go around the Earth.

   (ii) This was refuted by Copernicus, a Polish priest. He said that the Earth and other heavenly bodies move around the Sun.

   (iii) The theory of rotation of the earth on its axis and its motion around the Sun was proved by Copernicus. He also said that the earth was round.

    His theories aroused controversy and it was considered an attack on the authority of the Holy Scriptures.

Q. 7. With Reference to the impact of Renaissance in the field of Art, Literature and Science, mention the contributions of:

  (a) Mention the impact of Renaissance in the field of literature.

  (b) Write the details of any three famous works of Leonardo da Vinci.

  (c) Describe the achievements of Renaissance artists in the field of Architecture.

Ans. (a) Renaissance had a profound impact on the literature

   (i) Latin was the popular language which significantly changed in the age of Renaissance. Renaissance literature dealt much more with human characteristics and behavior, shifting away from religious and spiritual themes.

   (ii) There was an increased willingness of writers to satirize existing institutions such as the church and state and to write secular rather than religious works.

   (iii) The authors from the period of Renaissance also started concentrating on man and his problems.

  (b) Leonardo da Vinci is known as the Renaissance man. His impact in the field of art was immense. He was a very talented artist who painted Virgin of the Rocks, Mona Lisa, The Last Supper and many more famous paintings. His three famous works are:

   (i) **Virgin of the Rocks:** This painting exhibits Vinci's zeal for science, technical skill and his belief that the Universe is a well-organised place.

   (ii) **Mona Lisa:** This is a painting of a woman that echoes the various frames of mind of the human soul.

   (iii) **The Last Supper:** This painting highlights the psychological reactions of the people on the painting that range from horror, surprise to guilt.

  (c) The greatest impact of Renaissance was on art and its various forms such as painting, architecture and sculpture. The last quarter of the 15th century witnessed the glimmering inception of magnificent pieces in the sphere of art and architecture.

   (i) Most of the Renaissance architects were inspired by the Greco-Roman classical architecture.

   (ii) This adoption of the schemes led to the development of architecture that had its basis in cross-like plan for the floor that was adorned with arches, decorative columns and dome.

   (iii) In the architectural works of Renaissance, harmony, proportion and balance in the buildings were highlighted.

   (iv) One of the most popular architecture of this period can be seen in St. Peter's Basilica in Rome.

Q. 8. The Renaissance was a period of great intellectual activity. Give an account of the outstanding work of the following:

  (a) Niccolo Machivelli in the field of literature

  (b) Leonardo da Vinci in the field of painting

Ans. (a) Niccolo Machivelli is known as the father of modern philosophy. He is best known for writing:

    (i) The Prince, a handbook for unscrupulous politicians that inspired the term "Machiavellian" and established its author as the "father of modern political theory."

    (ii) His works outlines the political ideology of his age that prevailed in the Italian states during the close of the 15th and early 16th century.

    (iii) His ideas and suggestions was to separate political matters from religion.

(b) Leonardo da Vinci is known as the Renaissance man. His impact in the field of art was immense.

    (i) He was a very talented artist who painted Mona Lisa, the Last Supper and many more famous paintings.

    (ii) He changed paintings of the time from flat and disproportionate to impossibly graphic and real.

    (iii) His works were famous because of Leonardo's understanding of Linear Perspective, his integration of light and shadow and his outstanding understanding of anatomy.

Q. 9. The Renaissance was a period of intellectual activity. A lot of progress was made in different fields. In this context, write briefly on the impact of Renaissance on the:

(a) Progress of Literature   (b) Progress of Science

(c) Progress of Medical Science

Ans. (a) **Progress of Literature:**

Renaissance had a profound impact on the literature

    (i) Renaissance literature dealt much more with human characteristics and behaviour, shifting away from religious and spiritual themes.

    (ii) There was an increased willingness of writers to satirize existing institutions such as the church and state and to write secular rather than religious works.

    (iii) The authors from the period of Renaissance also started concentrating on man and his problems.

    (iv) English drama of this period was heavily influenced by the theatre of the ancient Greeks and Romans. Famous writers of this period were Francis Bcon, William Shakespeare, Ben Johnson, Edmund Spencer, etc.

(b) **Progress in Science:**

Major changes occurred in the fields of science and engineering during Renaissance.

    (i) Many new and exciting discoveries were made mainly in the areas of anatomy, astronomy and physics.

    (ii) Breakthroughs in engineering also paved the way for many of the world's most significant inventions, such as telescope, clocks and spectacles.

    (iii) The willingness to question previously held truths and search for new answers resulted in a period of major scientific advancement that ultimately resulted in the Scientific Revolution.

    (iv) Galileo Galilei and Leonardo da Vinci were pioneering renaissance scientists and inventors.

(c) **Progress in Medical Sciences:**

Great discoveries were made in medical sciences during Renaissance:

    (i) William Harvey discovered circulation of blood from heart to all parts of the body and back to the heart.

    (ii) Vesalius wrote a treatise on anatomy.

    (iii) Paracelsus proved a close connection between medicine and chemistry.

    (iv) Valerius Cordus, a German botanist prepared ether from alcohol and sulphuric acid.

    (v) Helmont discovered carbon dioxide.

Q. 10. Renaissance means revival of the freedom to think and act without being controlled by an external agency. In this context, answer the following questions:

(a) What role did progress in science play in fostering a spirit of enquiry?

(b) What was the role of Crusades in ushering in the spirit of inquiry?

(c) What role did the invention of Printing Press play in the spreading knowledge?

Ans. (a) In the age of faith, science had little scope for development. Many medieval scientists and scholars showed willingness to question previously held truths and asked their students to observe things in nature. This search for new answers resulted in a period of major scientific advancement. This scientific advancement created the spirit of enquiry and scientific temper. Roger Bacon contemplated the use of horseless carriages and flying machines. Copernicus proved that the earth moves round the sun. Galileo invented the telescope. These inventions broadened the mental outlook of the people and put an end to the old beliefs and traditions.

(b) The Crusades were the religious expeditionary wars with the goal of restoring the Church's access to holy places in and near Jerusalem.

  (i) These Crusades or wars fought between the Muslims and Christians between the 11th and the 13th century brought Europe in close contact with the economically and culturally rich Islamic world.

  (ii) The progressive ideas of Aristotle and Plato from the East migrated to the Western European nations that stimulated the imagination of their people who started questioning the blind faith.

  (iii) These Crusades were also responsible for re-establishing trade and commerce between the East and West, which was highly conducive for the rise of Renaissance.

(c) Invention of printing press with metal types acted as the most significant factor for ushering in Renaissance. Earlier, in the middle ages, books and manuscripts had to be copied manually and the cost of books was very high. But the invention of paper and a printing device brought about revolutionary changes in the growth of intellectual sphere. Books were made available on varied subjects at low prices to the masses. Superstition and blind faith was loosened and people developed self-confidence which brought a new awakening in the European continent.

Q. 11. Many new and exciting discoveries were made which revolutionized our ideas of the Universe. In this context mention the discoveries of the following men:

(a) Galileo   (b) Copernicus

(c) Issac Newton

Ans. (a) **Galileo Galilei:**

  (i) Galileo Galilei (1564-1642) was an Italian physicist, mathematician, astronomer and philosopher.

  (ii) He disapproved Aristotle's theory by proving the principle that the speed of a falling body depends on the distance it has to cover and not its weight.

  (iii) Some inventions of Galileo include the thermometer, hydrostatic balance and the improvisation of the telescope.

  (iv) He used the telescope to study the movements of heavenly bodies for Copernicus' theory.

(b) **Copernicus:**

  (i) Copernicus was a Polish mathematician and astronomer. He lived in the fifteenth century.

  (ii) He was the first person to prove that the earth is round and it revolves around the sun. He placed Sun rather than the earth at the centre of the universe.

  (iii) This is called the Heliocentric idea of the universe.

  (iv) Copernicus finished the first manuscript of his book, 'De Revolutionibus Orbium Coelestium' ('On the Revolutions of the Heavenly Spheres') in 1532. In it, Copernicus established that the planets orbited the sun rather than the Earth.

(c) Issac Newton :
  (i) Sir Issac Newton (1642-1727) was a physicist, mathematician, astronomer, philosopher and theologian.
  (ii) He discovered and described universal gravitational law. He carried Kepler's work forward and presented proof of heavenly bodies moving as per the gravitational law.
  (iii) He also developed the three laws of motion which form the basic principles of modern physics.
  (iv) His discovery of calculus led the way to more powerful methods of solving mathematical problems.

Q. 12. The Renaissance had a great impact on all aspects of life. In context of the above statement, answer the following: **[November, 2019]**

(a) Write about any three new trade routes discoverd by the Europeans during the 15th century AD.

(b) Sate any three contributions of Leonardo da vinci in the field of Art.

(c) How did the decline of feudalims lead to the growth of the Renaissance?

Ans. (a) The Turkish invasion that drove the Greek scholars westward, also made trade in the eastern Mediterranean too risky. Therefore, new trade routes to India and the East had to be found.
  (i) Vasco da Gama went round the Cape of Good Hope and reached Calicut, the coastal town of Kerala in 1498.
  (ii) Ferdinand Magellan, a Portuguese nobleman, went round the globe between 1520 and 1522.
  (iii) The new routes between Europe and the East brought great prosperity to Italian cities. As Italy became the centre of all trade routes, it led to the spread of Renaissance to the rest of Europe quickly.

(b) Leonardo da Vinci was a great sculptor and painter, musician and scientist.
  (i) His paintings of 'The Last supper' and 'Mona Lisa' are the great masterpieces of European art.
  (ii) New techniques were adopted in his paintings to give a fine feeling of reality.
  (iii) Painting of 'Mona Lisa' is a perfect depiction of beauty and harmony. It is more beautiful than any creation of nature. With a mild smile on the face and with half closed and revealing eyes, it reflects that she has something to say. The entire effect is such as any heart could desire.

(c) Under feudal system huge estates were owned by landlords, who exploited the peasants. The feudal system was opposed to progress and 'social mobility'. There was no freedom or equality of rights under this system.
  (i) The decline of feudalism in the 13th and 14th centuries developed the habit of free thinking.
  (ii) The feudal lords had always been fighting against each other.
  (iii) The peace and order that followed the decline of feudalism favoured the growth of New Learning.
  (iv) This led to the new developments in the fields of art, literature, science and philosophy.

Chapter 12. The Modern Age in Europe Reformation

Q. 1. State four of the important points in Luther's doctrine.

Ans. Important points in Luther's doctrine are as follows:
  (i) Man could attain salvation only by repentance.
  (ii) Salvation is a gift of God and can be had if the penance is done.
  (iii) He opposed indulgences.
  (iv) A baptised man cannot be condemned by sin but by unbelief.

Q. 2. With reference to Modern Age in Europe, answer the following questions:

    (a) What was the contribution of King Henry VIII in the Protestant Movement?

    (b) Who were the Anabaptists? What did they profess about Christianity?

    (c) What were the consequences of the Counter Reformation?

Ans. (a) At first, Tudor ruler Henry VIII was a devout Catholic Christian.

    (i) The reason he began changing the Catholic Church is because under catholic rules, it was not legal to annul his marriage. But, if the church was following protestant ideals, it would be legal to divorce his wife.

    (ii) So, he severed all relations with Rome, when the Pope refused to give him permission to divorce his wife, Catherine of Aragon.

    (iii) He championed the cause of Protestantism in England. In AD 1534, he passed the Act of Supremacy through Parliament to nullify Pope's power over the churches in England. By this Act he became the clergy and the Supreme Head of the Church of England.

    (b) The Anabaptists were one of the groups that arose from the religious reform movements of the 16th century.

    (i) They believed that baptism is valid only when candidates confess their faith in Christ and want to be baptised.

    (ii) They believed in adult baptism.

    (iii) They promoted separation of Church and State.

    (iv) According to Anabaptists, the government shouldn't have any power over matters of religion. The laws of the land shouldn't be imposed over Christians who followed the word of God.

    (c) Consequences of Counter Reformation were as follows:

    (i) Church leaders reformed the Catholic Church. Practices like selling Indulgences and violation of celibacy for the bishops and clergy were outlawed.

    (ii) It brought about the birth of Protestant church.

    (iii) The Catholic Church was further strengthened by the Society of Jesus; whose members called the Jesuits dedicated themselves to the service of people.

    (iv) Anti-Semitism increased and religious conflicts spread across Europe.

Q. 3. With reference to the Protestant movement, discuss the contribution of the following:

    (a) Ulrich Zwingli   (b) Erasmus

    (c) John Calvin

Ans. (a) Ulrich Zwingli brought in the Humanism of Erasmus into the Protestant movement.

    (i) He regarded the Bible as the sole guide to right living. He believed in simplicity and condemned idol worship and complicated ceremonies.

    (ii) The Swiss Reformation under Zwingli bore far-reaching repercussions in the social and cultural spheres.

    (iii) The Swiss Reformation emphasised the corporate character of the church, believing that clergy and laymen formed a 'holy community'.

    (iv) He was killed in AD 1531, in a religious war against the Pope.

    (b) (i) Erasmus was the greatest Renaissance scholar of Holland.

    (ii) He was the foremost advocate of the. New Learning and was deadly opposed to corrupt and immoral life of the pope and the clergymen.

    (iii) His influence extended to England, France, Germany and Italy also.

    (iv) 'Pocket Dagger', 'In praise of folly' and 'New Testament' are some of his famous works.

    (c) John Calvin was a leading Protestant reformer in France.

    (i) He popularised the Protestant movement in Switzerland and continued the work of his predecessors. Geneva became the centre of his religious activity.

(ii) He proclaimed that the Bible was the only source of salvation for the human soul and denounced the papacy and its doctrine of sacraments.

(iii) He was against all kinds of luxury, feasting, dancing, sports and games and wanted utter simplicity in the religion. This severe type of Protestantism was known as Calvinism.

(iv) Through his and his followers' efforts, Calvinism became an accepted form of the Christian faith.

Q. 4. The movement against the Roman Catholic Church is called Reformation. In this context discuss:

(a) What measures were taken to introduce reforms in Catholic Church?

(b) How did Reformation lead to the formation of Nation-States?

(c) How did Spirit of Inquiry contribute to the formation of 16th century Reformation movement?

Ans. (a) The Council of Trent took up strict measures to maintain discipline among the Church officials.

(i) Practices like selling Indulgences and violation of celibacy for the bishops and clergy were outlawed.

(ii) Preaching in local languages was allowed, seminaries or centres of learning for the priests were introduced.

(iii) Charging of fees for performing religious practices was forbidden.

(iv) The Society of Jesus was founded whose members were called the Jesuits. These members dedicated themselves to the service of the people.

(b) The concept of Nation-States emerged between 16th and 19th centuries. Several monarchs began to wield power by weakening the feudal lords and liaising with rising commercial classes. For example, France and Spain intervened in Italy at the behest of the Pope. However, many European kings now declared themselves as the Head of the Church as well of the Government leading to absolutism or absolute power. The concept of 'absolute states' assumed a new shape, which culminated in the development of national churches. This completed the structure of Nation-States.

(c) **Contribution of Spirit of Inquiry to Reformation:**

(i) The invention of printing press made it possible to print the Bible in vernacular languages. This enabled the people to question the Church's superiority as they began to feel they could reach God without the intervention of a priest.

(ii) The original thinking of certain scholars led to a rise of a spirit of inquiry.

(iii) People started feeling that the Church had numerous drawbacks owing to the factors like Renaissance movement, the revival of the secular and human spirit of ancient Greece to Rome, geographical discoveries, the Crusades, the contact with the east as well as the scientific inventions and discoveries.

(iv) Thus, people began asking many questions to satisfy their endless spirit of inquiry.

Q. 5. Reformation led to increased literacy, a renewed appreciation for education, and new ways of thinking about history. In this context discuss

(a) Why did religious persecution increase during Reformation?

(b) What was the impact of Reformation on economic development?

(c) How can we say that Individualism and Intellectualism were two important aspects of this phase?

Ans. (a) An immediate and unfortunate effect of the reformation was intolerance, which expressed itself in cruel persecution and religious wars.

(i) Instead of generating the true spirit of Christ, the Reformation made thousands suffer on account of their religion.

(ii) The subjects of the Spanish, Portuguese and Italian monarchs were forced to remain Catholic, or to suffer death or imprisonment at the hands of Inquisition.

    (iii) King Philip II of Spain, and Mary, Queen of Scots persecuted the Protestants. Similarly, the Protestant princes of Germany punished their Catholic subjects.

  (b) The Reformation is seen as a watershed in the history of Western Europe.

    (i) It ushered in the development of nation-states and the subsequent demolition of feudal-based monarchy.

    (ii) The nexus between Calvinism and economic development is highly mooted in the academic circles.

    (iii) In the midst of the 19th century, Karl Marx claimed that Protestantism won due to the capitalist values of thrift, self-discipline, diligence and rationality.

  (c) Individualism and Intellectualism were the two important aspects of this phase.

    (i) It had far reaching repercussions in the sphere of education. Reformation phase targeted mass at large and popularised humanist methods in varied schools and universities.

    (ii) Through the spread of liberal arts and humanist teachings, the concept of Individualism and Intellectualism were moulded in new ways.

    (iii) The debacle of old church resulted in the beginning of a chapter of secularism in Western Europe.

    (iv) It developed the ethic of Individualism. Some historians opined that Religious Individualism was just the opposite of Intellectual Individualism, which led to the birth of capitalism.

Q. 6. (a) What was meant by 'Sale of Indulgences'?

  (b) State any three contributions of Martin Luther.

  (c) Define 'Counter Reformation'.   **[February, 2020]**

Ans. (a) 'Sale of Indulgences' was one of the major causes leading to Reformation:

    (i) The 'Sale of Indulgences' allowed few people to receive pardon for their crimes.

    (ii) The letters were sold and money would be made to make people free from making penance. The clergy also claimed that those who bought these were pardoned by god for their sins.

    (iii) Few also collected money to construct elaborate and lavish churches and cathedrals.

  (b) Three contributions of Martin Luther were:

    (i) Martin Luther had thorough knowledge of the Bible and it led him to believe that man could attain salvation only by repentance. He questioned the authority to sell Indulgences and gained the support of common people and many princes.

    (ii) He questioned the powers of the Pope and the priests to forgive sins of all who paid even if they had no regrets for the sins committed.

    (iii) Luther burnt the Papal's Bull of Excommunication in the presence of the public at Wittenberg. His order for arrest was given at the Diet of Worms but was saved by the Duke of Saxony. He was forced to spend one year in hiding in a lonely castle and utilized the time in translating the Holy Bible from Latin to German.

  (c) Counter Reformation was the reformation of the Catholic Church in the 16th and 17th centuries:

    (i) The Churches began to improve their working, became more liberal and tolerant towards different opinions.

    (ii) Sale of Indulgences was stopped. Seminars were held, education was imparted and training was given to priests. Church services were to be made free and sermons were to be given in the language of the common people.

    (iii) This led to different religious orders to be founded. Ignatius Loyola founded a religious order by the name Society of Jesus with the permission of the Pope. He turned into a missionary and dedicated his life to spread the message of Christ.

    (iv) St. Francis Xavier, one of the founders of Society of Jesus, travelled widely to spread reformed Christianity.

    The dedicated and devoted service of the Jesuits helped to restore the prestige of the Roman Catholic Church.

Chapter 13. The Modern Age in Europe Industrial Revolution

Q. 1. What are the main difference between socialism and capitalism?

Ans. (a) Major difference between Capitalism and Socialism are as follows:

S.No.	Capitalism	Socialism
(i)	Country's trade and industry is controlled by private owners.	Country's trade, industry and wealth are controlled by the community or the government.
(ii)	The spirit of capitalism is 'market economy'.	The spirit of socialism is 'planned economy'.
(iii)	There is lesser influence of the government in the economic process.	Government controls the economic process.
(iv)	It focuses on self-interest.	It focuses on collective interest.

Q. 2. What were the political consequences of Industrial Revolution?

Ans. The political consequences of Industrial Revolution were as follows:

(i)   Rise of Capitalist.

(ii) Colonisation of weak countries by powerful countries.

(iii) Large scale migration of people from rural to urban areas.

(iv) Division of world into developed and under developed countries.

Q. 3. What were the negative effects of the Industrial Revolution?

Ans. Negative effects of the Industrial Revolution were:

(i)   The economic disparity between the rich capitalist and the poor workers led to gross social inequalities.

(ii) Due to migration cities became over populated and workers were forced to live in inhumane conditions.

(iii) Workers were exploited by the employers. They worked on very low wages and under extremely harsh conditions.

(iv) Extremely stressful working and living conditions led to a decline of moral values among the workers.

Q. 4. With reference to Modern Age in Europe, answer the following questions:

(a)   How did improvement in transportation ushered in the Industrial Revolution?

(b)   How did industrial Revolution led to increase in Slums?

(c)   Discuss how Industrial Revolution led to the growth of Capitalism.

Ans. (a) Transport and communication formed an important factor for the industrial growth and integration of markets.

(i)   Until mid-18th century, the condition of road transport was miserable and expensive. Mac Adam discovered a new process of road building using coal tar.

(ii) The use of coal tar facilitated hard roads and adequate use of waterways through steamships and steamboats extensively contributed to the development of the Industrial revolution in many European countries.

(iii) The invention of railways by George Stephenson in AD 1814 facilitated the transport of material from one place to another easing communication and accelerating Industrial Revolution.

(iv) The use of ship spurred the growth of industrialisation and subsequent development of imperialism.

(b) Industrial revolution led to increase in slums in the following way:

(i) With the invention of machinery and the advent of technology, factories could be built anywhere in towns and cities. Thus, people from the rural areas migrated to the urban areas looking for work, education, and other social benefits.

(ii) The cities became the centre of civilisation and culture, attracting many people from the nearby rural areas for better living standards.

(iii) Migration to cities led to an increase in slums.

(iv) Usually the factories were situated in areas near the coal-fields or sea-ports. Not much care was taken to provide house for the industrial workers.

They, therefore, were forced to live in slums.

(c) The Industrial Revolution triggered certain changes, due to which the arrival of Industrial Capitalism was witnessed by Britain.

(i) Industrial Revolution gave rise to capitalism because it enabled capitalists to build factories and earn profit. The profit earned would be reinvested to generate more profits.

(ii) The theory of free trade or Laissez-Faire came to the forefront, as a result of the Revolution.

(iii) Encouraged by this theory, the traders and capitalists wanted the least intervention of the state in economic affairs.

(iv) Owing to the Industrial Revolution, a new class of people was formed, known as the Capitalists.

(v) This would not have been possible if the industrial revolution had not created the technology and the machinery to create factories.

Q. 5. With reference to the impact of Industrial Revolution, mention:

(a) Urbanisation

(b) Mistreatment of Workers

(c) The formation of new social classes

Ans. (a) Urbanisation was one of the direct outcomes of the Industrial Revolution.

(i) With the invention of machinery and the advent of technology, factories could be built anywhere in towns and cities. Thus, people from the rural areas migrated to the urban areas looking for work, education, and other social benefits.

(ii) The cities became the centres of civilisation and culture, attracting many people from the nearby rural areas for better living standards.

(iii) However, this growth had major consequences; death rates in the cities grew significantly and overcrowding combined with poor sanitation led to the spread of diseases and epidemics.

(b) The capitalists exploited their workers thoroughly. The lives of the working classes grew miserable and burdensome.

(i) The workers did not get adequate wages. They had to work for fourteen to sixteen hours a day in poor working conditions.

(ii) They did not have safety guards on machines which led to frequent accidents and there were no provisions for the care of the injured and the sick.

(iii) The children and women employed in factories were also underpaid.

(c) Formation of New Social Classes

(i) The Industrial Revolution polarised the society into two main groups-the haves and the have-nots.

(ii) Some individuals became capitalist, meaning the owners of the main means of production. The capitalists had power, wealth and prestige.

    (iii) The other section of people created by the Revolution was the class of poor workers or proletariat. This class included those people who migrated to cities in search of employment and lived in inhuman living conditions or slums.

    (iv) Thus, the gap between the employees and the employers became very wide and remained unabridged.

Q. 6. With reference to the rise of Socialism, discuss

    (a) What were the reasons responsible for the rise of Socialism?

    (b) Mention any three key features of Socialism.

    (c) Who was Karl Marx and what was his contribution to Socialism?

Ans. (a) A number of factors led to the development of Socialism.

    (i) Firstly, it developed as a reaction to the evils of Capitalism. The society came to be divided into two different classes, namely, the Proletariat and the Capitalists. The socialists realised that the employers benefited from the mass production but the workers were living in poverty.

    (ii) Secondly, the British Government was forced by the strong Trade Union Movements to recognise the worker's rights. It was demanded that the workers should be provided better working conditions, security and should also be relieved of poverty.

    (iii) Lastly, the Chartist Movement that took place in the first half of the 19th century demanded a worker's right to vote. In the mid-19th century, the movement declined but offered a good model for further socio-political reforms.

    (b) The main features of Socialism are as follows:

    (i) Socialists believe in collective ownership. In socialism all means of production are owned by the community, that is, Government and no individual can hold private property beyond certain limit.

    (ii) Socialists have been great supporters of civil liberties, such as freedom of speech, freedom to form associations and freedom of religion, etc.

    (iii) In socialist economy, work is according to ability and wage according to need.

    (c) Karl Marx was a German economist and political philosopher. He is famous for his socialist ideology and considered the founder of modern Sociology.

    (i) In AD 1848, Karl Marx and Engles issued the Communist Manifesto which introduced the concept of scientific socialism or Communism.

    (ii) In AD 1867, Marx and Engles published the first of three volumes, entitled Das Kapital, in which they explained the sum and substance of Marxian Socialism or Communism.

    (iii) Many leading thinkers of the time were influenced by his ideologies and suggested the path to socialism.

    (iv) The ideas of Marx influenced world thought. Infact, the Russian Revolution in 1917 was inspired by Marx's ideologies. Later, many laws were passed by the capitalist nations to improve the condition of labourers.

Q. 7. Industrial Revolution marked change to machine work from hand work and to factory system of production from domestic system of production. In this context discuss:

    (a) Role of geographical location and availability natural resources in stimulating the Industrial Revolution.

    (b) Role of Enclosure Movement in ushering the Industrial Revolution.

    (c) Role of vast overseas market in stimulating the Industrial Revolution.

Ans. (a) The geographical location of England greatly helped in industrial revolution.

    (i) Its geographical position was suitable for world trade and all parts of the world were accessible to its ships.

    (ii) The rivers were beneficial for internal transport and its coastline offered excellent harbours.

(iii) The country had large deposits of coal and iron ores which greatly helped in the growth of many industries.

(iv) Location of coal and iron mines close to each other encouraged the English to evolve new techniques for the manufacture of iron and utilization of the coals.

(b) Enclosure was the legal process in England of enclosing a number of small landholdings to create one larger farm. It allowed wealthy lords to purchase public fields and push out small-scale farmers.

   (i) As a consequence of this movement big Landlords emerged and small farmers now became landless labourers.

   (ii) This forced several people to migrate to the cities in search of jobs.

   (iii) Thus the surplus supply of labour as a result of the Enclosure Movement greatly helped Industrial Revolution.

(c) Vast overseas market had a profound impact on the Industrial Revolution.

   (i) England started a vigorous accumulation of colonies like India and Canada in the 18th century.

   (ii) These colonies were not merely used as sources of cheap raw material but as a huge market for the industrially produced goods.

   (iii) The other factors that provided the incentive to produce more goods were the huge profits of expanding trade and the Napoleonic wars. The industry and trade of the continental countries were damaged by these wars.

   (iv) These countries were dependent on England for the manufactured goods thereby stimulating demand and providing goods thereby stimulating demand and providing fillip to Industrial Revolution.

Q. 8. Discuss the main principles of features of socialism.

Ans. The following are the main principles of features of socialism.

(a) Socialism favours collectivism, *i.e.,* collective good or social welfare which is of greater value than the good of an individual.

(b) Socialism promotes civil liberties such as freedom of speech and freedom to form associations.

(c) Socialism wants to reduce class division.

(d) Socialism belives that democratic means should be employed for achieving their objectives, *i.e.,* the good of socialism.

Q. 9. The Industrial Revolution in Europe had its impact. In the light of the above statement, answer the following:

(a) Define 'Socialism'

(b) State any three causes for the rise of 'Capitalism'.

(c) Write any two differences between 'Capitalism' and 'Socialism'

Ans. (a) Socialism emerged as a rection to Capitalism.

   (i) Socialism implies that "the land and other instruments of production shall be the common property of the people and shall be governed by the people, for the people."

   (ii) The other means of production included the mines, factories, means of transport and communication, banks and consumer stores, etc.

   (iii) The Socialists belived that such a system alone can create conditions in which everyone would have opportunity to benefit from the country's wealth.

(b) Three causes for the rise of 'Capitalism' were:

   (i) Industrial Revolution increased national wealth and living standards. It checked various diseases and increased population. Therefore, large number of people began shifting to the cities in search of work.

(ii) The Enclosure Laws required the farmers to put fences of hedges around their farms to prevent common grazing on the land. The big farmers consolidated their holdings. Small farmers, who could not afford to do this, sold off their land. They became landless labourers. They had to move to the cities in search of work in the factories.

(iii) New manufacturing towns and cities grew fast. Many factories were located near the coalfields and also near sources of power as power could not be distributed very far. Industrial towns like Glasgow, Manchester, Leeds, Sheffield, Birmingham, etc. grew as there was a sharp rise in the population when they became important centres of capitalistic economic activity.

(iv) Mass production led to the destruction of domestic system of production.

(Mention any three causes)

SECTION : A (CIVICS)

Chapter 1. Indian Constitution

Q. 1. Look at the picture and answer the following questions:

(a) Who is this personality? What was his contribution to framing the Constitution of India?

(b) When was the Constitution adopted? What were the views of BR Ambedkar after completing his work?

(c) How was the Constitution of India adopted, enacted and enforced?

Ans. (a) The personality shown in the picture is Dr. B.R. Ambedkar. He was a renowned social reformer, politician and jurist. He is also called the Father of Indian Constitution.

    (i) B.R. Ambedkar was appointed as the Chairman of the Drafting Committee.

    (ii) Under the Chairmanship of Dr. B.R. Ambedkar, the Constitution was drafted and introduced in the Constituent Assembly, which later came into force on 26th January 1950.

(b) The Constitution was adopted on 26 November 1949. B.R. Ambedkar felt that:

    (i) The Constitution was workable.

    (ii) It was flexible and it was strong enough to hold the country together both in peace time and in war time.

(c) The Draft Constitution was published on 26 February 1948, after many deliberations and amendments.

    (i) It was published in all the leading newspapers of the country in order to seek wide-ranging consultations and opinions.

    (ii) The Assembly considered the views of judges, lawyers, private individuals and public bodies and decided to revise the Constitution.

    (iii) The Draft Constitution was discussed in detail by the Drafting Committee. On 26 November, 1949, the Constitution was enacted and adopted by the Constituent Assembly.

    (iv) At the time of its signing, the Constitution comprised 8 schedules and 395 Articles.

Q. 2. In the given picture Jawaharlal Nehru is signing the Indian Constitution. In this context answer the following questions.

(a) What was the role of Jawaharlal Nehru in framing of our Constitution?

(b) Why was 26 January thought to be an appropriate day for the declaration of the Constitution?

(c) What were the objectives highlighted in the 'Objectives Resolution'?

Ans. (a) The idea of an independent Constitution for India was first mooted by Pt. Jawaharlal Nehru, expressing his views in 1938. He advocated the formation of an elected Constituent Assembly to frame the Constitution of a free India without interference from outside sources. On 24 March 1946, the British Government sent a delegation (Cabinet Mission) of three Cabinet Ministers. The Cabinet Mission proposed the formation of Constituent Assembly for framing the Constitution of free India.

(b) In the Congress Session at Lahore it was decided that 26 January should be observed as the 'Purna Swaraj Day' meaning complete independence. For the first time the Complete Independence Day was celebrated on 26 January 1930 and continued to be celebrated till 1947. But after India achieved Independence on 15th August 1947, it came to be known as Independence Day and 26 January as the Republic Day of India. Therefore, these factors made the Assembly select 26 January as the commencement of the new Constitution of India.

(c) The work of drafting the Constitution was started by the Constituent Assembly and on 13 December 1946, Pandit Jawaharlal Nehru moved the Objectives Resolution, which formed the preamble of the Constitution. The Resolution proposed:

(i) Free India will mean being 'republic'.

(ii) The republic would grant Fundamental Rights to citizens.

(iii) The ideals of political, social and economic democracy would be guaranteed to all people.

(iv) The state would safeguard the rights of backward classes and minorities.

Q. 3. The given picture is a comprehensive document of Indian Constitution. In this context answer the questions that follow:

(a) What do you mean by single citizenship?

(b) How can we say that Indian Constitution is partly rigid and partly flexible?

(c) Why is Indian Constitution considered as the lengthiest in the world?

Ans. (a) Under a federal system, there is generally a dual citizenship, that of the State to which an individual belongs and of the Nation that represents a Union of States.

    (i) In India, our Constitution provides single citizenship despite the federal structure. Single citizenship means Indians cannot be citizens of another country.

    (ii) Citizens of other countries cannot take Indian citizenship.

    (iii) In India all citizens, irrespective of the state in which they are born or reside, enjoy the same political and civil rights and no discrimination is made between them.

(b) The Constitution of India is neither wholly rigid nor wholly flexible. It is partly rigid and partly flexible. It is because of the fact that for the purpose of amendment, our constitution has been divided into three parts:

    (i) Certain provisions of the constitution can be amended by a simple majority in Parliament like ordinary laws of the land. (Flexible)

    (ii) Certain provisions can be amended by a two-third majority in Parliament and ratified by at least fifty percent of the states. (Rigid)

    (iii) The remaining provisions can be amended by Parliament by two-third majority. (Rigid)

(c) Our constitution is regarded as most lengthiest in the world because

    (i) Our constitution has tried to incorporate good points of all the constitutions of the world.

    (ii) Ours is a vast country with diverse languages, customs, traditions, races, religions, etc. As such justice was to be done to all of them and more and more deliberation and thinking was required, and hence more space.

    (iii) Provisions of safeguards for minorities, scheduled castes and scheduled tribes have also been provided in our Constitution.

    (iv) It covers all the details and descriptions of all the powers which are enjoyed by the executive, legislature and judiciary.

Chapter 2. Salient Features of the Constitution

Q. 1. Study the given picture and answer the questions that follow:

(a) Which fundamental Right do the given symbols in picture signify? Why is this freedom given to Indian citizens?

(b) State any three freedoms given under the 'Right to Freedom of Religion'.

(c) Can state funds be utilised for religious instruction in educational institutions?

Ans. (a) The given symbol in the picture signifies the 'Right to Freedom of Religion'.
   (i) India is a multi-religion nation. Therefore this right is given to Indian citizens to give all religions equal respect and recognition.
   (ii) This right says that all Indian citizens have the freedom and right to profess, practice and propagate their religion.

   (b) The right of freedom of religion includes:
   (i) **Freedom of Conscience and the Free Profession and Propagation of Religion:** Article 25 guarantees to every Indian citizen the freedom of conscience and the right to practice, profess and propagate any religion.
   (ii) **Freedom to manage Religious Affairs:** Article 26 of the Constitution guarantees the right to establish and maintain institutions for charitable and religious purposes and to manage its own affairs regarding matters of religion.
   (iii) **Freedom as to Payment of Taxes for Promotion of any Particular Religion:** Article 27 states that no person shall be compelled to pay any taxes, the proceeds of which are meant for the promotion or maintenance of any particular religion.

   (c) Article 28(1) states, "No religious instruction shall be provided in any educational institution wholly maintained out of State funds."
   (i) It means that public funds cannot be utilised by any institution to propagate religious instruction, especially the institution is wholly maintained out of State Funds.
   (ii) In case of State-recognised or State-aided educational institutions, there is no bar to giving religious instruction.
   (iii) But no individual can be required to take part in any religious instruction without his/her consent and in case of a minor, the consent of his/her guardian has to be obtained.
   (iv) Thus, the constitution aims to establish a Secular State by allowing equal freedom of worship and faith to all.

Q. 2. The given picture is of the Supreme Court of India. There is a right in India which states that a person can move to Supreme Court if he/she wants to get their fundamental rights protected. In this context answer the following questions.

   (a) Which right in India gives a citizen the right to move to the court? Briefly explain that Fundamental Right.
   (b) What is the writ of habeas corpus and why is it important?
   (c) What is the difference between a writ of certiorari and a writ of mandamus?

Ans. (a) Right to Constitutional Remedies-Article 32 provides the right to move the Supreme Court for the enforcement of the Rights conferred by Part III of the Constitution.
   (i) It provides writs or legal remedies for the protection of our Fundamental Rights against the arbitrary actions of the State.
   (ii) The High Courts are also empowered by the Constitution to issue orders or writs for the enforcement of any of these rights.

   (b) The writ of Habeas Corpus protects the safety of any person held in prison or taken into custody.

    (i) This writ can be issued where a person is illegally held even by a private individual.

    (ii) By issuing this writ, the court can order the detaining authority to bring the detained person to the court to explain why such a prisoner is being held.

    (iii) This writ also acts as a deterrent to unlawful imprisonment of people under trial.

    (iv) The writ of habeas corpus is reckoned as "the popular and effective writ, as far as illegal confinement is concerned".

(c) Writ of Certiorari

    (i) The word 'certiorari' means 'to be fully informed'.

    (ii) By this writ, the lower court has to hand over all the relevant records of a case to the higher court.

Writ of Mandamus

    (i) The Latin word 'mandamus' means 'we command'.

    (ii) The writ is issued when a petition is filed against any public official or unit who is not performing its duty.

Chapter 3. Elections

Q. 1. Look at the given picture and answer the questions that follow:

(a) What is shown in the picture? What is its importance in election process?

(b) Why is election needed in India?

(c) In what circumstances repoll is done in a constituency?

Ans. (a) It is an Electronic Voting Machine (EVM) that uses electronic means to either aid or take care of casting and counting votes. EVMs are important in election process because :

    (i) It is used to record votes. The machine shows the names of the candidates and the symbols.

    (ii) It eliminates the possibility of invalid votes, makes the counting process faster and reduces the cost of printing.

    (iii) An EVM can be used in areas without electricity as it runs on alkaline batteries.

(b) Elections are needed in India for the following reasons:

    (i) These elections give an opportunity to the voters to indirectly participate in the administration of the country.

    (ii) It is the best way by which the representatives of the people can be chosen and sent to legislature.

    (iii) By contesting elections either as members of a political party or as an independent candidate, people get a chance to participate in government formation and enact laws and execute policies for the good of the people and their country.

(c) Under following circumstances, the Election Commission orders repoll in a constituency:

    (i) In case of booth capturing.

    (ii) In case ballot papers or boxes are destroyed.

    (iii) Election Commission can suspend polling when it fears a threat to voter's security or other genuine reasons. In this situation the Election Commission orders a repoll which takes place within two or three days after the first polling.

Q. 2. Study the picture and answer the questions that follow:

    (a) Where is this building situated? With what objective this whole setup been made?

    (b) State the composition of the Election Commission. What is the difference in the status of the Chief Election Commissioner and other Election Commissioners?

    (c) What is the function and powers of this body?

Ans. (a) This building is the headquarters of the Election Commission of India.

       (i) It is situated in New Delhi.

      (ii) The main objective is to conduct all kinds of elections in free and fair manner in India.

    (b) According to the Article 324 of the Indian Constitution, the Election Commission in India shall comprise:

       (i) A Chief Election Commissioner, and

      (ii) Two Election Commissioners.

         Though the Chief Election Commissioner is the chairman of the election commission, however, his powers are equal to the other election commissioners. But the Chief Election Commissioner can be removed from the office of Election Commission through impeachment of the Parliament. At the other end of the spectrum, other Election Commissioners can be removed by the President at the behest of the Chief Election Commissioner.

    (c) Some of the important functions and powers of Election Commission are as follows:

       (i) To superintendence, direction and control of elections.

      (ii) To improve the accuracy of the electoral rolls and prevent electoral frauds.

      (iii) To give recognition to political parties as All India Parties or Regional Parties on the basis of the voter received by them in the last elections.

      (iv) To allot election symbols to various political parties and independent candidates. The Election Commission is also responsible for hearing and settling all disputes with regard to such symbols.

Q. 3. The given picture is the logo of Election Commission of India. In this context answer the following questions:

    (a) Mention the manner of appointment of members of Election Commission.

    (b) Explain their conditions of service.

    (c) Discuss the manner of the removal of members of Election Commission.

Ans. (a) According to the Article 324 of the Indian Constitution, the Election Commission in India shall comprise:

       (i) Chief Election Commissioner and   (ii) Two Election Commissioners.

The Chief Election Commissioner and Election Commissioners are appointed by the President of India. Regional Election Commissioners assist the Election Commission in its functioning.

(b) Conditions of service of members of Election Commission:
  (i) They have tenure of six years, or up to the age of 65 years, whichever is earlier.
  (ii) They enjoy the same status and receive salary and perks as available to Judges of the Supreme Court of India.
  (iii) They do not hold any office of profit after retirement.
  (iv) The Constitution ensures the independence of the Election Commission in its functioning.

(c) The members of the election Commission can be removed in the following manner:
  (i) The Chief Election Commissioner can be removed from the office of election Commission only through impeachment by the Parliament.
  (ii) At the other end of the spectrum, other Election Commissioners can be removed by the president at the behest of the Chief Election Commissioner.
  (iii) The grounds of removal of the Chief Election Commissioner are the same which are applicable to a judge of the Supreme Court.

Q. 4. Look at the pictures of the Party symbols of various parties. In this context answer the following questions:

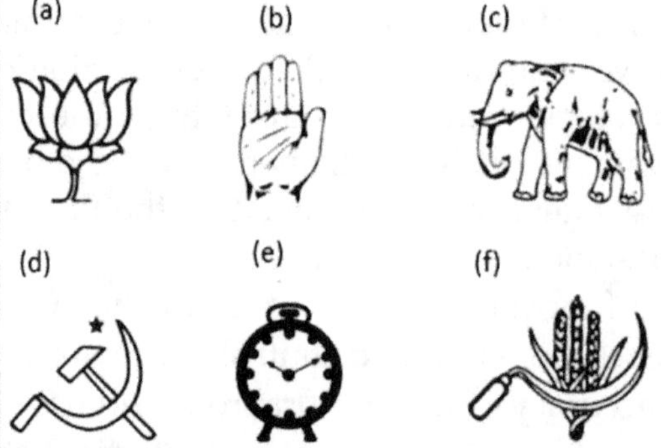

(a) Identify each party symbol and mention the name of the party.
(b) What is the main purpose of allotting symbols to political parties?
(c) How is a political party recognised as a National Party?

Ans. (a) These are the party symbols of the following parties:
  (a) Bharatiya Janta Party (BJP)   (b) Indian National Congress (INC)
  (c) Bahujan Samaj Party (BSP)   (d) Communist Party of India (CPI)
  (e) Nationalist Congress Party (NCP)
  (f) Communist Party of India (Marxist) (CPI)(M)

(b) Political parties are allotted reserved common symbols, while the independent candidates may select them from a list of free symbols.
  (i) Main purpose is that these symbols may be easily recognised by illiterate people.
  (ii) Allotment of symbols helps the party in election campaigning.

(c) For any political party to be eligible for recognition as a National Party, it has to satisfy any of the three conditions listed below:
  (i) Secure at least 6% of the valid vote in an Assembly or a Lok Sabha General Election in any four or more states.
  (ii) And won at least 4 seats in a Lok Sabha General Election from any State or States.
  (iii) Win at least 2% of the total Lok Sabha seats in a Lok Sabha General Election and these seats have to be won from at least 3 states.
  (iv) The party is recognised as a State Party in at least four states.

Q. 5. Look at the picture and answer the questions that follow:

(a)   What is the importance of issuing voter's identity card?

(b) How can we say that Elections are barometer of Democracy?

(c) What is an electoral roll? How can we say that updating of electoral rolls is a continuous process.

Ans. (a) Importance of Voter's Identity Cards:

    (i) A voter's identity card, also known as Electors Photo Identity Card (EPIC) is a photo identity card, which is issued by the Election Commission of India.

    (ii) The photo identity card is given to all the citizens of India who are entitled to vote.

    (iii) To improve the accuracy of the electoral rolls and prevent electoral frauds, the Election commission ordered the making of photo identity cards for all voters in the country in August, 1993.

(b) Elections are barometer of Democracy.

    (i) They are the indicator of the efficiency of our democracy.

    (ii) Elections at regular interval are a striking aspect of democratic polity.

    (iii) If there are no elections people would not be able to choose their leaders.

    (iv) Elections display sovereignty and integrity of all the citizens of the nation.

(c) The electoral roll of a constituency is a list of all those people in that constituency who are registered to vote in the elections.

    (i) Only those people whose names are there in the electoral rolls are allowed to vote as 'electors'.

    (ii) The electoral roll is normally revised every year to add the names of those who are not less than 18 on a qualifying date years as on the first day of January of that year, or have moved into the constituency, and to remove the names of those who have died or moved out of the constituency.

    (iii) The updating of electoral rolls is a continuous process, which is interrupted only at the time of the elections during the period from after the last date of filing nominations till the completion of the elections.

Chapter 4. Rural Local Self-Government

Q. 1. The given picture shows members of Gram Panchayat conducting a meeting. In this context, explain:

(a) Civic facilities and Welfare functions

(b) Developmental Functions

(c) Functions related to the regulation and General Administration

Ans. (a) Functions of Gram Panchayat with respect to civic facilities and welfare are:

    (i) Providing safe drinking water that includes measures like building and maintaining wells, tanks and drains for the public.

    (ii) Health Care Facilities like setting up of health centres and dispensaries by the Panchayat.

    (iii) Maintenance and construction of roads, good drainage, street lights, culverts, footpaths, bridges and car tracks.

    (iv) To look after the well-being of expecting mothers and their children.

    (v) Introducing welfare programmes for youth, children and women.

(b) Developmental functions of Gram Panchayat are:

    (i) Undertaking schemes for irrigation and arranging for fertilisers and seeds.

    (ii) Preparing and executing various agricultural plans.

    (iii) Electrification of the rural areas.

    (iv) Provision for education at primary and secondary levels.

    (v) Developing and fostering small scale and cottage industries that include industries related to food processing.

(c) Functions of Gram Panchayat related to the regulation and General Administration are:

    (i) Registering marriages, births and deaths.

    (ii) Maintenance of burial grounds for the cremation rites.

    (iii) Upkeep of watch and ward services like Chowkidars, etc.

    (iv) Collecting and maintaining of records and statistics of villages' purchases, sales, land grants, etc.

    (v) Maintaining public property of the village.

    (vi) Extending help to the government in preserving law and order.

Q. 2. Look at the given picture below and answers the following questions:

(a) What does this image show?

(b) Qualification for elections.

(c) Composition of Gram Sabha.

(d) Functions of Gram Sabha.

Ans. (a) The image shows members of gram sabha meeting in a village.

(b) In order to become members of the Panchayat, the following criteria have to be fulfilled by the aspiring members:

    (i) As per the Act, a candidate has to attain a prescribed age.

    (ii) The name of the candidates must be registered as voters in that particular Panchayat.

    (iii) The candidates must be mentally sound.

    (iv) The State Legislatures must not have disqualified the candidates under any law.

    (v) The candidate should not hold any office of profit under the government.

(c) A Gram Sabha consists of all the adult citizens and is constituted in every village with a population of not less than 1500.

   (i) All the adult members of the Gram Sabha elect the Gram Pradhan or Sarpanch for a period of five years.

   (ii) The number of members in Gram Sabha differs from one state to another.

   (iii) The state government, depending upon the population of the village determines the number of Panchas in a Sabha. However, the number generally varies between 7-15 members.

   (iv) Out of the total seats, one-third is reserved for women. Some of the seats in the Panchayats are also reserved for the Scheduled Castes and Scheduled Tribes in accordance with the total population of the village.

(d) The main functions of Gram Sabha are as follows:

   (i) It keeps an eye on the working of Gram Panchayat, which is the administrative body of the Gram Sabha.

   (ii) It elects Gram Pradhan (Sarpanch) and other members of the Gram Panchayat.

   (iii) It prevents the Gram Panchayat from wrong doing and can seek clarifications from the Sarpanch and Panchas regarding any matter.

   (iv) It implements government schemes related to generation of employment in the village.

   (v) It oversees all the activities of village like the construction and maintenance of water sources, roads, drainage systems, schools buildings, etc.

Chapter 5. Urban Local Self Government

Q. 1. The given picture is of Municipal Committee of Pahalgam. In the context of Municipal Committee, discuss:

(a) Their composition

(b) Their optional functions

(c) Their obligatory functions

Ans. (a) **Composition of the Municipal Committee:**

Since, this Committee is smaller in size, it has three wings namely,

   (i) **The General Body or the Council:** The members of the General body or Council are called Councillors and the adult citizens residing in a particular Municipal ward elect them.

   (ii) **The President/Chairman:** The Councillors of a Municipal Committee directly elect their President, a Senior Vice President and a Junior Vice President from amongst themselves.

(iii) **The Chief Executive Officer and other Officers:** The Chief Executive Officer is responsible for managing the administrative section of the Municipal Committee.

(b) The Optional functions of Municipal Committee are carrying out activities like founding reading rooms and libraries, arranging exhibitions and fairs, building stadiums for sports activity, offering conveyance facilities and other services for the welfare and comfort of the people. The Municipalities are expected to adopt schemes that plan to provide work for weaker sections of the society.

(c) Following are the Obligatory functions of Municipal Committees:

(i) **Health and Sanitation of the Public:** It is the responsibility of the Municipality to maintain numerous hospitals and dispensaries in the city or town.

(ii) **Providing Electricity and Supply of Water:** One of the most important functions of Municipal Committee is to provide electricity and safe drinking water for use in domestic as well as commercial circles.

(iii) **Public Works :** This largely includes building of roads, community halls and shopping centres.

(iv) **Registering Births and Deaths:** An account of the number of births and deaths in the city is also to be maintained by the Municipal Board.

Q.2. The given pictures shows functions of Municipal Corporation. In this context, explain :

(a) Public works undertaken by Municipal Corporation.
(b) Obligatory functions related to health and sanitation.
(c) Obligatory functions related to education and sports.

Ans. (a) The duties of the Corporation related to Public works are:

(i) Providing buildings, roads, bus-shelters and public urinals for the convenience of people.

(ii) Issuing notices and demolishing various structures and buildings those are in miserable condition.

(iii) Setting of rules with regard to the building of hotels, restaurant and shopping centres.

(iv) Planting trees.

(b) Obligatory functions of Municipal Corporation related to health and sanitation include:

(i) Measures like establishing and maintaining hospitals, centres for child welfare, maternity homes and dispensaries.

(ii) Organising vaccinations and inoculation camps for eradication of infectious diseases.

(iii) Making provisions for the safe disposal of garbage.

(c) Obligatory functions of Municipal Corporation related to education and sports include:

(i) Setting up of schools up to primary and secondary levels, along with centres for educating adults, setting up libraries, museums and night schools.

(ii) It is the duty of the corporation to ensure that all children below the age of 14 years go to schools.

(iii) They also organise and embark on the promotion of games and sports among young boys and girls.

Q. 3. The given picture shows Nagar Palika of Mawana. In this context, explain:

(a) Tenure and composition of Nagar Palika.

(b) Compulsory functions of Nagar Palika related to health and Sanitation and Public works.

(c) Optional or discretionary functions.

Ans. (a) According to the new Nagar Palika or Municipality Councils Act, 1992, every Municipality will have a uniform tenure of five years. The membership for the municipality depends on the population of the city or town.

Since this Committee is smaller in size, it has three wings namely:

(i) The General Body or the Council

(ii) The President/Chairman

(iii) The Chief Executive Officer and other officers.

(b) Compulsory functions of Nagar Palika related to

(i) **Health and Sanitation:** It is the responsibility of the Municipality to maintain numerous hospitals and dispensaries in the city or town. Other responsibilities of the Committee that come under this head are cleaning public lanes, putting a stop to the sale of foodstuffs that are rotten and selling of adulterated milk, etc.

(ii) **Public Works:** This largely includes building of roads, community halls and shopping centres.

(c) The discretionary functions of Municipalities are:

(i) These functions range from carrying out activities like funding reading rooms and libraries, arranging exhibitions and fairs, building transport facilities and other services for the welfare and comfort of the people.

(ii) The Municipalities are expected to adopt schemes that plan to provide work for weaker sections of the society.

(iii) For encouraging self-employment to the small artisans schemes like Nehru Rozgar Yojana exist to provide financial help to small artisans.

(iv) Provisions are also in place to cater to the clearance of the slum areas and various constructive housing programmes.

SECTION : B (HISTORY)

Chapter 1. The Harappan Civilisation

Q. 1. Study the picture given below and answer the following questions:

(a) Identify the figure with the site from where it is excavated.

(b) What does this picture signify?

(c) State any two remarkable features of this figure.

Ans. (a) (i) The picture identifies the figure of a nobleman or a 'priest king'.

   (ii) It was excavated from the sites of Mohen-jo-Daro.

(b) (i) This figure indicates the outstanding skills of sculptor belonging to the Indus Valley civilisation.

   (ii) Some historians signified this figure as a statue of a yogi due to its posture.

(c) (i) This male figure is draped in a shawl over the left shoulder and the right arm.

   (ii) It also featured a well-trimmed beard and half-closed eyes.

Q. 2. Study the given picture and answer the following questions :

(a) Identify the picture. What does it reflect?

(b) State any two feature of this picture.

(c) Write short notes on the seals of Harappan civilisation.

Ans. (a) (i) The above picture identifies the unicorn seal.

   (ii) It reflects the mythical beliefs of the Harappan people.

(b) (i) The seal is engraved with the figure of the mythical animal unicorn, featuring a single protruding horn.

    (ii) This seal shows that at a very early stage of civilisation, humans had produced many creations of imaginations in the shape of bird and animal motifs that survived in later art.

(c) (i) About 2000 different types of seals have been excavated from the various sites of the civilisation.

    (ii) Most of these seals were rectangular or square shaped. However, some were circular also.

    (iii) Most of the seals are engraved with the images of real animals while a few were engraved with the most common mythical animal (unicorn).

    (iv) Historions believe that these seals were probably worn by people as armlets to protect themselves from evil spirits.

Q. 3. Study the given picture and answer the following questions :

(a) What does the given image identify?   (b) What does it depict?

(c) By which animals it is surrounded?

(d) What was the significance of this image?

Ans. (a) The given image identifies the Pashupati seal.

(b) The Pashupati seal depicts a yogi, probably shiva.

(c) (i) The Shiva is surrounded by a rhino, a buffalo, an elephant and a tiger.

    (ii) Under his throne are two deer.

(d) This seal signifies that Shiva was worshipped and he was considered as the lord of animals.

Q. 4. Study the picture and answer the questions:

(a) What does the given image signify?

(b) From where was this site structure excavated?

(c) Write any three feature of the underground drainage system of the Indus valley civilization.

Ans. (a) The above image identifies an underground drain in a street.

(b) This structure was unearthed from Mohenjo-Daro.

(c) (i) The drainage system of the Indus valley civilisation was very advanced.

(ii) The draines were always covered with slabs.

(iii) Housewives were expected to use pite in which heavier parts of the rubbish would settle down while only sewerage water was allowed to drain off.

Chapter 2. The Vedic Period

Q. 1. Study the picture and answer the following questions :

(a) What does the picture depict? What phase of life does it signify in an Aryan's life?

(b) State any four basic features of the system.

(c) Did an Aryan spend all his adult life in the above environment? If not, write about the other phases in his life.

(d) State any two features of the above system that are totally different from the system you all are familiar with.

Ans. (a) (i) The picture depicts the Gurukul system of education in the Vedic Period.

(ii) It signifies the Brahmacharya phase of an Aryan's life.

(b) (i) The Gurukul was the residence of the guru in which the young Aryans lived with the guru's family during the entire period of their education.

(ii) Apart from Vedic literature, other secular subjects like mathematics, law, grammar, logic and astronomy were also taught orally.

(iii) No fee was charged, however, students voluntarily paid gurudakshina on the completion of their education.

(iv) Along with studying, the students did the routine household chores like gathering fuel, tending cattles, etc.

(c) (i) No, the Aryans did not spend all their adult life in the Gurukul.

(ii) They only had to spend their Brahmacharya stage of life in Gurukul.

(iii) Apart from Brahmacharya, the other phases of the Aryans' life were Grihastha, Vanaprastha and Sanyasa.

(d) (i) Unlike the Gurukul system from which we are familiar, the students had to live with in the Vedic gurukulas for entire period of their education.

(ii) During the Vedic period, the students were also taught to go out and beg for alms, in order to learn about humanity.

Q. 2. Study the given picture and answer the following questions:

- (a) What does the picture depict?
- (b) When did it start in India?
- (c) What was the basis of this division in the Vedic Indian Society?
- (d) Was this system rigid in the Vedic Period? Discuss.

Ans. (a) The picture depicts the four fold division of the Vedic Society.

- (b) The four fold division was established in India when the Aryans defeated the non-Aryans and established their settlements in India.
- (c) With the coming of Aryans, the Indian Society was divided in the two classes namely, the Aryans and the non-Aryans, on the basis of their complexion, *i.e.* varna, meaning colour.
- (d) (i) No, initially this system was not rigid as occupations were not yet hereditary.
  - (ii) With the growth of population and complexities of social life, the society came to be divided into four classes on the basis of division of labour.

Q. 3. Study the given picture and answer the following questions:

- (a) What does the given image depict?
- (b) Why was this performed?
- (c) When did this performed?
- (d) Who was the god of fire in the Vedic Age? Why was he worshipped?
- (e) Apart from the god of fire, name the other gods who were worshipped during the early Vedic period.
- (f) Write any three features of these performances.

Ans. (a) The given picture depicts the performance of Yajnas.

- (b) These Yajnas were performed to please the gods.
- (c) The yajnas were performed on all the important ceremonies, like marriages and cremations.
- (d) (i) Agni was the god of fire.
  - (ii) He was considered to be an intermediary between gods and men, thus worshipped.

(e) Besides Agni, Indra (god of strength, rain and thunder), Varuna (god of water), Surya (the Sun), Yama (god of death), Vayu (god of winds), Prithvi (goddess of Earth) and Usha (goddess of Dawn) were also worshipped.

(f) (i)   All members of a family took part in the Yajnas.

   (ii)   Small sacrifices like offering milk, juice, grains, ghee and flesh were performed in every house as a part of the daily ritual.

   (iii) These Yajnas were performed by learned Brahmin.

Chapter 3. Jainism And Buddhism

Q. 1.   Study the given picture and answer the following questions :

(a) What is shown in the given picture? In which state it is situated?

(b) With what religion is this hall associated?

(c) What is the purpose of this hall?

(d) Give any three distinctive architectural features of this excavated hall.

Ans. (a) (i)   The given picture depicts the cave temples of Chaitya hall found at Karle.

   (ii) It is situated at Karle in the Pune district of Maharashtra.

(b) The Chaitya Hall is associated with the Buddhist religion.

(c) The Chaitya Hall was used for prayers and meetings.

(d) (i)   The Chaitya or a worship hall was a rock cut cave which consisted of a rectangular hall with a semi-circular side at one end.

   (ii) There was a large window above the main door through which light was admitted.

   (iii) There were long rows of pillars in the hall and the entrance was decorated with Sculptures.

Q. 2. Study the picture and answer the following questions:

(a) Identify the picture. Where is it located?

(b) Who built it? With what religion is it associated?

(c) Why was this structure raised there?

(d) How many lions figures are on the top of the structure? What do these lions signify?

(e) Explain the significance of the wheel below the lions.

(f) Name the four animals sculptured on the abacus.

Ans. (a) (i) The given picture identifies as the Lion capital of the Sarnath pillar.

(ii) It is located in Sarnath, near Varanasi in UP.

(b) (i) The Sarnath pillar was erected by the Mauryan emperor Ashoka, in the 3rd century BC.

(ii) It is associated with the Buddhism.

(c) It was erected to honour the place where Buddha preached his first sermon with the Dharma Chakra.

(d) (i) There are four lion figures standing back to back on the top of the structure.

(ii) The depiction of four lions indicates the supremacy of Buddha in all corners of the world.

(e) The solar wheel alternating these animals signifies the true law, spreading to all four corners of the world.

(f) The round abacus of the capital is sculpted with four dharm chakras alternating with an elephant, a bull, a horse and a lion.

Q. 3. Study the given picture and answer the following questions:

(a) What is the name of the structure given in the above picture? When and by whom was it originally built?

(b) In which state is this situated? Which school of art does it represent?

(c) Mention three important features of the stupa.

(d) What events are depicted on the panel of the gateway of the stupa?

Ans. (a) (i) The given picture depicts the image of Sanchi Stupa.

(ii) It was originally built during the 3rd century BC by emperor Ashoka.

(b) (i) It is situated near Vidisha, 60 kilometres away from Bhopal in Madhya Pradesh.

(ii) It represents the Shunga School of Art.

(c) (i) The relief features of this stupa depicts the story of Buddha which covers all the portions of the gateways.

(ii) It is a solid hemispherical dome-like structure carved by using the wood carving technique.

(iii) Buddha is represented in the form of symbols like a wheel, a lotus and royal umbrella, etc.

(d) The panel of the gateway of the stupa depicted the human figures that illustrate the Jataka stories and other episodes in Buddha's life.

Q. 4. Study the picture given and answer the following questions:

(a) Name the person you see in the given Picture. Write his birth and death date.

(b) How did he achieve enlightenment?

(c) Enlist the Buddhist Councils.

Ans. (a) (i) The above picture depicts the image of Gautam Buddha the founder of Buddhism.

(ii) He took birth in 563 BC in Lumbini in the Sakya of kapila-vastu.

(iii) He died at the age of 80 in 483 BC at Kushinagar in the Gorakhpur district.

(b) (i) At the age of 35, Siddharth meditated under a Pipal tree located in Bihar's Bodh Gaya.

(ii) Here he attained spiritual enlightenment and came to be known as Buddha or the 'enlightened one'.

(c) List of Buddhist Councils:

(i) First Buddhist Council took place around 400 BC at Rajgriha in Bihar.

(ii) Second Buddhist Council took place around 4th century BC at Vaishali in Bihar.

(iii) Third Buddhist Council occured around 251 BC at Pataliputra in Bihar.

(iv) Fourth Buddhist Council was held around 1st century BC in Kashmir.

Q. 5. Study the picture and answer the following questions:

(a) Whose image is this? When and where he born?

(b) What is Kaivalya? When did he achieve Kaivalya and become a Jina?

(c) When and where did he attain Nirvana? Which religion he founded?

Ans. (a) (i) The above picture shows the image of Vardhaman Mahavira.

(ii) Lord Mahavira was born in 599 BC in a Kshatriya family in Kunda-grama at Vaishali near Patna in Bihar.

(b) (i) Kaivalya means supreme knowledge.

(ii) At the age of 13th, Mahavira gained supreme knowledge or Kaivalya.

(iii) After that he came to be known as Jina that means a person who has conquered self, curbing all desires.

(c) (i) Lord Mahavira achieved Nirvana or salvation at the age of 72 at Pavapuri in the Patna District of Bihar.

(ii) Lord Mahavira founded the Jainism sect.

Chapter 4. The Mauryan Empire

Q. 1. Study the picture and answer the following questions:

(a) Identify the given picture.
(b) What was his contribution in the foundation of the Mauryan Empire?
(c) Write in brief about his renowned work.

Ans. (a) (i) The above given picture identifies the image of Chanakya or Kautilya whose real name was Vishnugupta.
    (ii) He was the advisor and Chief minister of Chandragupta Maurya.
(b) (i) Chanakya, the learned Brahmin of Taxila met young Chandragupta and identified his capabilities.
    (ii) Chankya taught Chandragupta the art of warfare and governance so that together they could destroy the Nandas.
(c) (i) Kautilya composed 'Arthashastra' in 1st millenium BCE in Sanskrit.
    (ii) This book is divided into 15 segments, 180 subjects and approx. 6000 shlokas.
    (iii) It also provided a detailed account regarding duties of the king and ministers, his foreign policy, organisation of spies, civil and criminal laws, guilds and corporation, etc.
    (iv) It further patronizes the principles of interstate relations and suggests methods to win wars.

Q. 2. Study the given picture and answer the following questions:

(a) Identify the person given in the picture.
(b) Which religion did he adopt?
(c) What was his contribution in the Buddhist architecture?
(d) How did the Kalinga War affect him?

Ans. (a) The person given in the picture identifies as the great Emperor of the Mauryan Empire, Ashoka.
(b) Ashoka adopted Buddhism.
(c) Ashoka built about 84,000 stupas and monasteries across the length and breadth of India to spread Buddhism.
(d) (i) Ashoka won the Kalinga War but it marked a major turning point in his life.

(ii) He was immensely moved by the sufferings of people and this made him give up the war.

(iii) Ashoka who was a great worshipper of lord Shiva, embraced Buddhism after this war and became the ardent follower of Lord Buddha.

(iv) After the war, he devoted himself fully for the welfare of his subjects.

Chapter 5. The Sangam Age

Q. 1. Study the picture and answer the following questions.

(a) What does this picture remind you of?

(b) List some things that have been excavated from the graves.

(c) Why were these objects placed on the graves?

Ans. (a) This picture reminds us about the megaliths.

(b) Following objects have been excavated from the graves:

    (i) Human bones,   (ii) pieces of pottery,

    (iii) iron objects such as hoes, sickles, arrow heads and spear heads.

(c) (i) These objects were placed on the graves in the belief that the dead persons would need them in the next world.

    (ii) They believed in the life after death.

Q. 2. Study the picture and answer the following questions:

(a) Identify the person given in the picture. Which famous work he has written?

(b) In which period of time did he write his book?

(c) Give a brief note on his famous work.

Ans. (a) (i) The picture identifies the image of the great Tamil poet Thiruvalluvar or popularly known as Valluvar.

    (ii) He authored the most famous and greatest of all Tamil classics, Tirukkural.

(b) (i) The poet Thiruvalluvar who is believed to have lived between the 2nd and 6th century AD composed Tirukkural.

    (ii) However, the period of the composition of Tirukkural was disputed.

    (iii) It is believed that it was created in the late Tamil sangam period around 5th century BC.

(c) (i) The book Tirukkural consists of 1330 Tamil couplets organized into 3 main sections and 133 chapters.

(ii) Each chapter contains 10 couplets associated with a specific subject, ranging from 'ploughing a piece of land' to 'ruling a country'.

(iii) The text has been translated into many languages across the world.

Chapter 6. The Age of Guptas

Q. 1. Study the picture and answer the following questions.

(a) What does this image signify?

(b) Where was it situated?

(c) Who established it and in which period?

(d) Who destroyed it?

(e) Give three of its special features.

Ans. (a) This image identifies the ruins of Nalanda University.

(b) The Nalanda is situated near Rajgriha in Bihar.

(c) (i) A Buddhist tradition revealed that sakraditya established this centre of learning.

(ii) Initially it was established as a Buddhist monastry probably during the reign of kumara Gupta I around AD 414-445.

(d) This centre of learning was destroyed towards the end of the 12th century by Muhammad Bin Bakhtiyar Khilji, general of Mohammad Ghori.

(c) (i) The Nalanda University was supported by the revenue from many villages donated by the kings and also by donations from merchants.

(ii) It was a residential university where the staff and students had free boarding, lodging and education.

(iii) It was specialised in Mahayana Buddhism but also offered many subjects for study such as grammar, philosophy, astronomy, literature, Buddhism and Hinduism.

Q. 2. Study the picture and answer the following questions:

(a) Identify the given image, where is it located?   (b) To which period does it belong?
(c) To which deity is the temple dedicated?   (d) Write four features of this place.

Ans. (a) (i) The given image identifies the Vishnu temple also called Gupta temple or the Dashavatara temple.

(ii) It is situated at Deogarh, about 112 kilometres from Jhansi in Uttar Pradesh.

(b) It was built in the beginning of the 6th century AD.

(c) The temple is dedicated to lord Vishnu, who is depicted to be sleeping on a giant serpent that is coiled underneath lord Vishnu.

(d) (i) The temple has an ornamented doorway which has statues of Ganga and Yamuna.

(ii) There is an outer wall around the temple and figures of a lotus are sculptured on the gates of the temple.

(iii) This temple is built of red stone on a 1.5 metre square terrace with a flight of steps in the middle on all four sides.

(iv) The basement has sculptured niches on all sides depicting events from Ramayana.

Q. 3. Study the picture and answer the following questions :

(a) Identify the person in the given image.   (b) Under whose court did he live?
(c) Name his four major poetic works.
(d) Name his three dramatic works for which he is renowned.

Ans. (a) The given image is of the greatest of all Indian poets ever, Kalidasa.

(b) Kalidasa lived in the court of Chandragupta II in the 5th century AD.

(c) (i) Raghuvansa   (ii) Ritusamhara
(iii) Kumarasambhava   (iv) Meghaduta

(d) (i) Vikram Vashiyam   (ii) Abhijnanashakuntalam
(iii) Malavikagnimitram

Q. 4. Study the picture and answer following questions :

(a) What does the given image identify?   (b) Where is this statue located?
(c) To which period does it belong?   (d) Of which material is it made?
(e) What does it show?

Ans. (a) The given image identifies the seated Buddha.

(b) It is situated at Sarnath near Varanasi.

(c) It belongs to 5th century AD.

(d) This statue is made of Sandstone with a texture of shining smoothness.

(e) It shows sitting Buddha in a yogic position and preaching his first sermon to his disciples.

Q. 5. (a) Identify the given image. Which dynasty was he founded?

(b) How did he extend his empire?

(c) Who was the last ruler of this empire?

Ans. (a) (i) The given image identifies Chandragupta I (AD 320-335), the son of Ghatotkacha.

(ii) He founded the Gupta Empire.

(b) (i) He strengthened the power of his dynasty by a matrimonial alliance with the Lichchhavi clan.

(ii) His marriage with Kumara Devi, a Lich-Chhavi princess helped him in amassing great political gains by adding the Lichchhavi clan to Magadha and thereby extending his dominion over Awadh as well as along the Ganges and as far as Prayag.

(iii) The Chandragupta's empire included a part of Bengal, Bihar and eastern Uttar Pradesh.

(c) The line of the Imperial Guptas is supposed to have ended with the last known king, Vishnugupta.

Chapter 7. The Cholas

Q. 1. Study the picture of a famous temple and answer the following questions:

(a) Identify the monument and explain when and by whom it was built.

(b) To which deity is it dedicated to? Where is it located and who declared it a world heritage site?

(c) Why this temple is so famous?

Ans. (a) The monument is Brihadeshwara temple. It was built in AD 1000 by Chola King, Rajaraja I and was completed in 1035 AD.

(b) This temple is dedicated to Lord Shiva. It is located at Thanjavur (formerly known as Tanjore). It has been declared a world heritage site by UNESCO.

(c) The Brihadeshwara or Rajarajeshwara temple at Thanjavur is the best example of the Chola architecture.

    (i) The entire temple structure is made of granite. It consists of an inter-connected Nandi mandapa, a pillared portico and an assembly hall.

    (ii) The temple has a massive colonnaded prakara (corridor) and one of the largest Shiva lingas in India.

    (iii) The 57 metres high tower or vimana comprises thirteen storeys and its top is crowned with an 8.6 metres high single block of stone that weighs 80 tonnes.

    (iv) The temple's interior walls are decorated with magnificent sculptures and elaborate paintings.

    (v) In this temple, a carving of a man's head with a European hat is located (in a subsidiary structure) who is interpreted at Marco Polo (13th century Venetian traveller).

Chapter 8. The Delhi Sultanate

Q. 1. Study the picture of a famous monument below and answer the following questions:

(a) Identify the monument and explain when and by whom it was built. Why was it constructed?

(b) How is it an important archeological source to reconstruct the history of Delhi Sultanate?

(c) Mention any four architectural features of this monument.

Ans. (a) This is the Qutub Minar. Its construction was started by Qutub-ud-din Aibak but its construction was completed by Iltutmish. It is believed that its construction was started in around 1192 AD and was completed in 1230 AD. The tower was built to celebrate Muslim dominance in Delhi after the defeat of Delhi's last Hindu ruler.

(b) Qutub Minar is one of the most magnificent archeological sources constructed by the Turks. The Minar contains numerous inscriptions in Arabic and Nagari characters, which narrates its history. The construction of the Qutub Minar was started by Qutub-ud-din Aibak, but he only constructed the basement. The construction of the tower was later taken over by his successor Iltutmish who constructed three more storeys. The last two storeys were completed by Firoz Shah Tughluq. The different architectural styles from the time of Aibak to Tughluq are clearly visible in the Qutub Minar.

(c) Architectural features of Qutub Minar:

    (i) The circular tower of the minar that rises to a height of 72.5 metres was dedicated to the Sufi saint Qutub ud-din Bakhtiyar Kaki.

    (ii) It has five storeys. Each storey is separated from the other by balconies, which encircle the tower.

    (iii) Inside the tower there are 379 stairs, which lead to the top.

    (iv) Red sandstone, marble and grey quartz have been used to construct the tower. It is the tallest stone tower in India.

Q. 2. Epigraphic records are a valuable source of information. In this context, study the picture given and answer the questions that follow :

(a) On what epigraphic source have records regarding the sultanate period been found?

(b) In what language are these records?

(c) Why are these recoreds valuable?

Ans. (a) Inscriptions belonging to the Sultanate period have been found on coin, seals and walls of monuments such as mosques and tombs.

(b) Majority of epigraphic records are in Persian and Arabic.

   (i) Some inscriptions are in Sanskrit and Urdu also.

   (ii) Some are bilingual, that is in Arabic or Persian both.

   (iii) Some are in local language.

(c) These records are valuable as:

   (i) They give information about the political, economic and social life of the period.

   (ii) They also provide information regarding the boundaries of the kingdom.

   (iii) Epigraphy on coins carries the dates and names of the rulers.

   (iv) Its deciphering helped to know the date of the muslim conquest of Delhi.

Q. 3. Delhi sultanate ruled during the period of 1206 to 1526 and they contributed greatly to Architecture and Administration. In light of this statement, answer the following :

[November, 2019]

(a) (i) Identify the monument given in the picture above.

   (ii) Who began erecting this monument? Where is it located?

   (iii) Name the saint after whom the monument is named.

(b) Write any three steps taken by Alauddin Khilji to regulate prices.

(c) Explain two reasons for the failure of Muhammad Bin Tughluq in his attempt to transfer the capital from Delhi to Daulatabad.

Ans. (a) (i)   This is Qutub Minar.

    (ii)   The construction of the Qutub Minar was started by Qutub-ud-din Aibak in 1199 AD. It is located in Delhi.

    (iii)   Qutub Minar is named after Qutub-ud-din, Bakhtiyar khaki a Muslim saint of Ush, near Baghdad.

(b) Alauddin khilji tried to regulate the prices of goods, and control of markets was an astonishing achievement of Alauddin Khilji. As he maintained a large army on relatively small pay, he had to ensure that essential commodities were available at low prices. He achieved this by regulating the prices of:

    (i)   Foodgrains, sugar and cooking oil   (ii) Cloth, and

    (iii) Horses, cattle, slaves and other commodities

(c) Muhammad Bin Tughluq had a huge empire to rule. In 1327, he decided to shift his capital from Delhi to Daulatabad, situated in the middle of his Kingdom. Also, Delhi was under continuous threat from the Mongols. He wanted his capital at a safer distance. However, his scheme failed.

    (i)   The sultan did not merely shift his court. He demanded that the entire population shift from Delhi. Many resented the forced movement.

    (ii)   Daulatabad was more than 1500 km away from Delhi. The people suffered greatly from fatigue, hardship and mental torture of the long journey. Many people perished during the journey.

    When the Sultan realised the failure of his scheme, he ordered the people to return to their homes in Delhi.

Chapter 9. The Mughal Empire

Q. 1. Study the personalities shown in picture A and B and answer the following questions.

(A)   (B)

(a) Name the personalities and their period of rule. Mention any one monument each constructed by both the men.

(b) How are these both personalities similar?

(c) How were both personalities different from each other?

Ans. (a) (i)   Picture A is of Mughal ruler, Akbar and Picture B is of Mughal ruler, Aurangzeb.

    (ii)   Akbar ruled from AD 1556-1605. Aurangzeb ruled from AD 1658-1707.

    (iii) Akbar constructed his father Humayun's Tomb in Delhi. Aurangzeb constructed the Moti Masjid (Pearl Mosque) in the Red Fort complex in Delhi.

(b) Similarities between Akbar and Aurangzeb:

   (i) Both were Mughal rulers and great leaders.

   (ii) Both were expansionists and wanted to build a vast empire and rule whole of subcontinent.

   (iii) Akbar is very well-known today and so is Aurangzeb. At that point in time these leaders were known in the farthest parts of the world.

   (iv) Akbar was feared by his opponents and so was Aurangzeb. Aurangzeb was considered to be the last powerful and effective ruler of the Mughal Dynasty.

(c) Differences between Akbar and Aurangzeb:

   (i) The rule of Akbar was primarily focused on tolerance. He was a secular ruler and was not focused on the Islamic aspects of the empire. He made changes to the way non-muslims were treated. He abolished the tax on non-Muslims and allowed them administrative positions within the government. Akbar was a great patron of art and literature.

   (ii) Aurangzeb's rule was quite different. Aurangzeb was a devout Muslim and wanted to re-establish the importance of the faith at the center of the empire. He also implemented new taxes on non-Muslims and imposed restrictions on their ability to achieve positions within the government. Unlike Akbar, Aurangzeb was not a great patron of art and literature.

Q. 2. Study the picture of the famous monument and answer the following questions:

(a) What monument is it and where is it situated?

(b) When and by whom was it built? What makes this monument famous?

(c) Mention any four features of this monument.

Ans. (a) (i) This monument is Jama Masjid.

   (ii) It is situated near the Red Fort in the ancient town of old Delhi.

(b) (i) Mughal Emperor Shah Jahan built it.

   (ii) It was built during AD 1650-1656.

   (iii) Jama masjid is famous because it is the biggest mosque in India.

(c) Features of Jama Masjid:

   (i) The mosque is built on a high platform with three domes of white marble decorated with stripes of black colour.

   (ii) Its courtyard is 99 meters wide and can accommodate as many as 25,000 people at a time.

   (iii) The mosque has three great gates, four towers and two 40-metre tall minarets constructed of strips of red sandstone and smooth white marble.

   (iv) The face of the massive prayer hall consists of eleven arches. This is the most spectacular feature of this magnificent construction.

Q. 3. Study the picture of the famous monument and answer the following questions:

(a)

[Februry, 2020]

    (i)   Identify the outstanding monument in the picture above.

    (ii) Where is it located?

    (iii) Name the Mughal Emperor who built it.

(b) State any three features of Emperor Akbar's Mansabdari system.

Ans. (a) (i)   The monument in the picture is the Taj Mahal.

    (ii) It is located in Agra, Uttar Pradesh, India.

    (iii) Taj Mahal was built by the Mughal Emperor Shah Jahan.

(b) Akbar was an efficient and a brilliant administrator. He created the mansabdari system, an imperial service based on merit and graded according to military rank.

    (i)   The mansabdars were directly appointed by the emperor.

    (ii) They got their remuneration in cash and not in land grants.

    (iii) The mansabdars, out of their salary, had to maintain a required quota of horses, elephants, mules and carts. The mansabdars played the dual role of military commanders and civil administrators.

Q. 4. Study the given picture and answer the questions that follow :

(a) Identify the picture.   (b) Where is it located?

(c) Who built it?

(d) Which important buildings are constructed within this enclosure?

(e) How many gateways does this monument have? Name one.

(f) How is this monument connected with free India?

Ans. (a) The picture is of Red Fort.   (b) It is located in Delhi.

(c) Shah Jahan built this fort.

(d) Some of the important buildings within the Red Fort are the Diwan-i-Aam, the Diwan-i-Khas and the Rang Mahal.

(e) There are two gateways. The western gateway, known as the Lahori Gate. It is the principal and ceremonial entrance.

(f) Every year on 15th August, the Prime Minister of India addresses the nation from its rampart to commence the Independence Day celebrations.

Chapter 10. Emergence of Composite Culture

Q. 1. Study the picture and answer the following questions:

(a) Who are they and what did they preach? What is the basis of this cult?

(b) Who were Vasudevaka? What was the theme of their hymns?

(c) How did bhakti movement bring social change in India?

Ans. (a) They are Bhakti saints.

    (i) They preached oneness of God, equality of all human beings without any discrimination on the basis of colour, caste, creed, religion and complete surrender of self to God.

    (ii) The basis of this cult has been traced to the Upanishads, the Puranas and the Bhagawad Gita.

    (iii) It also has its roots in the Shankaracharya's revival of the Hindu philosophy.

(b) (i) The devotees associated with the cult of Krishna are called Vasudevaka. They worshipped Lord Krishna as an incarnation of Vishnu.

    (ii) The main theme of the bhajans or religious hymns of the saints were the childhood escapades of Krishna known as Krishna Leela.

    (iii) The cult of Krishna Vasudeva is an archaic form of worship in the domain of Vaishnavism.

(c) (i) The bhakti saints preached universal brotherhood. The teachings of Ravidas, Guru Nanak and Kabir helped in reforming Indian society.

    (ii) By denouncing caste distinctions and following the principle of equality, they tried to evolve a new social order.

    (iii) Also, they did away with the domination of priests exposing the futility of empty rituals. Thus, this movement brought social change in India.

Q. 2. Look at the picture and answer the given questions:

(a) Name this Bhakti saint.

(b) Whom did she worship?

(c) Where did she live?

(d) What did she preach through her devotional songs?

Ans. (a) This Bhakti saint is Mira Bai.

(b) She was an ardent worshipper of Lord Krishna. She renounced all worldly comforts and dedicated her life to Krishna.

(c) She was the queen of Prince Bhoj Raj of Mewar, Rajasthan.

(d) Through her devotional songs (bhajans) she taught people how they could surrender themselves to Lord Krishna. Her bhajans are still sung all over India.

Q. 3. Look at the following picture and answer the questions that follows.

(a) Identify the monument of Sufi saint.

(b) Where is it situated?

(c) Why is it considered a sacred place?

(d) Why was the saint called a 'siddh'?

(e) What do you know about Khanqah?

(f) What other names are given to him?

Ans. (a) The monument is the tomb of Nizam-ud-din Auliya.

(b) It is situated in Delhi.

(c) His tomb is considerd a sacred place because every year the Urs (a religions fair) is celebrated in the memory of the holy saint.

(d) He was called a 'siddh' because it is said about him that he had mastered some of the yogic sidhis.

(e) Nizam-ud-Din received a divine revelation that he should live solitary life away from whole crowd of people, so he built his khanqah also known as ribat, (a building designed specifically for gatherings of a sufi brotherhood) in a village Ghiyaspur outside the city where he lived for more than 60 years and sometimes lost in meditation.

The Khanqah turned into a place of pilgrimage and is visited by Nizam-ud-Din's disciples and followers till now.

(f) Nizam-ud-Din Auliya is being called by many names such as Mehboob-i-llahi (the beloved of God) and Jag Ujyare (the light of the world).

Q.4. Look at the picture and answer the questions that follow:

(a) Identify the monument which is the oldest European Church in India.

(b) When was it originally built?

(c) Where is it located?

(d) With what material was it built originally?

(e) With what material was it rebuilt later?

(f) Who converted it into a Protestant Church?

(g) To whom was it voluntarily surrendered in 1804 AD?

(h) At present, by whom has it been taken over?

Ans. (a) The monument is Francis Assisi Church.

(b) It was originally built in 1503.

(c) It is located in fort Kochi (Cochin).

(d) It was built originally of wood.

(e) Later it was rebuilt with stone and was roofed with tiles by 1516 AD.

(f) The Dutch converted it into a protestant Church.

(g) It was voluntarily surrendered to the Anglican Communion in 1804 AD.

(h) At present, it has been taken over by the Church of south India.

Chapter 11. The Modern Age in Europe Renaissance

Q. 1. The painting shown is of Mona Lisa. In this context answer the following questions.

(a) Who painted this? To which country did the painter belong? Besides painting what were his other interests?

(b) Mention any two of his outstanding works other than Mona Lisa.

(c) Why is this painting so famous?

Ans. (a) Leonardo da Vinci painted the painting of Mona Lisa. He belonged to Italy. Though he is famous for his painting of Mona Lisa, he had other interests too. He has been described as a man of 'unquenchable curiosity'. His interests ranged from painting, sculpting, architecture, science, music, mathematics, engineering, astronomy, history and cartography.

(b) Leonardo da Vinci's two outstanding works other than Mona Lisa are:

   (i) **The Last Supper:** This painting highlights the psychological reactions of the people on the painting that range from horror, surprise to guilt.

   (ii) **Virgin of the Rocks:** This painting exhibits Vinci's zeal for science, technical skill and his belief that the Universe is a well-organised place.

(c) Leonardo da Vinci's painting 'Mona Lisa' is a perfect depiction of beauty and harmony. She is dressed modestly in a translucent veil, dark robes, and no jewelry. One of the commonly cited reasons for her fame is the 'Mona Lisa's Smile'. There is a mild smile on the face with eyes, half closed and half revealing as if she has something to say. Da Vinci painted Mona Lisa in such a way that the eyes are the center of the viewer's attention. The nature of the landscape also plays a role.

Q. 2. Look at the given picture and answer the questions that follow:

(a) Identify the personality shown in the picture who's a famous English poet and dramatist of the 16th century.

(b) Mention how many plays, sonnets and long poems were written by him.

(c) List any five of his works.

(d) Mention the impact of Renaissance on literature.

Ans. (a) The personality shown is William Shakespeare.

(b) He wrote 38 plays, more than 150 sonnets and two long poems.

(c) Five of his famous works are as follows:

   (i) Hamlet   (ii) Macbeth

   (iii) The Merchant of Venice   (iv) As You Like it

   (v) All's Well That Ends Well

(d) The Renaissance in Europe ushered in a new era in literature. The use of native languages for literary writings was the outstanding impact of the intellectual revival. For centuries, Latin was used by the scholars which could be understood by very few educated people. Due to Renaissance, modern European languages replaced Latin as the language of poetry, drama and fiction.

Q. 3. The personality shown in the given picture is Copernicus who rejected Ptolemy's theory and gave a new theory which is accepted.

In this context, answer the following questions:
(a) What was Ptolemy's theory about all heavenly bodies which was believed for centuries? Mention the theory given by him.
(b) What was the view of John Kepler?
(c) Who confirmed the theory given by Copernicus?

Ans. (a) For centuries, it was believed that all heavenly bodies, including the sun, go around the earth once in 24 hours. Copernicus rejected this theory and proved that it is the earth and other planets which move around the sun and that the earth is round in shape.

(b) John Kepler proved that the planets move around the sun in an elliptical orbit, not in a round circle.

(c) Galileo confirmed the theory propounded by Copernicus.

Chapter 12. The Modern Age in Europe Reformation

Q. 1. This is the picture of Martin Luther who was the first to initiate the Protestant Movement in Germany. Answer the following questions related to this personality and his role in Protestant Reformation.

(a) Why did Martin Luther rose in revolt against the Church?
(b) Explain Martin Luther's literary work 'Ninety-Five Theses'. What was its contribution?
(c) What is Diet of Worms? Why was Martin Luther called by Diet of Worm? What did it decide about Luther?

Ans. (a) Martin Luther, a German clergyman and professor of theology at the Wittenberg University was the first to initiate the Protestant Movement in Germany.

    (i) In AD 1514 Luther became priest at Wittenberg's Church. He observed that the practice of granting 'indulgences' to provide absolution to sinners became increasingly corrupt.

    (ii) In AD 1512, in a pilgrimage to Rome, he found the clergymen living a luxurious life.

    (iii) He turned strongly against the Church and openly criticised the papacy for selling indulgences. He pointed out that no one on earth was capable of forgiving sins.

    (iv) He wrote 95 theses in revolt against the difference between beliefs and practices.

(b) Martin Luther (1483-1546) openly challenged the Church, on the basis of false practices and drawbacks practiced by the Church and clergymen.

    (i) Acting on his belief, he wrote Ninety-Five Theses that were statements highlighting the difference between the beliefs and the actual practices of the Church. He later nailed them on the door at Wittenberg castle Church in AD 1517.

    (ii) Luther questioned the powers of Pope and priests to forgive sins of all who paid, regardless of whether they sincerely regretted their actions.

    (iii) In addition to the criticisms of Indulgences, he emphasised the primacy of The Bible rather than Church officials as the ultimate religious authority in Ninety-Five Theses.

(c) Diet of Worm was a Council of high dignitaries and Princes of the Holy Roman Empire. Martin Luther, the chief catalyst of Protestantism, defied the Holy Roman Emperor Charles V by refusing to recant his writings. In 1521, the pope excommunicated him and he was called to appear before the emperor at the Diet of Worms to defend his beliefs. The Diet of Worms ordered writings of Luther to be burned and banned. Refusing to recant or rescind his positions, Luther was declared an outlaw and a heretic.

Q. 2. Look at the picture of the great Church Council and answer the questions that follow:

(a) Who summoned this Church Council? When and where was this Council summoned?

(b) Why was the great Church Council summoned?

(c) What were the four decisions made here for reforming the Catholic Church?

Ans. (a) This is the Council of Trent.

    (i) It was summoned by Paul III.

    (ii) It was summoned in the Italian town of Trent.

    (iii) It was summoned between 1545 and 1563.

(b) The great Church Council was summoned for following reasons:

    (i) It introduced reforms in the Catholic Church without changing its basic doctrines.

    (ii) It defined the doctrines of the Church in the light of the changing times.

    (iii) Anti-Catholic books were banned.

    (iv) The Pope was declared as the head of the Catholic Church and the final spokesman of the Christian doctrines.

  (v) The Church through the Inquisition punished all heretics.

 (c) The Council of Trent took the following measures for reforming the Catholic Church:

  (i) The sale of indulgences was stopped.

  (ii) The sale of Church offices was stopped. Church officers were to be appointed on merit.

  (iii) No fee was to be charged for religious services.

  (iv) Seminars were to be conducted for educating and training priests.

  (v) Sermons were to be preached in the language of the people.

Q. 3. Study the given picture which shows the sale of indulgences. In this context, answer the following questions:

 (a) What was an indulgence?

 (b) Besides the sale of Indulgences, what were other practices for the collection of money in Church?

 (c) Mention the reasons behind the corruption in the Church.

Ans. (a) An indulgence was a piece of paper issued by the Pope that said that a person would not be punished for his sins as an indulgence was a 'pardon certificate'.

 (b) Besides the sale of indulgences, the following practices were also followed :

  (i) **Simony:** Many priests received their appointment by buying offices known as Simony.

  (ii) **Sale of Dispensation:** By giving money to the Church, people were exempted from Church rules and obligations such as fasting.

  (iii) **Annate:** It was known as the first fruit. First year income was given to the Pope by the chief of the Church in every state.

  (iv) **Tithe:** It was one/tenth of the income of each family. It was paid like a tax to the Chruch.

  (v) **Peter's Pence:** It was the payment made voluntarily to the Church. It was called Peter's Pence because a penny from every house was collected on 1 August, the feast day of St Peter ad Vincula. However, it was said to be not a tribute to the Pope but for the maintenance of the English school or College at Rome.

 (c) During the early middle ages, the pope and the Churchmen led a pious and simple life. But some degree of negligence occurred with the passage of time. As a result, high positions in the Church were occupied by priests and officers. They often paid huge money and them to make up that more. They started charging different kind of taxes.

  This ultimately led to the corruption in the Church.

Chapter 13. The Modern Age in Europe Industrial Revolution

Q. 1. Look at the given picture and answer the following questions:

(a) The personality shown in the picture is Karl Marx. What was his contribution to the socialist movement?

(b) Define the term 'Socialism'? Who first used this word?

(c) Who has been called the 'father of British Socialism'? Explain his role in the history of socialist movement?

Ans. (a) Karl Marx (AD 1818-1833) is the most outstanding figure in the whole socialist movement. He was a German economist and political philosopher.

   (i) He is famous for his socialist ideology and considered the founder of modern Sociology. He was a famous advocate for communism.

   (ii) Marx, in conjunction with Frederick Engles published The Communist Manifesto in 1848; later in life, he wrote Das Kapital which discussed the sum and substance of Marxian Socialism or Communism.

   (iii) Ironically, Marx was eloquent in describing the exploitation of the working class while personally failing to maintain a job for a significant period of time. Many leading thinkers of the time were influenced by his ideologies and suggested the path to socialism.

(b) The term socialism refers to any system in which the production and distribution of goods and services is a shared responsibility of a group of people. Socialism is based upon economic and political theories that advocate for collectivism. In a state of socialism, there is no privately owned property. Socialism aimed at eliminating the capitalist class and substituting some form of working class ownership and control of the means of production. The term socialism was created by Henri de Saint-Simon.

(c) Robert Owen played a prominent role in the interest of the laboring class so he came to be seen as the 'the Father of British Socialism'.

   (i) He was a Welsh textile manufacturer, philanthropic social reformer.

   (ii) It was he who first used the word 'Socialism' and maintained that the object of government was to make the people happy.

   (iii) He is best known for efforts to improve working conditions of his factory workers.

   (iv) He reduced the working-hours of the factory workers, paid the good wages and helped the Trade Union Movement to grow.

Q. 2. The starting point of the Industrial Revolution was the invention of machinery and its application to its process. Look at the picture and answer the questions that follow.

   (a) The picture shown is of spinning Jenny invented by James Hargreaves. Mention any three such inventions that gave a boost to the Industrial Revolution.

   (b) How can we say that English scientists had a very practical bent of mind?

   (c) How did Britain's policy contribute to the spread of the Industrial Revolution?

Ans. (a) Some of the inventions that gave a boost to the Industrial Revolution were:

     (i) Kay's flying shuttle not only helped the weavers to weave wider cloth, but also doubled their output.

     (ii) Inventions in iron and coal industries, textile production and in the field of communication and transport brought radical changes in industry and commerce.

     (iii) With the invention of the steam engine by James Watt, running big factories became possible. This discovery of steam as a power source ushered in the Industrial Revolution.

   (b) Another factor which contributed to Industrial Revolution was that the English scientists and engineers had a very practical bent of mind.

     (i) They made inventions keeping in view the needs of the time.

     (ii) They concentrated mainly on those inventions of science which had practical utility.

     (iii) This was a complete contrast to the continental scientists who concentrated on research in electricity, chemicals, etc. which were not of immediate applied relevance.

   (c) Industrial Revolution, spanning from 18th to 19th centuries, was a crucial event in Europe, Great Britain and the World history. It signifies a series of revolutionary changes that took place in the field of industry and production due to the use of machines.

     (i) A policy of commerce, trade and empire-building was followed by the British Government.

     (ii) Instead of undertaking trade and commercial activities, the Government left them to private entrepreneurs.

     (iii) Extraordinary zeal and spirit of enterprise was shown by the traders, private manufacturers, colonists and sailors. Besides earning huge profits for themselves, they brought immense wealth to their country.

     (iv) Thus, the British progressive policy proved crucial in the success of the Industrial Revolution.

Q. 3. The 'machine' was nothing but the extension of the tool. With the help of machines, more things could be produced in lesser time. The changes in methods of manufacture were drastic indeed, and hence, worthy of the title of a 'Revolution'.

   (a) Towards which 'Revolution' are the above lines indicating?

   (b) Why did the change through machines take place first in England?

   (c) The rise of capitalism was the impact of machine age. Give your views.

Ans. (a) The above lines are indicating towards Industrial Revolution.

(b) There are several reasons for why the change took place first in England.

(i) The most important reason was that England was a big colonial power, which controlled large countries like India and Canada. England, therefore, had a big market for its machine-made goods.

(ii) Besides this, iron and coal were available in England in large quantities.

(iii) The feudal system broke down in England earlier than any other country of Europe.

(iv) The agrarian revolution preceded the industrial revolution. As a result, large number of peasants were thrown out of employment, because new peasants were easily available at low wages.

(v) Naval supremacy of England was also helpful.

(vi) Above all, raw material was available from the countries like India at cheaper rates.

(c) With the coming of industrialisation, a lot of money and assets were needed for factory production. The workers under this system did not own anything. They worked for a wage. The owner of the factory invested and made huge profits. This accumulated wealth which is known as individual capital. So, its impact was the rise of capitalism.

●●